P9-CCZ-792

The LAST *of the* HIGH COMEDIANS

THE INCOMPARABLE REX

The LAST *of the* HIGH COMEDIANS

THE INCOMPARABLE

REX

A Memoir of Rex Harrison in the 1980s

PATRICK GARLAND

FROMM INTERNATIONAL

NEW YORK

First Fromm International Edition, 2000

Copyright © 1998 by Patrick Garland

ISBN 0 88064 216 5

A CIP record for this book is available from the Library of Congress

10 9 8 7 6 5 4 3 2 1
Manufactured in the United States

This memoir of Rex Harrison and the revival of *My Fair Lady* in 1980–81 is dedicated to the two producers, Don Gregory and Mike Merrick – christened by Rex, 'The Flying Wallendas' – because without them, the show would never have taken place, and this book would never have been written.

'. . . the chief thing he remembered was Socrates compelling the other two to acknowledge that the genius of Comedy was the same with that of Tragedy, and the true artist was a true artist in Comedy also.'

from the *Symposium* of Plato

'The Actor's medium is himself . . .'

Max Beerbohm

CONTENTS

LIST OF ILLUSTRATIONS

Prologue
ICE

'THEN THERE'S ALWAYS the question of Ice . . .'

'Ice?' queried Rex. The internal window between ourselves, in the back of the sound-proofed black limousine, and the uniformed chauffeur in the front, magically and soundlessly closed. We were travelling uptown, between 45th and 44th on Madison, Rex Harrison seated in the middle, and on each side two large wide-shouldered Broadway producers; let me call them, in homage to Moussorgsky's *Pictures from an Exhibition*, Samuel Goldenberg and Schmuyle. I sat on one of the jump seats, facing the liveried chauffeur's squashed cap and burly neck.

'I mean,' pursued Rex, 'the idea of Ice has not truly entered the subject of conversation.'

'Up to now,' agreed Goldenberg, 'but it might be a fruitful avenue to explore.'

'If that's the route we want to go,' added Schmuyle, drawing on his habitual cigar.

'Well . . .' interposed Rex, but with a cautious tone to his voice, 'I suppose it might be. It's a possibility.'

The two producers veered off the topic as the driver took an equally abrupt right turn into the shabby street where the Algonquin Hotel stood and where we were due to lunch.

Turning to face them I asked Goldenberg and Schmuyle to explain to me what 'Ice' was.

'Ice,' said Schmuyle patiently through his cigar, 'is when management gives the star several pairs of complimentary seats to a smash hit he's starring in as part of his deal. Somebody in the know from management gets the wink from box-office, and they slip them to a ticket tout. The tout sells them on to the concierges of the smart

1

hotels, the Plaza, the Drake, the Carlyle, at double or triple the cost, and splits the profit five ways, management, box-office, front of house, tout and star – there's nothing the Revenue can do about it—'

'The top dollar on a smash is fifty dollars. On a show you can't get into—' said Goldenberg.

'Which is New York's definition of a smash—'

'You can double or treble it.'

'When *Chorus Line* was a smash, tickets on the street were going for two hundred dollars—' said Goldenberg.

'With *Phantom* it was three hundred—' added Schmuyle.

'Business people,' explained Goldenberg patiently, 'don't care how much they spend to see a smash, if the smash is big enough, and there's a star. Say the star is getting twenty pairs a night, you're talking twelve hundred dollars already. For a single stall. Now multiply that by twenty and that's twenty-four thousand, double *that* and you're comfortably talking forty-eight thousand. Okay you divide it by five so everybody gets their cut, and you're still talking nine thousand, every week, in untaxed dollar bills, untraceable on your dressing-room table.' Rex was chuckling softly:

'Nine thousand dollars every week, untraceable and untaxed! Good heavens . . .!'

'Do many stars accept Ice?' I asked, contented to play the straight man.

'They've always accepted Ice. In the twenties and the thirties, they all did, Al Jolson, Fanny Brice, George M. Cohan, Flo Ziegfeld, they were all taking Ice.'

'Did it go back that far?'

'Ice came in with the thirties. It started in burlesque, in vaudeville, years ago. The Mozarts invented it, David Belasco refined the art. Even Flo Ziegfeld knew about Ice . . .'

'Who knows when it started, or who started it,' said Schmuyle as the low black limousine drew up in front of the Algonquin. The bell captain had his hand on the passenger door, saluting Rex as he carefully extended a well-trousered leg into the sharp New York air.

'Good day, Mr Harrison.'

'All I know is,' said Goldenberg, stubbing out his cigar, 'first there was Ice, then there was Theatre.'

2

Chapter 1

BEAUCHAMP

I FIRST MET Rex Harrison in the summer of 1976, in the
picturesque Old Harbour of Nice. In those days (no longer alas)
the ferry-boats from Corsica landed and departed from the picturesque waterfront, reminiscent of Marcel Pagnol's trilogy of films
starring the imposing Raimu and concerning Marseille, *Marius*,
César, and *Fanny*. The *Napoléon*, pride of the Corse-Med Transat,
swerved left-handed into the Mediterranean, out of Bastia, passing
Cannes on her stern side, and what Scott Fitzgerald in 1934
described so perfectly as 'the bright tan prayer rug of a beach',
before steaming soundlessly into the green waters of Nice. I had
been on holiday in Corsica, and an arrangement to meet, to
discuss a secret project, had been made on the wildly undependable
village telephone.

Mr Harrison was waiting for me, having arrived early, standing apart from the huddle of Corsican-Niçoises greeting their
relatives returning from the Île de Beauté. The island, after the
holidays, had retreated to its habitual indolent pace, and the last
tourist, bearing bottles of *eau de vie*, rich sausage, known as *coppa*,
and jars of 'Miel du Maquis', had departed. The Corsicans did not
appear to recognize Rex. He was dressed in summer clothes,
creamy and white, as if reduced from brighter colours left to fade
in the sun. He wore a light shirt with a yellow sheep's wool tie,
pale yellow I recall, and a floppy straw hat which lightly freckled
his forehead. Beside him, at his heels, and rather incongruous for
so Mediterranean a scene, sat a mournful and unmistakably
English basset hound. Behind, and parked where it ought not to
be, right in the centre of the embarkation-dock stood a classic
open-roofed blue Bentley, which could only belong to him. It was

unlikely to have belonged to the Corsicans. The basset hound and the Bentley caused a great deal more attention than the solitary, nonchalant figure. From the second deck I waved down, and received an airy flutter of a hand in reply. That was the closest we ever came to an introduction.

Safely on the quay, while the Corsicans wept and embraced each other, argued and plucked imaginary grapes from the air, we said a reticent English how d'you do, and I presented my leggy Californian girlfriend, Susan Miller. She had sun-bleached white fuzzy hair, the fashion of the times, inexcusably long legs, short pants of sailing-cloth, one of those girls who seem to spring full-breasted and sun-blessed, from California or New South Wales, out of the sea. Six foot tall, bosomy and supremely fair, she had been christened by John Betjeman, who took a shine to her, 'the Icelander'.

'I'm going to drive into the little town,' announced Rex, 'pick up some grub and booze on the way, and I thought we'd all have lunch in a nice old-fashioned pub I know in Beaulieu. This, by the way,' he added, looking down to the basset at his heels, 'is Homer. One of my closest chums.' Later, I heard him confess he far preferred Homer to any of his wives.

The Bentley was, naturally, old-fashioned, English and right-hand drive, but Rex had little difficulty steering it around the Lower Corniche, where it and he attracted envious stares. He enjoyed Susan's tall, windswept figure beside him in the front; I lounged happily in the back with Homer, relishing the familiar swaying ride along a much-admired coastline. Rex, who was living on his own at this stage, explained that he had purchased Beauchamp from an English exile some years earlier, with his fifth wife, Elizabeth, and how happy it made him, in the company of Angélique, his housekeeper, and Marcel, the gardener. It was true, the purpose of the visit was a working weekend on the play we were due to rehearse later in the year at Chichester, a modest comedy by Eugène Labiche, called *Le Voyage de M. Perrichon*, but initially Rex had in mind a few days of indolence, swimming, luxury and charm. He wanted me to bring a companion, as at the time he was running a splendid society hostess called Princess

Maria Obolensky, who turned out, unusually, to be an entrepreneur in organized tournaments of Blackjack, a fashionable pursuit of the day. He seemed to wish for Susan and me to act as chaperones, and form a respectable quartet on outings.

All appeared to go well, although I became aware that Rex was driving in rather an eccentric manner for the Lower Corniche. It was as if he were seated somehow in the middle of the car, rather than under the steering wheel, and was attending to the actual driving of the Bentley at one remove, as it were, somewhat to his right hand. This dilemma became manifest when we actually deviated away from the main road, and drove through the tormented alleyways leading to St Jean itself. First of all, with cars parked, French-fashion, up on the pavements, the Bentley seemed to occupy whatever little space there was left, and Rex, responding instinctively to the position of the wheel, was driving down the left-hand side of the narrow street. This proved unimaginably complicated for the Citroëns and Peugeots attempting to approach the old town from the opposite direction. Most curious of all, Rex was totally unrepentant about this casual unawareness of the code of the country. He simply drove forward, slowly, sedately, as if he was at home in a quiet English village, occupying the left-hand way, oblivious to all the klaxons and vocal protests around him. Finally, there was a total breakdown at a modest crossroads, and a French gentleman in another open-tourer, without any rancour that I could see, bent out of his car almost into the Bentley, and rather patiently, considering the situation, explained to Rex in a fairly restrained outpouring of indignation how he was totally at fault. Rex, relaxedly poised over the wheel, seemed to be unaware of the intellectual authority of the argument, and when the Frenchman paused for breath, murmured: 'Yes, well, I can't think what all that is about . . .' and drove steadfastly forward. 'I think it's possibly to do with driving on the left-hand side,' I ventured. 'How extraordinary,' was all Rex volunteered, and he calmly proceeded to drive all round the market-lanes of St Jean, without paying the slightest attention to the fact that he was driving in an illegal way. This was the first time I noticed Rex was not always familiar with the conventions or legalities of anything. When we arrived near the hotel, at which he had suggested we enjoy our first glass of Burgundy, he parked in a convenient space beside a fierce 'Stationnement Interdit' sign, and commenting 'That's handy,' led us confidently to the bar. 'Bonjour, Monsieur 'Arrison, et bienvenu,' said the barman, reaching for the wine-list.

And that was how we met, on the French Riviera, in the summer of 1976. Even had I wished it, it would be quite wrong to say this launched a friendship which was to last until his death fourteen years and four productions later on, but certainly it initiated a relationship which was constantly to delight and frustrate me, perhaps more than anything I can remember before or since. So many memories efface themselves, or blur, but I can never forget that sight of Rex Harrison, coolly attired in white cotton, carefully and composedly driving through the alleyways of St Jean, on the wrong side of the road, and parking against a No Parking sign.

As Susan reminded me, that same evening, after dinner almost silently sitting over the green figs and goats' cheese, in the haze of unending chilled Sancerre, the peacefulness was sweetly disturbed by an amorous bullfrog. Rex wandered to the far end of his lovely stone-terrace, in the direction of the sound: 'Arrête!' he cried out. The bullfrog stopped.

Chapter 2

'MYSELF WHEN YOUNG . . .'

'I WAS BORN in a family of three,' said Rex. 'I had two sisters and myself. I was the youngest, and I was born in a little village called Huyton, outside Liverpool, and it was really a very tiny, little village then where I was born. Now I understand it's grown up and is almost part of Liverpool.'

We were sitting in the stalls of the Haymarket, the prettiest nineteenth-century theatre in London, formerly known as 'The Little Theatre in the Hay', and the scene of several of Rex's later triumphs. And one or two catastrophes. 'My family lived up in Huyton for a long time, and my grandfather had been extremely wealthy. He had a lovely great house called Belle Vale Hall, and I used to get taken over there as a little nipper, and my grandfather was dead by then, but my grandmother was still alive, living in great state in this great big Georgian house. I used to love going over there, because there were lots of things I remember. They had a great big cricket field where all the boys used to play, and they had wonderful croquet lawns, and lakes, and hard and soft tennis courts, and a rookery. I remember hearing the rooks make a marvellous noise. My grandmother, who was then terribly aged, lived in a very large mechanical bath chair, an electric bath chair, I think, wheeling herself around and she kept saying: "Have to eat hash, have to eat stew, no money, no money, no money." That must have been what my grandfather said, I suppose, before he died, because he lost all his fortune, and having had seven boys, I think, or something like that, as they were apt to do in the Victorian age, it didn't leave my father very much. So he was never brought up in any great style, any more than I was, as a matter of fact. So, the idea of a family fortune is only a memory for me, and a remote one. I was brought up in this semi-detached house in Huyton, and went to a little kindergarten there, and then to a private school, and finally to the Liverpool College, which was a fairly well-known minor public school. There I met a man called Fred Wilkinson, who was a classics master, and very keen about the theatre. Now, being on my own, as a child, I'd been making up all sorts of games and things by myself, and I had a sort of imagination about plays. I hadn't been to the theatre, ever. But I, for some reason, felt that the theatre was the only thing I wanted to do. It's a strange thing what a calling is. Without knowing really what it was, I just felt determined to go on the stage. So after I met Fred Wilkinson, I did some amateur dramatics at Liverpool College. My first appearance was as Thisbe in *A Midsummer Night's Dream*. I played it with a lisp, and my mother, I remember, made me a rather large blond wig for it, and this was my first appearance. My first taste of the theatre. I then went to the Liverpool Repertory Company. I joined it as a student, thirty shillings a week, well, I could manage on thirty shillings a week, because I was living at home. And William Armstrong was the man who ran the Liverpool Playhouse in those days. He took rather a dim view of me right away from the very start. The first thing I ever did there was a little play called *Thirty Minutes in a Street*, which was really just people passing in the street. I was given this tiny little part of a dishevelled husband, who has to run across the stage and say: "Fetch a doctor. Baby!" I thought, this is rather a cinch. So, on the opening night, I ran across and said: "Fetch a baby. Doctor!" That was not so very good. And so, I thought my career was at an end. The company went up to London, and they had a little success at the Everyman Theatre, came back slightly depleted; so rather reluctantly, William Armstrong took me on in the company. Three pounds a week I got then, and he took me on as a sort of, not student exactly, but a minor member of the company, and I got my first decent speaking part. I had one other bit part in a play called *Abraham Lincoln* by John Drinkwater.' This is a play of modest ambition, but very famous in its day, whose chief distinction was that the last line – 'He's with the angels now' – is so peculiarly stressed that it can be pronounced any of five ways.

'I played the messenger who ran on, absolutely exhausted and out of breath. I came on, incredibly out of breath, and a voice from the stalls, William Armstrong, said: "You all right, Harrison?" I said: "Yes, Mr Armstrong, yes. I'm acting."

'"Oh," he said, "I thought you were having a heart attack."

'You can see how bad I was, and so at the end Armstrong said to me: "Oh, please, Harrison," almost on his knees, "oh, give it up," he said, "please, give it up. Go into your father's business, please. Do *anything*, but for God's sake, don't try the theatre."

'But, I was determined, and so I asked my mother if I could go to London, and she took me up to London. And I stayed with an aunt in Leinster Gardens, Notting Hill Gate, and looked around for work.'

It was an interesting period – insecure, bohemian, days filled with frustrated auditions for parts, the companionship of fellow-actors, theatrical landladies, thirty shillings all in, the conspiracy of unemployment, frugal coffee-shops to scrounge a meal, and occasional tours where, every Sunday, itinerant repertory companies met at Crewe Railway Station for their connections, carriages marked 'Actors' and 'Fish'. It was a long way from the craft supremely learnt, and the effortless high comedy of Professor Henry Higgins. One evening reminiscing, Rex said to me, nostalgically: 'I learnt my craft, leaning over the balcony at the Alhambra, Liverpool, and from ten years hard in the third division.' And with a rare sense of achievement, 'The volume of work done is monumental. I'm amazed I'm still alive.'

Chapter 3

LOTUS EATING AND CHOKING

ONCE, WHILE WAITING to complete the final sequence of his *Farewell to the Haymarket* that we were filming, Rex talked of the events which led up to his acceptance of Higgins, in what eventually came to be called *My Fair Lady*. In the spring of 1944, Rex was given an honourable discharge from the Royal Air Force because the Air Ministry wanted him to return to entertainment duties. He was released to make *Blithe Spirit*, produced by the Rank Organisation and directed by David Lean. Noël Coward was disappointed with the result. So was Rex. 'I found this rather tough going; unless a piece of material is actually made for the screen, just to put it on as a stage play never works very well, and David, I must say, Lean, whose humour is not his strong point, just put it up as a stage play, and I wasn't terribly pleased with it.' But during the making of *Blithe Spirit*, there arrived at the Savoy Hotel an agent from America with an offer for Rex to go to Hollywood on a seven-year contract, with 20th Century Fox, with one film named, and that was *Anna and the King of Siam*. Rex demurred. 'I knew that if I went to Hollywood,' he said, 'it was a vast step to take. Talk about roads taken and not taken. I could easily have·stayed on in London, wandering from theatre to theatre, and done my plays. I didn't know what was going to happen to my career, and as a matter of fact, it turned out strangely, because I didn't make an enormous number of films, and the move took me to Broadway almost as much as it took me to Hollywood.'

I asked Rex whether he had ever been a particular believer in the Roman goddess, Fortuna, and the mysterious enigma in everybody's life of 'the road not taken'. This unleashed an agony of characteristic insecurity: 'No, not really. But I'm a Pisces. And that means that it's awfully difficult for me to make up my mind. Shall I do it? Shan't I do it? Shall I? Shan't I? It's really been an agony all my life to make decisions, because I know how important decisions are in the theatre. They can make or mar an entire career. So, I worried away for about three weeks about whether I should go to Hollywood, and finally I made up my mind that I ought to have a crack at it.'

Rex underestimated the perceived view of himself at this time. Actually his career was known in America from *Night Train to Munich*, which had had quite a success in the States, in which he played a British spy frequently, and rather dashingly, attired as a Nazi officer.

By now the war was over. A new feeling was in the air – not so much of peace, as the austerity continued in England for years, but of some undefined and imprecise change: 'Well, it was very strange,' he said, 'I had to go and get a permit from the Board of Trade to leave, and then I went across on the *Queen Mary*, and she was still trooping; so I had a little cabin tucked away somewhere, but the troops were sleeping on the decks. I mean, the GIs were swarming all over the *Queen Mary*. We were getting the boys back as quick as we could, and it was very exciting.' Rex travelled with his second wife, Lilli Palmer, and they were the only two civilians on the vast Cunarder and 12,000 GIs. 'There was a boozy disembarkation in New York and a heroes' welcome to all these boys coming back, and they had wonderful things called "ha! ha!" boats, which were really tugs that came out to New York Harbour, with brass-bands and jazz-bands on them, streamers, fire-boats with hoses spouting, people cheering and waving. I remember seeing Paulette Goddard singing in the docks. And all the GIs joined in. It was really extraordinary!'

Then they went directly, with no luggage other than two suitcases, to Grand Central Station, and got on board the Super Chief (there were no airplanes yet flying East to West across the continent). The train voyage took three nights: 'And so the Super Chief arrived to my delight through the orange groves of Pasadena.

Marvellous. I had arrived in Hollywood. It was all very overwhelming and very exotic, and very hot, and it was all open shirts and open cars. Great luxury, I must say, but they started me to work fairly soon on my first film, *Anna and the King of Siam*.'

From the austerity of England at war, it was almost inconceivable for Rex suddenly to find the steaks, and the unlimited wine, and the brilliant heat, and the swimming pools. 'The luxury was unbelievable. I suspected it highly, I thought it was going to do me damage in some way.'

Although he had always been suspicious of the 'lotus-eating' aspect of Californian life (having maintained just before he left, to Roland Culver, that 'Hollywood was finished and on its last legs'), he was swiftly seduced by the poolside ease of the social life.

'I didn't do much of that while I was making *Anna and the King of Siam*, but later on I thought that I'd indulge a little bit in it, and also the studio bosses couldn't find anything for me. They didn't know where to place me at all. They didn't know what to make of me. They didn't think I was a comedian. They thought I was a character man, I think, in Hollywood. So they were offering me scripts that they didn't want to do; and there were great soirées on Saturday night in all the stars' homes, which I was invited to. And one suddenly found one's self sitting next to Gary Cooper or Clark Gable, or Spencer Tracy or Edward G. Robinson, and people you had only ever seen at the Empire Leicester Square. I mean for a Huyton boy, it was overwhelming, and I couldn't quite believe it was going on, because I'd seen them on the silver screen, but that was all.'

'Did they strike you as behaving like actors?' I asked. 'I mean, as theatrical actors on the West End or Broadway stage?'

'Not really, no. They were much more interested in sports. They were talking about their last hunting trips, and how their guns behaved, their favourite fishing rods, which I'd never heard actors talking about before. They weren't really talking about acting as such. It was an enormous change for me, and of course the atmosphere was very, very lush and exotic.'

In fact, it all got a little too lush and exotic, and after a hectic love affair, with Carole Landis (who fell deeply in love with him –

too deeply – and committed suicide with a handful of barbiturates), and a mere half-dozen movies, none of them especially riveting, Rex and Lilli returned to New York. His final verdict on Hollywood was as of 'simply, incredible, preposterous boredom'. It did not exactly endear him, neither to the proprietorial studio bosses, nor the likes of the gossip queens who made or wrecked careers, like Hedda Hopper. But then Rex was impervious throughout his life to public opinion.

Chapter 4

L'INVITATION AU VOYAGE

IT WAS SOME years after his success in the film of *Anna and the King of Siam* – which was easily the best of his forties Hollywood years – that one of the supreme roads *not* taken offered itself as a genuine *invitation au voyage*. Just as he was about to rehearse T. S. Eliot's *The Cocktail Party* in London, two gentlemen, Richard Rodgers and Oscar Hammerstein, said they were going to make a musical of *Anna and the King of Siam*, to be called *The King and I*.

'Gertrude Lawrence was going to play Anna,' said Rex, 'and she was very anxious to have me play King Mongkut, if I could sing it. I said that I really hadn't thought of anything like that before, so again my Pisces instinct jumped to the fore and I said: "Well, wait a minute, I mean . . . do a musical?" They said: "Yes, would you? Would you mind coming and singing?" I didn't want to go and sing for them in the least. That was the last thing I wanted to do. Go and sing for Rodgers and Hammerstein. So I said: "Yes, all right. What theatre do you want me to go to?" And they told me what theatre, Her Majesty's I think, and there they were sitting in the stalls, and I can't even think what I sang. Anyway I sang something and they said: "Oh, very nice. That's very nice, Rex. Thank you." – "We'll let you know later," sort of thing! – Well, thank God, of course, I never heard a word, because if by any mischance they had liked what I did, which they obviously didn't, and offered me *The King and I*, I might have been tempted to do it, and what a mess that would have been. I mean, I might have missed an even greater opportunity, and a much more suitable triumph, of Higgins in *My Fair Lady* than ever an Oriental potentate could be.'

Yul Brynner, who did win the part of King Mongkut, and

14

made it his own in much the same way Rex did with Professor Higgins, played it virtually up until his death. One evening in New York, in 1980, Rex and I went along to see him play it. Yul was having trouble with the top notes too, but had hit on an excellent way of dealing with it. Boiling up to the top C of 'Shall We Dance', as the band hit the note flat out, Yul Brynner opened his mouth, and lifted his right hand high above his head, finger outstretched giving the illusion he was hitting the top C. Rex and I were not, but two and a half thousand customers that night were entirely convinced. We were filled with genuine admiration. Rex said, 'That's the way to deal with that infernal top G in "Danced All Night".'

Chapter 5

HOW IT ALL BEGAN

'THE FLYING WALLENDAS' was Rex's affectionate way of referring to the producers, Don Gregory and Mike Merrick. When they were not busy flying around the world making deals, they discovered each other sharing two adjoining offices in California, in the summer of 1978. They knew one another from some years back, when they had produced together, and very successfully, a couple of high-class one-person star vehicles for Julie Harris and Henry Fonda: *The Belle of Amherst*, about Emily Dickinson, the reclusive New England poet, and *Clarence Darrow*, about the forthright liberal lawyer, celebrated for his brilliant and radical defence of the Leopold and Loeb child-murderers. When Don and Mike discussed the idea – which seemed entirely remote at the time – of trying to pick up the rights for *My Fair Lady* and *Camelot*, neither of them could possibly have imagined the journeys they would accomplish, when eventually they settled into their first-night seats at each major revival. Alan Lerner, who had employed Mike Merrick as press officer throughout the production of *On a Clear Day You Can See Forever*, made it axiomatic that Rex Harrison, and only he, *had* to be Professor Higgins, and as Don knew Rex socially he was to ask him. In fact, more than socially. They had met in Paris several years earlier, and enjoyed a series of rendezvous 'getting drunk together and hysterical with laughter' while enjoying the favours extended from the high-class *filles de joie* to be enjoyed at Madame Claude's.

Because they got on well together, Don flew over to London to sound him out. The timing was both fortunate and perfect – Rex was not so much in demand as he had been in the movies, and so a financial deal was struck, greatly to Mr Harrison's advantage, offering him all kinds of control – especially, although they were bitterly to regret it, all-important, casting-control. So Rex agreed, and in due course, so did Alan Lerner. Fritz Loewe was around, but a little forgetful at this time. Around the same year, Alan also let it be known he would only release the rights of *Camelot* if Richard Burton could take on his original role of King Arthur. Mike always felt more at ease with Burton than Harrison, and Don, the other way about, and so he fielded Burton, at that time enjoying life with his enchanting new wife, Susan. The two producers could hardly believe their good fortune when they realized they had signed up the two most glamorous and heady British star-performers-in-exile for each of their shows, and the publicity was sensational, the length and breadth of America. The provincial managers were ecstatic. Potentially, they would clean up a fortune on the tour, pay off the costs – astronomical – of both productions, and go into New York well ahead of the game. The rest would be sheer profit. Mike felt it was tactful to warn Rex that there was a second musical on the agenda, and every bit an equivalent superstar 'helming the show' as *Variety* puts it. So Don dutifully rang Rex with the news about Richard Burton, thinking he might be pleased. 'Burton!' came the astonished cry. 'That drunk, Burton? Fuck him. You arseholes better get yourselves another BOY!' and the phone slammed down. Mike and Don, holding the empty receivers in their hands, gaped at each other in silence. This was only the first of countless setbacks.

Chapter 6

LADY LIZA

WHILE REX AND I sat away from the heat and brightness of the lights, when we were filming a documentary at the Haymarket of his early life, and as he seemed in an unusually reminiscent mood, I asked him how Bernard Shaw's *Pygmalion* was originally translated into *My Fair Lady*, in 1956.

'I was doing a play in London called *Bell, Book and Candle*,' he told me, 'when three gentlemen arrived staying at Claridges – Fritz Loewe, Alan Lerner and Herman Levin, who was the producer of a play then called, believe it or not, *Lady Liza*. And they had, I believe, after a lot of argument with Shaw obtained the rights, but they had very little music. They had, I think, one number of mine, possibly two, and they asked me if I would play it. I was very worried – as usual. I mean, my friends all advised me very strongly not to touch a musical of *Pygmalion*, they said it's sacrilege. "You can't do that to Shaw." So, I said: "Oh, I think you're right, you know." I was terrified that somewhere in the shuffle Shaw would be lost and somebody, I don't know who, but certainly not up to Shaw's standard of literary talent would be brought in "to fix" up the book. I was convinced this was going to happen. It was my one nightmare; so I thought I mustn't do this; so I demurred again. Finally, I did a half "yes", and I said: "Well, listen. I've got a voice problem. I don't think I can sing it. So let's tackle it the other way round." They said: "Well, if you don't commit yourself, Rex, how can we write you the numbers?" That's always the come-on. "We can't write numbers for you, if we don't know they're for *you*." So I said: "Well, let's start off by going to a teacher, a voice teacher." And so that's what I did. I went and looked up a man in Wigmore Street and I went to try and learn to sing. He was a tiny little man,

18

and real singer of *bel canto*. Anyway he used to say: "Now you stand at that window, Mr Harrison, and belt out a note and try and hit the house opposite on the other side of the street." I was no good at hitting the other house opposite. I thought, well, this is ridiculous. If I worked for ten years with this chap, I'm not going to be any good as a singer. So, I rang Alan Lerner and I said: "Listen, Alan, this is no good. I can't do it. I'm never going to learn to sing, not in that sense of the word, and so let's call it off." So, Alan said: "No, wait a moment. Let's think of something else. Maybe there's somebody else you could go to. Maybe there's another man we can think of." Then he rang me back and he said: "There's a chap I think you ought to see, who's a conductor in the Coliseum Pit, who would like to come and talk to you about methods of dealing with musical numbers." So I had a piano put in the suite at the hotel I was staying and Bill Lowe, his name was – no relation of Fritz – Bill Lowe came in and he started to go over the one or two numbers that I had on the piano and he began, slowly to teach me the art of 'speaking on pitch', which is, I gather quite an old-fashioned thing. The people who played in the music-halls used to do it. It is actually using the lyrics, and using the music, but using the words to hit the middle of the note and you've got to hit it plum in the middle because you can also talk flat, unless you're very careful, and I've seen people talking flat since. You've got to be on the pitch; so I said okay I'll try that, and I worked with Bill Lowe and it seemed to be going rather well. So I rang Lerner and Loewe and said: "Listen, I think that maybe this 'speaking on pitch' is going to work." So I finally decided that I'd better give it a try. So we went to America and when I got to America, they met me with "I've Grown Accustomed to her Face", which is a beautiful number, and cheered me up a lot because it really was the last number in the show and a great number and it was very cleverly devised. It was built almost like an opera piece at the end of the play and it was lovely to do. I could believe in it.

'Rehearsals seemed to plod along quite well, and they cast Julie Andrews as Eliza, and Stanley Holloway as Alfred Doolittle. So we opened in New Haven on a Saturday night in February 1956. They sprung a Saturday night on me – I was supposed to open on the Monday – and I said: "I can't go on. I haven't had enough rehearsals with the orchestra." They don't like giving rehearsals with the orchestra, I discovered. It's far too expensive for them. So, I said: "How can I go on?"

'"Oh, well," they said, "you've got to go on, it's snowing, the house is full. It'll get into the press. It'll be a scandal." So I staggered on, and they gave me just a ten-minute rehearsal with the orchestra, and somehow I got through it. We were very over-length. I sang one number in there called "Come to the Ball", which I only sang once, and we did a ballet trying to get Eliza to come to the Ball, called "Lady Liza", which was also only danced once; so the whole thing in New Haven ran from half past eight to half past twelve. We cut it down from half past eight to sort of half past eleven, and so we worked away on it. It was by no means a success when we opened. We went on next to Philadelphia. We worked and worked and worked on it. I kept on annoying them by walking around with this Penguin version of Shaw's *Pygmalion*. It drove them mad. I had to see that Shaw was still there. I thought it was my duty to do so. So we kept a lot of Shaw in, and we went on to Philadelphia, and Alan wrote me another number called, "Why Can't A Woman Be More Like A Man", which was great fun – that was a new one on the road. So we put it all together, and we got to the Mark Hellinger Theatre, and we opened and it was, of course, a tremendous success. It really was the biggest success of my career – very exciting. It took the place by storm. Like a sort of "happening" in New York, extraordinary, I mean, weird things happened like in dead winter, when you went out of the stage door, there would be a long queue waiting round the theatre. I said: "What are all those people waiting there for?" They were waiting with thermos-flasks and rugs, for standing room for the following night!'

'And a lot of distinguished people came to see you?'

'Oh, yes. They did. It was rather marvellous from that point of view. I remember having Marilyn Monroe in my dressing-room, looking at herself in two mirrors at the same time – rather spectacular. And Spencer Tracy came in with Frank Sinatra, and said: "You made the little wop cry." Louis Armstrong came in and

20

said with that famous crackly voice: "You hit each note right down the middle, man." Very proud of that. And also people like Charles Laughton came and asked if he could stand in the wings and watch it one night.

'Cole Porter used to visit it often. I didn't see much of him, but I was told he had a seat in the stalls, I think, and used to see it regularly twice a week.'

'No musical has ever had a book like that, you know. Nor since. It's a wonderful play. Plus the fact that the music was absolutely excellent and Alan Lerner's lyrics stood up to Shaw's dialogue, perfectly. It was a remarkable blend.' Later on, I noticed, Rex was not always so polite.

'However, we had one or two very strange occurrences there. I had to run round the back of the stage to make my re-appearance in front of the dropped cloth, which was "The Street Where You Live" to sing "I've Grown Accustomed To Her Face", and as I went round the stage manager said: "Don't worry Rex if you hear a noise." I said: "What do you mean, hear a noise?" and went on. In the number, no noise at all, no laughter, no applause, dead silence. I came off to my stage manager, Biff Liff, and I said: "What do you mean, 'don't worry if you hear a noise'". "Well," he said, "we'd a message from the Mad Bomber." (There was a Mad Bomber around in New York, he used to leave bombs all over the place.) "The Mad Bomber," said Biff, "was going to place a bomb under the front row of the stalls during your last number. We didn't like to tell you" – "Thank you very much," I said, "I see I'm dispensable, am I?"

'Another thing that happened, which was really very strange and alarming too was that – it must have been in the second year – because behind this front cloth, I had a very large piece of scenery which was flown, up on to the pulleys, and which was the Library set, which was the basic set for the whole play, really. And during my solo number, the ropes broke, it collapsed behind me. The front cloth bellied out. I was covered in bits of wood. The stage was covered in bits of wood. It was totally ruined, the Library set, all in little bits, and when I recovered from the shock of this noise, I looked down and I saw that the conductor Franz

Allers wasn't waving his stick around at all. The orchestra stopped. The whole thing had come to a dead halt. I thought, well now what do I do, I can't go on without an orchestra. What do I do now?

'Very quickly on my feet, I knew that I had one instrument that plays my melodies and that was the clarinet and so I thought, I've got to get the clarinet in somehow. I bent down to Franz and I said rather firmly: "Clarinet!" And the clarinet picked up the tune, and I continued the number, but I knew all the time I was finishing the number that I wouldn't be able to finish the play, because that set was the set that I finished the play and said to Julie Andrews, "Where the devil are my slippers?" So I had to think of something ... so Julie came on and I explained to the audience what had happened that the Library set had crashed to the ground and was no longer in existence, but at the end Eliza came back and picked up the slippers, and finished the scene. The audience loved that. So that was the end of that rather catastrophic experience.'

By the time the film came out, to great acclaim, there was an awkward and uncomfortable ceremony with the Academy.

'The Oscars. Yes, that was a rather trying evening, because Audrey Hepburn made the film and her PR people had advised her that it would be very nice if she would go to the awards in case I won it; so she could give me the Best Acting Award, but unfortunately she didn't realize that at the same time Julie Andrews was also going to be nominated for a different film, *Mary Poppins*. So, I was up there for the photographs with two Eliza Doolittles – one of whom had *not* played Eliza Doolittle in the film, but won it for something else, and the other one who *had* played Eliza Doolittle, and wasn't awarded anything. You can imagine what sort of a night I had! I was very grateful to win the Oscar for Henry Higgins, but it wasn't the sort of evening I would like to repeat.'

I reminded Rex he had corrected me when I spoke of light comedy, instead of *high* comedy, which was a very important distinction and that I thought his performing Chekhov's *Platonov* was an illustration of exactly what was meant by high comedy at its most delicate. His particular gift of turning from almost-farce to near-tragedy, and back again was never in greater evidence.

'Yes, there's a great distinction between high and light comedy, I think. High comedy is equivalent, by contrast, to low comedy. Low comedy is very broad, and high comedy can be quite raw too. *Light* comedy is something quite different – light comedy is almost like a sort of musical-comedy dancer; not Fred Astaire, I don't mean, but the average musical-comedy dancer performs light comedy. David Niven is a light comedian, without the musical element. The high comedy is something a lot of actors have tried to achieve, and certainly I have tried to achieve and it's marvellous if you can actually use that expertise in Chekhov. Because I've got a feeling that's the way Chekhov would have liked to have seen it done. High comedy teeters on the edge of tears – even on the edge of tragedy, if well done. The farcical element in Chekhov is a peculiarly Russian thing; I never feel the English can manage that, or if they have, I've never seen it. But I always think in every perfect comedy, whether it's Wilde, Congreve, Shakespeare or Molière, there should always be what I call "the Seymour Hicks moment".'

Rex had told me before, not only was Seymour Hicks one of his private models or mentors, as well as Ronnie Squire and Gerald du Maurier, but he had befriended him when he was an old man, and Rex something of a beginner. It was the young Seymour Hicks who attended the third and tragic Oscar Wilde trial – one of the few members of the theatrical profession who behaved with generosity and loyalty, as opposed to the shabby behaviour of George Alexander, who plastered over Wilde's name on the billboards as soon as the playwright was in trouble. Was it Seymour Hicks, perhaps, up in the gallery of the Old Bailey, who – at the Judge's sentence – called out 'Shame, Shame!'? A genial portrait, in the upstairs bar of the Garrick Club, of Seymour Hicks in dazzling white-tie emblazoned by a gardenia in his buttonhole and glittering watch-chain and gold-topped cane has always delighted me. Quite simply, the Seymour Hicks moment is that towards the end of the comic denouement, no matter how funny events and the collision of characters may be, there must be a moment of *absolute seriousness*. One thinks of Malvolio at the end of *Twelfth Night*, the last scene of *Tartuffe* or *L'Avare* – the finale of *Cosi Fan Tutte* – and, oddly enough, in contemporary terms (the only one I can think of) almost any episode of *Men Behaving Badly*.

Chapter 7

THE CONDUCTOR FOLLOWS ME!

PREPARATIONS FOR THE revival of *My Fair Lady*, on tour and eventually on Broadway, occupied most of 1979–80. They began with a quest for Eliza.

Kingsley Amis, whilst explaining that malice makes for good copy, said a misguided sense of mercy shouldn't stand in an artist's way – and Rex was a manifestation of that. This was something I had occasion to witness many times, and although many of the incidents are funny now in retrospect, I cannot pretend that they were necessarily very funny at the time. Rex was frequently at his least charitable when talking about his fellow artists, in particular whoever played Eliza Doolittle. Cyril Ornadel the first English conductor of *My Fair Lady* joined us for general auditions at the Globe Theatre, and was giving an enthusiastic account of a singer who was just about to perform for us. 'Now this girl used to be Julie Andrews's understudy and she looks just like her and she's got a lovely natural singing voice of her own, but if asked to she can produce exactly the Julie Andrews sound.'

Rex beckoned Cyril to bend close down to him, and I heard him reply: 'Cyril that's exactly what I don't want.'

Another time he said: 'I can't bear any of those suburban girls – I don't want anybody coming in looking like or talking like Audrey Hepburn, or . . . or . . . oh Christ, what's her name . . . that *other* girl.' Presumably he was referring to Julie Andrews.

On another occasion he said about Audrey Hepburn: 'Eliza Doolittle is intended to be distinctly ill at ease in European ballrooms. Bloody Audrey has never spent a day of her life *out* of European ballrooms.' Which was true in a way. What Rex really felt was that Eliza Doolittle should be performed by a back-street

25

girl who works her way into the middle classes (like him, perhaps?) and not – as it always was, from its first interpreter, Mrs Patrick Campbell to Julie Andrews or Audrey Hepburn – by a refined middle-class girl, inventing a theatrical cockney accent for Act One.

Alan Lerner who knew his own show with remarkable accuracy, and on many occasions was of enormous value and help to me about the specific demands that the show made at different points in the evening, always nagged me to find an Eliza who knew how to hit the top G effortlessly. 'Otherwise,' he would say, 'there's nothing between "The Rain In Spain" and whatever follows "I only know when he/Began to dance with me . . ." You know, Ascot. Once you can get the girl who sings that top G, you're home and dry. That gets the hand, the hand buys you time to bring the Ascot front-cloth in, that gets a further hand, and by *that* time you've got the old lady on. But if you miss the top G, everybody stands there waiting for something to happen, and nothing does.'

When I explained all this to Rex one evening, all he said was: 'Oh I wondered what accounted for that ghastly glazed look that used to come over Julie Andrews's face once we had finished "The Rain In Spain" scene; it was obviously the prospect of that imminent top G that she had to sing a few pages later on.'

Nor was he particularly complimentary about Wilfred Hyde-White, whom theatrical tradition always agreed was the definitive Colonel Pickering. Rex refused to have him in the revival, because, he said: 'Wilfred is essentially an amateur – well, that doesn't matter very much, but Wilfred jealously preserves his amateur status.' Wilfred's own view of himself was endearing in its candour – after George Cukor persuaded him to stay in California after the success of his work with Marilyn Monroe in *Let's Make Love* the work offers poured in. Trying to justify his absences from Ascot and Epsom and Whites to his cronies, Wilfred explained: 'I couldn't turn the offers down when you consider what a lousy actor I am.' He was particularly near the mark when he responded to William Douglas-Home's criticism that he underplayed Colonel Pickering, 'Well, what's the point in trying to compete with that crafty old bugger, Rex?'

When the Deputy conductor, in Detroit, Bob Kriese, came round to see Rex after the show, which he habitually did to share a glass of wine, and exchange comments or criticisms if there were any, Rex in a positively benign mood congratulated him: 'My dear Bob, I feel absolutely safe and secure in your hands, and I think you're doing a marvellous job, I always appreciate the wonderfully muted sound you achieve in the pit.' Bob accepted the somewhat enigmatic compliment with customary grace but just as he was about to go out of the door Rex stopped him. 'Oh Bob, by the way, there is one thing, if you don't mind me pointing it out – if you don't mind, Bob, don't wear a tail-coat in the pit, old boy.'

'But Mr Harrison, I always wear a tail-coat, out of respect for you.'

'I know Bob,' said Rex, 'that's the trouble. If you wear too much white, I can see you.'

Once during auditions we were sitting around discussing the recent spate of musical revivals ahead in New York; there was talk of *West Side Story*, *Most Happy Fella*, and *Oklahoma*. Rex asked suddenly: 'Talking of tired old commercial revivals, how's Burton?'

But Rex reserved his chief contumely for the venerable and distinguished conductor Franz Allers. Franz had conducted the original *My Fair Lady* on Broadway, subsequently *Camelot*, and *Gigi*, he had also conducted the Vienna State Philharmonic Orchestra and was a renowned interpreter of Mahler and Bruckner. It was an act of considerable generosity and sacrifice on his part to come out of retirement (he was in his eighties at this stage), and conduct the revival of *My Fair Lady*, which he did out of great friendship and reverence for the artistry of Rex Harrison. It was, if you like, although a professional engagement, an act of genuine loyalty and affection on his part to come over to New York. All of this fell on stony ground. When I explained this sentimental background to the arrival of Franz Allers to act as Musical Director, Rex's only comment was: 'I don't like the look of that Nazi in the pit!'

Later he summoned the two producers, 'The Flying Wallendas', one evening on the telephone to say: 'I insist on a special private orchestral rehearsal with Franz Allers, in order for me to tell the conductor exactly how I want it done.'

PATRICK GARLAND

On another occasion he said to me quite severely: 'Patrick, I
don't have to pay attention to anybody in this show except the
conductor, and I *never* pay *any* attention to *him*.'

One day in desperation when Franz and Rex were both of
them desperately out of synchronization with the very complicated
opening solo in the study – 'I'm An Ordinary Man', Franz was
imploring Rex to look in his direction: 'Rex, if only you would
look even *once* over here, I am leaning forward in the pit, with the
baton upraised, and if you will glance a look in my direction I can
take you out of "I'm a very gentle man" and into the up-tempo
"But let a woman in your life", and all will be well and from then
on you can follow me . . .'

'I don't follow the conductor,' snapped Rex, 'the conductor
follows *me!*' That there was a certain degree of right and wrong on
both sides was indisputable, and as much as I privately cherished
every musical remark which fell from Franz's lips, I recognized
that there was something perhaps over-imperious and autocratic in
him for a musical comedy, and there was indeed something in
what Rex said when he declared: 'Franz always has the baton in
his right hand, even when he's at lunch.'

It was when we were due to leave San Francisco and go into
Chicago that Rex made his most incautious remark. The Associate
conductor, Bob Kriese, whom Rex greatly preferred to our distinguished Musical Director, because he was more easy-going, and, it
must be said, more humorous, raised our sense of anticipation by
promising that we would have the best pit band of all when we
arrived in Chicago; the reason being that the local musicians were
all former instrumentalists in the old speak-easy days in the 1930s
of Chicago's heyday, when it was one of the jazz capitals in the
United States. 'Rex,' said Bob, his eyes gleaming with anticipation,
'you're going to love the bright, brassy sound of the Chicago pit
band!' I also was a great lover of early Chicago jazz, without Rex's
expert knowledge, but certainly with a similar amount of enthusiasm. I, every bit as much as Bob Kriese was looking forward to
the much-vaunted 'bright, brassy sound' of which we had been
told. I thought of Bix Beiderbecke and his Chicagoans, Mez
Mezzrow, Johnny and Baby Dodds. Came the day of the first *sitz*

28

pröbe, and Rex and the cast were introduced to the musicians, myself coming forward to do so at the edge of the pit and looking down on the eagerly up-turned faces of the twenty-six or so jazzmen we had been so famously promised by Bob Kriese. With customary American politeness and friendliness, the pit musicians all applauded Rex warmly, and with affectionate murmurings of appreciation, and tapping on the floor with their feet. Rex towered above them from the stage and gazed benevolently down: 'Ladies and Gentlemen of the orchestra, it gives me great pleasure to be here as a representative of the *My Fair Lady* Company which has enjoyed splendid success playing your magnificent and appreciative cities. Now we have come to Chicago, where I am reasonably informed you are going to contribute "a bright, brassy sound": of which I hope we will hear very little, as to my experienced ear I believe Mr Fritz Loewe has composed a romantic all-string score.' To this day I can never forget the astonished but soundless gasp which greeted this tactfully delivered hand-grenade and the row of up-turned faces staring towards the oracle, who, with a deprecating and respectful bow of his head, turned lightly on his heel and elegantly made his way upstage, and back towards his dressing-room. When he saw me a few moments later, with an enthusiastic smile he commented dryly: 'I think my little speech went down rather well with the musicians, don't you, Patrick?'

Chapter 8

'*YOUR* FRIEND LARRY OLIVIER'

I HAD NEVER been able to discover exactly what lay beneath the submerged hostilities between Rex Harrison and Sir Laurence Olivier, or in Rex's tireless phrase '*your* friend Larry Olivier'. In fact, whereas I could not call Sir Laurence a friend exactly, he was certainly somebody I had the thrill of working for both at his own National Theatre, and on subsequent occasions, albeit minor ones, evening-dress Galas for either the going-into or the coming-out of the Common Market, or for various birthdays of the Queen at the Royal Opera House. Socially, I knew him well, especially when he lived in his Sussex farmhouse, and when I was taking over his seat at the Chichester Festival Theatre. Above all, I belonged to that generation of actors, directors, playwrights, designers, and indeed, public, who worshipped at his shrine. For me he was the David Garrick, or the Charles Dickens (the creator of dozens of familiar characters) of our day, and I happily go on record as saying I have never seen, not even remotely, performances in the classical plays to match the exhilaration and dramatic intensity of his. Nor do I expect to in the future. All of this earned him the soubriquet, in Rex's view, of '*your* friend Larry Olivier'. Whether their mutual resentment was based on simple rivalry, or not, is a matter of conjecture. Certainly, it is beyond dispute that Sir Laurence resented Rex Harrison's international superstar status, and it is even possible that he resented Rex's superiority as a screen actor, which to my eye and ear seems quite clear. Equally, on his part, Rex resented ferociously the adulation Sir Laurence received, not only as the supreme all purpose actor of his generation, but also as a national figure, honoured by State and Crown, and given the unreserved eminence in the Presidential Chair of the theatrical hierarchy. Rex, both as a movie actor and a tax exile was always on the fringe of that society, no matter how familiar his face when he walked down the street.

Am I wrong, I sometimes wonder, in imagining that there might have been a personal reason underneath all this? Certainly Rex was in his prime, both as film star and sexual adventurer, when he played opposite the ravishing Vivien Leigh in a curious melodrama with Charles Laughton (and Tyrone Guthrie in a minor role) called *St Martin's Lane*. Rex was always evasive whenever the subject cropped up, and I was too reserved to probe the issue, but I wondered whether Rex had either made a pass at Vivien Leigh during the time of their filming, or, perhaps more to the point, had even had a full-blown love affair with her. No evidence of this crops up in either his memoirs or indeed hers, or Laurence Olivier's, not that it ever would, but it has always been at the back of my mind that the hostility between these two fierce tigers of the theatrical world of the thirties and forties had a profoundly personal source. It is not improbable, although I suppose by now the world will never know. The truth was, for whichever of these reasons, Rex and Sir Laurence, who were similar in many ways as men, egocentric, supremely gifted, insecure, envious, deeply attractive to women, actually disliked one another a very great deal.

Several anecdotes, even if speculative, testify to their mutual animosity. The second assistant on a bizarre film of 1980, called *Clash of the Titans* about the Greek deities, had Olivier as Zeus he told me – when asked to join the cast, Rex declined, saying: 'I'm not going to play a subordinate god to that bastard!'

Apparently, when he was running the Old Vic, Sir Laurence invited Rex to play opposite him in *The Dance of Death*. Rex replied with one sentence on an open card: 'Dance of Death? Only on your grave, dear boy.'

This was, I believe, hearsay, because there is no suitable opposing role in the play – but Simon Callow (who was an usher at The Old Vic in the 1960s) told me he went to wake up a member of the public slumped in his seat after a matinée, only to discover he was dead. The play was the same *Dance of Death*, and

31

when Olivier was told, he said: 'Oh my God, I must have killed him.'

At one of Laurence Evans's parties, which were held annually in his beautiful house and grounds at Chesworth, near Horsham, a domestic Tudor home which once belonged to the family of Katherine Howard, I remember seeing Sir Laurence sitting with a group of his chums at one end of the ornamental gardens, while Rex sat equally at home with his cronies in the other. I, in a Pandarus-like manner, found myself hovering apprehensively between the two camps, as it were of Hector and Achilles. When I walked over to Sir Laurence, he peered melodramatically at the distant form of the seated Rex wearing fastidious summer clothes and resting beneath a pale cream Panama hat. 'Good God,' said Olivier, 'is it really that shit Rex Harrison sitting over there? I can barely recognize him, he's gone off terribly.' And at a later point in the afternoon finding myself seated beside Rex, when he stared almost sightlessly over in the direction where Olivier and his party were grouped, he said scathingly: 'I think *your* friend Laurence Olivier is sitting over there. I must say he looks frightfully decrepit.'

The impresario Duncan Weldon told me of an alarming time when he was going to visit Manchester in order to see Rex Harrison who was appearing at the Palace Theatre in his production of *Heartbreak House*, where he was playing the part of Captain Shotover. I had visited the play on tour at Brighton, at the Theatre Royal, when Rex played there, and was very impressed with his performance. Unexpectedly, he seemed totally at home with the long and difficult text – he was always a superb Shavian actor, having just the right lightness of touch to deal with all the bogus philosophizing, so that it sounded as witty as when Shaw spoke it himself, with a delicate brush stroke – also he looked magnificent, with a wild white shovel beard, home-grown for the role, that suited him and the character of Captain Shotover down to the ground. At the same time, Laurence Olivier was also in Manchester, where he was rehearsing and performing his final, great classical role on television, namely *King Lear*, and both he and Rex Harrison were booked at the same hotel, where all theatrical celebrities stay, the Midland Hotel. Laurence Evans, who was agent to both of them, tactfully warned Duncan Weldon to be very careful and to make sure that one did not bump into the other; Weldon accepted the warning, but thought it would be unlikely. For his characterization of King Lear, Sir Laurence had short cropped white hair, and had also grown a large white bushy beard. When they were checking in at reception, Duncan and Rex were shown a suite of rooms on the fifth floor. It was customary for Rex to check into a hotel, look at the rooms allotted to him, and by definition, and without apology, to reject them. Coming back from this inspection, Duncan and Rex were waiting at the junction of the fifth floor for the lift when it stopped; the lift doors opened, and there right in the middle was the unmistakable form of the great man himself, the Lord Olivier resplendent in cropped head and white beard, looking every inch the tyrannical King Lear, glaring in front of him. Rex stood motionless outside the lift and glared back. Of course, by this time as is well known, Sir Laurence's illness had afflicted him considerably, and that brilliant, clarion trumpet of a voice had lost a great deal of its splendour. With a somewhat ancient treble, the voice from this raging figure enquired: 'Can you inform me – are we on the ground floor, by any chance?'

Rex rasped back, 'No, this is the fifth floor,' at which point Olivier pressed the button of the lift doors, they closed, and he disappeared from sight. Duncan Weldon was momentarily stricken with dread that the two unrepentant enemies had recognized one another. However, Rex failed to comment, and when Duncan later saw Olivier, he failed to comment also; it only occurred to him then that in fact Laurence Olivier and Rex Harrison had indeed confronted one another face to face, on the fifth floor of the Midland Hotel, Manchester, three feet apart, but neither had remotely recognized the other.

It hadn't always been like this. Years before, in 1952, Sir Laurence had directed Rex Harrison in a production in London of *Venus Observed*. Taking over the role of the Duke of Altair, Laurence found it difficult to interpret – and in a long thirty-page letter from his dressing-room in New York, had this to tell the author, Christopher Fry, about Rex's quality on stage: 'Rex is the most attractive actor imaginable, he has a style, presence and personality that is most original, brilliant and extraordinarily winning in its individuality. I really love his performance, and I know you would be captivated by it. If one wished to be scathing, which I really do not' – here it comes, the little touch of Larry in the night! – 'the worst one would say would be that it smacks of Berkeley Street rather than St James's. His lack of vocal range and equipment makes it very hard for him to keep the *sound* of the part rich and refreshing in tune . . . This is all very poetic, but what I really mean is, at times, it's a little boring to listen to.' So even as long ago as that, subversive cracks and fissures of envious competition were beginning to appear!

Chapter 9

WIVES – ELIZABETH

IT WAS ELIZABETH Rees-Williams, later Harris, later still, Harrison, who first told me that Rex was the only man she had ever known who sent back the wine in his own house. Elizabeth succeeded Rachel Roberts as wife number five ('the Katherine Howard part', Rex once confided to me), and years after their divorce, always kept on excellent terms with him. I remember several tender, almost romantic meetings with them both, drinking champagne on her elegant terrace overlooking Cadogan Square, where I also lived. John Betjeman maintained happiness was a flat in Cadogan Square. At one stage, I got the impression that Rex was considering a reconciliation, even a second marriage Burton–Taylor style, especially when he borrowed my apartment overlooking the leafy square for a summer; but that was an illusion. 'I was very fond of Rex before we were married, and even more fond of him *after* we were married,' Elizabeth told me once, 'it was the bit in between which got so difficult.'

One thing she could never forget about him, she told me, something so unusual, something extremely rare in all other men – throughout their years as a couple, living together, and in married life, Rex was always, always, impeccably well dressed. She never remembered him once scruffy, dishevelled, unshaven, unwashed, anything other than beautifully and fastidiously turned out. I remember that unaffected refinement also, and agree, with Elizabeth, fastidiousness in dress is a quality all too lightly disregarded in our slovenly age. Nor was it ever self-conscious, or irritatingly apparent, as it is, alas, in so many women, forever concerned about the way they appear to *other* people. Rex was only preoccupied about the way he looked for himself. He was self-centred, but not, I think, vain. In addition, good dress was instinctive to him, as unforced as breathing. He had excellent taste in clothes, formal or informal, and affected most of the time a delicious state of 'undress', beautifully tailored shirts, neatly fitted 'bags' as he called them, pale colours, silks, cashmeres, linens, light cottons. Some of this fastidious attention may be commonplace for a dandy; it was, after all a signature of Rex Harrison, 'the look, the cut' of *le milord anglais*, and might be considered a part of his public image, calculated for the outside world and the press. But Elizabeth Harrison's point was precisely that in his own home, at his ease, when there was no pressure to make an effort, no spectators even, early in the morning, last thing at night, Rex always appeared relaxed and elegantly turned out. This was part of his innate allure for women, a sensitive maleness, complemented by the low, enticing timbre of his cascading voice, which could 'roar you as gently as any sucking dove', and the choreographic grace of his movement.

In our eccentric age, everything seems brutally restricted to the visual, the way things *look*, decorative, trivial, fleeting: Rex looked well enough, of course, but it was the eloquent music of his sinuous voice, the swoops and barks and sudden, heart-stopping plunge of his tone, and the pantherine grace of his half-pouncing, half-floating walk which ploughed such furrows in feminine hearts – even though, much of the time they were unaware of it. Rex possessed the efficacy in sensual terms of the Ghurka's *kukri*. 'Missed!' 'You shake your head and see.'

One evening in Portofino, early on in their married life, Rex and Elizabeth were enjoying an al fresco dinner together, overlooking the peaceful harbour beneath them. It was an occasion Rex wanted to work well, both romantically, and gastronomically. Unfortunately, from the very first, everything went wrong. The food was not properly cooked, the fish underdone, the meat overdone, the white wines were served chambrés with the red meat, and the red wines, arrived frozen with the fish. The whole evening was a catastrophe, exacerbated by total incomprehensibility on the part of the Italian servants. Tempers flew, unforgivable insults were exchanged. 'I've lived in this country for fifteen years,' complained Rex bitterly, 'you'd have thought the little buggers would have learnt to speak English by now.' But then languages were never Rex's forte. When at Portofino, he could never learn Italian – and at Beauchamp, he never mastered French. Once, when we ate at a steak-house in Nice, he summoned the *maître d'hôtel*: 'Ce bifstek' he complained, 'est brûlé comme la buggère.'

On a later occasion, when their relationship was at a lower ebb, Rex had been filming in Paris, and Elizabeth was still resident in Cadogan Square. Returning from a shopping expedition, Elizabeth entered her apartment, the telephone ringing urgently at the exact moment two or three burglars pushed roughly past her. Surprised by the owner's unexpected return, there followed one of those farcical scenes of confusion and crisis as the burglars half-apologized for their sudden exit. Half-dazed with the shock of the incident, Elizabeth automatically picked up the telephone. A distressed voice shouted: 'Elizabeth! This is Rex! Look, you've got to help me. I'm in Paris – I'm at the Georges Cinq . . . !'

'Rex, can I ring you back, I've just got in, and my flat's being burgled . . .'

'No, Elizabeth, *don't* hang up! You've *got* to help me! I'm at the Georges Cinq Hotel . . .'

'Yes, I know, Rex, but let me call you back when . . .'

'No, you can't. Elizabeth – you've got to help me now. I've got an important plane to catch, and all these frightful hall porters, and *maître d*'s, and concierges are lined up in front of me . . . !'

'I understand that, Rex, but my flat's being burgled, I'll call you back . . .'

'But you *don't* understand! All these little buggers are lined up in front of me, all wanting tips, and I don't know how much I ought to give them . . . !'

'Let me call you back!'

'No, don't call me back! There isn't time! Just tell me how much I'm expected to give these bastards!'

In desperation, Elizabeth blurted out some rough idea of the sort of gratuity they might content themselves with, and got off the telephone as quickly as she reasonably could.

'Thanks so much, Elizabeth, you see there's this plane to

catch, and all these frightful little buggers are all lined up and shouting away. I can't understand a bloody word they say – and I don't have the faintest idea what to do about it. I'll call you when I get to Rome. Goodbye.' And, without a word referring to her own predicament, and any dismay she might feel surrounding the burglary, he hung up. The next morning, while Elizabeth was still recovering, and counting the cost of a fairly disruptive robbery, even in spite of coming home in time, Rex telephoned again: 'Elizabeth, this is Rex. I'm so sorry about yesterday, but I've just been reading in the English newspapers all about your flat being burgled. I say – I had absolutely no idea I'd bought you so much expensive jewellery . . .'

Elizabeth was always so beautiful, and impeccably turned out, it was not difficult to imagine her as the perfectly cast consort for Rex. And at the beginning of their marriage, probably Rex thought so too. Dulcie Gray told me, when she met Rex at that tremulous stage in his life, he assured her this time (after four misfires) he'd found real love and contentment at last, and nothing could threaten or evaporate it. Dulcie believed the sincerity of his sentiments, and seeing Elizabeth later on, told her exactly what Rex had said. Elizabeth enthusiastically agreed, and added, to confirm her feelings, 'Yes, I really think Rex and I *have* found one another, and the first thing I mean to do is get rid of that horrid little house in Portofino.' Dulcie said she didn't think it augured very well.

A man may be counted for the quality of his wives, even if there are rather more of them than is conventionally thought appropriate in this day and age, and Rex has to be admired for his. There is a huge distinction, it must be clearly said, between Rex Harrison and his wives, and Elizabeth Taylor, for instance, and her husbands. With the solitary exception of 'my friend Burton', they are a questionable bunch, compared, that is, with Lilli Palmer, Mercia Tinker, Collette Thomas, Kay Kendall, Rachel Roberts and Elizabeth Harris – all of them alluring, all of them intelligent, all of them elegant, all of them refined. By contrast, the actor Edward

Duke told me he was staying for a country-house weekend with Lord S— at some grand estate, whose fertile lands seemed to flow without obstacle from Herefordshire and Carmarthenshire to the sea. Elizabeth Taylor and her most recent acquisition, Larry Fortinsky, were house-guests at the same time, and at breakfast, Edward assured me, looking out at acres of finely sculptured lawns, as far as the eye could see, Fortinsky said: 'Well, my Lord, may I congratulate you, sir, on your elegantly manicured back-yard.'

For myself, I was overjoyed on one occasion to join both Rex Harrison and Alan Lerner at lunch at Chez Victor in Wardour Street. While the two Titans reminisced I wondered silently how many other young men had the privilege I had, since the Middle Ages, to sit down to a meal with two men, who had married fourteen women between them. Even Rex was muddled by his marriages at times. The story is told that once after a furious row with Lilli Palmer, in the forties, she stormed out of the house (probably on account of Kay Kendall) and ran away from him, down the garden path. Rex came stamping out of the house in a volcanic eruption of marital indignation.

'Come back, come back . . .' he stormed, and then hesitated, as he couldn't be entirely sure which wife it was. 'Come back,' he cried out, '. . . *You.*' But then, Rex always had, like Henry Higgins, 'my *own* soul, my *own* spark of divine fire!'

When Lady St Just, an old friend of Rex, first met Elizabeth, she chastised Rex for his insensitivity towards his beautiful and unhappy fifth wife.

'Rex, you've got to do something about Elizabeth; I've never met a more unhappy woman in all my life.'

'Oh, haven't you, Maria,' he said, 'I have. All my other wives.'

Chapter 10

'*MY* FRIEND BURTON'

WHEN THE PRODUCERS Mike Merrick and Don Gregory first met Richard Burton it was in order to invite him to play King Arthur in the musical revival of *Camelot*. The problem was that Rex Harrison although considering himself a great friend of Richard Burton also thought of him as a rival and 'The Boys', or 'The Flying Wallendas' (and, in a bad mood: 'those Bus and Truck Merchants'), soon realized they had merely exchanged one dilemma for another. It was Don who took the responsibility of ringing Rex up – it was not an enticing task. In the past ever since they had engaged Rex Harrison to star in their revival of *My Fair Lady* both Don and Mike telephoned Rex on a weekly basis just to see how he was getting on.

'The Boys call me every week,' said Rex genially to his lawyer, Harold Schiff, 'but I think it's just to check that I'm still alive.' He was considerably less genial when Don broke the news that they had also contracted Richard Burton to play the lead in *Camelot*. It was as if he took offence by proxy.

Whenever Rex was crossed in any way by the producers, or indeed even if he and I had a faint argument, his initial line of antagonistic defence was as previously said, to snap: 'Then you better get yourselves another boy!' That for him appeared to settle every argument, and it must be said that in general it did. But most of the time The Flying Wallendas and Rex got on rather amiably together. Don Gregory in particular was permanently mesmerized by Rex Harrison, and his style of living, his high-class manner of acting, dressing, and dining, and indeed his astounding marital status. Once, he told me, he and Mike Merrick and their two wives were taking a taxi to go to Euston Station before visiting the provincial tour of the English production of *My Fair Lady*, which was in the Royal Alex Theatre in Birmingham. The much married Alan J. Lerner and Rex got into the second taxi, with Mercia, Rex's sixth wife. Don said he felt an overwhelming and almost irresistible desire to call out to the pedestrians and passers-by: 'Hey, do you people realize there are fourteen marriages in that car!'

Although Rex professed a long-standing and genuine friend-ship with Richard Burton, as with so many of his friends, that relationship was ambiguous. Richard Burton, whom I hardly knew at all, was speedily consigned to the not unfamiliar role, along with Laurence Olivier, Dirk Bogarde, and David Niven, of '*your* friend Burton'. I had met him only on one previous occasion, and that was many years before, when he came to visit his friend John Gielgud in my production of *Forty Years On*, when he was recently married to Elizabeth Taylor. They caused a great stir to those in the audience, and it must be said, to the boys on stage, who delighted in observing Miss Taylor's prominent Diamond as Big as the Ritz, which she displayed rather ostenta-tiously on her left hand. I was to meet Richard Burton on several subsequent occasions, because we were in fraternal productions touring America, and often one preceded the other, and most of those occasions were in the company of Rex. Richard Burton upon these occasions was the spirit of generosity and friend-liness, however I cannot say quite as much for the attitude of Rex. There was one occasion, that Richard Burton told me about himself, when he had invited Rex and Mercia over to have dinner with him and his then wife Suzy. It was a very agreeable occasion and they enjoyed an excellent dinner, exchanged dozens of comical stories – most of them directed against Hollywood and producers – and they drank a good deal of excellent claret. To keep the cheerful atmosphere going Rich-ard Burton, without any thought casually put a record on to the turn-table which happened, quite by chance, to be the original long playing record of *Camelot*. Nobody commented on this at the time, and Richard Burton was not even conscious of having put on any particular record, it was simply for background effect.

However when the Harrisons were leaving and Mercia was walking towards the limousine which had been waiting outside to collect them, Rex in shaking his friend's and host's hand warmly, paused, and on departing said: 'When you have friends to dine with you Richard, do you always play your own fucking recordings!'

At one stage in his career, a little low on his luck, and empty-handed in his film career, at a three-handed table with Burton and his agent, the conversation lingered too long over the subject of Richard playing first Tito in one film, and then Trotsky in another. Rex snarled:

'Yes, you'd be very good as Tito, Richard, and Trotsky. It takes a peasant to play a peasant.' At which, Burton laughed good-humouredly. But he was used to that kind of comment by then. In his Old Vic days, Burton was lingering in his dressing-room after a play, *Coriolanus* probably, and surrounded by his Welsh family, all gabbling in Welsh together. John Gielgud, who had a dinner date with him, burst in without knocking, and after a horrified look around the Welsh relatives, said: 'Oh, I'll come back later, Richard, when you're better. I mean, *ready*!'

Burton had his own story about Rex and the occasion of a vivid altercation with an Italian *bersagliere*, over-enthusiastic at the customs desk, when Rex and one of his many wives were on their travels. Not surprisingly Rex travelled with a great deal of baggage wherever he was going, and on this occasion – in Rome airport during the filming of *Cleopatra* – Rex resolutely refused to unpack his bags when asked by a somewhat officious Italian customs officer. Voices were raised to a hysterical level, and as Rex never spoke a word of any language other than his own the argument was unsatisfactory on all sides. Nor was the confrontation helped by the fact that Rex was very tall and the Italian customs officer comically small, and finally, towering above him, Rex snapped furiously: 'And *take your hat off* when you're talking to *me*! You pompous buffoono!' This caused a row of international status, and rose up to the highest possible diplomatic levels, as the Italians maintained that Rex Harrison by insulting an officer in uniform had deliberately insulted the Italian flag. Eventually it was only settled by Rex making a formal apology to the officer, the Italian president, and finally to the entire Italian nation.

But, it must be acknowledged, that 'my friend Burton', as Rex would have it, also had a difficult, even duplicitous side. When *Camelot* began rehearsals, according to the two producers, both Richard Burton, and the director, Frank Dunlop, expressed themselves completely satisfied with the courageous casting of an unknown girl, fresh out of the chorus, as Queen Guinevere, and to the producers' dismay she swiftly proved herself virtually hopeless. She sang sweetly enough but was unable to act at any level. It was not her fault, she was perfectly happy with a role in the chorus, she was a singer not an actress, and profoundly inexperienced. When they delicately sounded out Richard Burton's opinion, as the star, he announced himself totally confident, and in a vote of solidarity and commitment, suggested that if he were ever to play Othello in the near future he would like this girl to be his Desdemona. A few more days passed by, and not only did she not improve, it seemed she steadily got worse. A week later, however, Burton spoke to his agent, and the agent telephoned Don Gregory that the great man no longer wanted to be treated like Richard Burton but insisted on being 'directed'. 'What does that mean?' asked Don to the agent, 'he *is* being directed.'

The agent replied, 'Well, I think it means he's unhappy.'

'Unhappy with what?'

'The girl playing opposite him.'

'Guinevere?'

'Yes, I guess so.'

'But *he* chose her.'

'Well, I think he wants to let her go.'

'So,' said Don Gregory, 'whenever the star says, "don't treat me like the star, but give me direction", what he really means to say is you must recast Guinevere. Or, conversely, if the guy playing Othello wants an unknown kid from the chorus to be his Desdemona, what he really is trying to say is "get rid of the girl".' They got rid of the girl.

When I arrived in New York to begin rehearsals for *My Fair Lady*, the rehearsals for *Camelot* had been going on for several

43

weeks. Some of the stage management team from *Camelot*, having achieved all they needed to achieve, were now moving on to my production, which was rehearsing in 55th Street. Several of them were sitting around in rehearsal during a pre-production meeting, among them Bud Whitney, who was one of Alan J. Lerner's most intimate friends, and who had worked as an assistant twenty-five years earlier on the original Moss Hart production of *My Fair Lady*. At this stage in rehearsals, the unknown chorus girl who everybody had been so keen on to play Guinevere, by this time had been painfully sacked (or, euphemistically 'let go') and the principal role of Guinevere had been taken over by a fairly well-known New York actress called Christine Ebersole. This young lady was every bit as striking in her looks as she was accurate in the top Cs and Gs that the role of Guinevere asked for. It had not escaped the notice of the production team, presently sitting round with paper cups of coffee in the *My Fair Lady* rehearsal room, that Christine Ebersole, whether knowingly, or indeed quite innocently, had caught the eye and attention of the seven-times married but now safely divorced lyric writer of the show, Mr Alan J. Lerner himself. Bud said sagely that he was quite convinced that Alan was crazy about her. I felt something of a new boy with these disenchanted Broadway musical veterans sitting all round me, and I didn't feel it was my place to bend their ears with the latest gossip, so adopting a somewhat timid note I ventured to say that the word around the British musical comedy circuit made claim that Alan J. Lerner had very much fallen for the beautiful Eliza of the London stage-version, namely Liz Robertson. This comment was greeted with a chorus of scorn by my colleagues: 'No, it's the American Guinevere he's crazy about,' they chorused, 'he's mad about Christine Ebersole. Every time she's up there on the stage rehearsing a song, Alan's up there with her taking her through it, teaching her the lyrics, darting back into the stalls again, and behaving in every way like he's crazy about her.' I doggedly stuck to my version, which I knew was the right one and beyond mere showbiz gossip. 'No,' I said, 'I think you'll find that the reality is Alan is very much in love with the English Eliza, and without being in the slightest bit chauvinistic, I think you'll find that this romance has been in the British newspapers, and in fact just before I came over to New York, I read in the *Daily Mail* that Alan and Liz Robertson are engaged to be married.' There was a short pause, and then Bud Whitney ventured to observe: 'Patrick, there's something you ought to know. When Alan J. Lerner asks a girl to marry him, it's his way of saying goodbye.'

A few weeks later while we were still ploddingly rehearsing, *Camelot* opened in, I believe, Toronto, at the O-Keefe Centre, a draughty Barn which seats three and a half thousand people. So vast is it that when the Royal Ballet dance there, one of the principal dancers told me, the Company have to stagger the choreography and slow it down, as there is a distinct time-lag between the sound waves from the point in the orchestra pit when they leave the stage, and the acoustic at the back of the vast auditorium. I knew, from an unmistakable note of glee in his voice, when Rex telephoned me from his apartment overlooking the Hudson river the morning after the show had opened, that the reception of *Camelot* could not have been all that happy. 'I see that your friend Burton has opened in *Camelot*,' he announced, 'and the reactions are not all that good for him!'

'Have you read some New York notices for it?' I asked.

'No, but I've spoken to The Boys up in Toronto, and I hear they fired the girl and fired the director. They say the show overran by at least an hour, the scenery jammed, and the reception wasn't as good as they'd hoped.'

'And what was the response to Richard Burton?' I enquired.

'Well,' and here Rex had a rather puzzled note in his voice, 'according to The Boys, Mr Burton spoke it very well when he could remember his lines, and did the last scene very movingly, and apparently he got a great response from the customers, but according to Mike Merrick, there was something the matter with his arm. I couldn't make out what Merrick was trying to say, or what his arm had to do with it.'

There was a short pause and Rex began again, 'Maybe Burton acts with his arm.' 'Burton's arm' became something of a running gag with Rex, and every time he met The Boys, he always enquired about the state of Burton's arm. But this was not the only drama going on in Toronto. Richard Burton hadn't been married for a very long time to his fourth and (as it turned out) penultimate wife Susan, and Don Gregory told me that all had gone quite well at the previews until the moment came when he and his wife were sitting next to his partner Mike Merrick, and his wife, Annie, with Suzy Burton in the middle. They were all talking animatedly together, having been the best of friends through the difficult technical rehearsals and try-out period, and as they leafed through their souvenir programmes, Don's wife Kaye noticed something which made her blood freeze. In the souvenir programme among the many illustrations, there was a reproduction of a newspaper photograph of Richard Burton and Elizabeth Taylor shortly after they were married. Kaye had noticed Suzy Burton's eye fall on to the same offending photograph, and from that moment on the laughter and good cheer vanished and she remained ominously silent. At the interval instead of joining them for drinks in the bar she muttered some mild excuse and disappeared. All of them feared the worst. It was not long in arriving. The next morning Richard Burton's agent telephoned to insist that they would have to reprint the souvenir programmes for the run at the O-Keefe Centre. He was very sorry about it, but the photograph had deeply offended the new Mrs Burton, and the star of the show was insisting that changes had to be made. Don Gregory had only one course of action before him, and he took it, even though in his heart he felt certain it was a battle he would lose. The next day he went round to see Richard Burton in his dressing-room. 'I suppose you've seen the souvenir programme, Richard?'

'Yes.'

'Do we really have to destroy all those programmes just for that photograph of you and Liz Taylor?'

Richard Burton looked uncomfortable, and sympathetic, but explained there was really nothing he could do about it. It was not his will, but his wife was absolutely insistent. Don tried hopefully to appeal to his decent side.

'But Richard, leaving musicals and show business and everything out of it, don't you agree that it is quite justifiable that the management should print a picture of you and Elizabeth Taylor. Don't you think that's reasonable?'

Richard said, 'I'm sure that it's entirely reasonable, Don, but there is nothing I can do about it. I'm afraid you're going to have to reprint the programmes.'

'But Richard,' pleaded Don, 'don't you realize there are 79,000 programmes printed for the entire run?'

'Yes.'

'Richard, that means we would have to reprint 79,000 souvenir programmes.'

'Yes.'

'But why? I appeal to you – not as producer to star – but as a friend, man to man . . .'

Richard Burton turned thoughtfully and morosely on his dressing-room chair and stared gently at his producer.

They had always got on very well together, and they understood one another at this moment.

'Don, you have to understand that I'm deeply uxorious.'

'What does that mean Richard?'

'It means Don, that I'm totally dominated by women. Completely in awe of my wife. I have been all my life. Submissive to every woman I've ever been married to. And I'm afraid to tell you that the result of my being uxorious is that you are going to have to pulp 79,000 souvenir programmes.'

And so it happened. The very next day the two producers, and the managers of the O-Keefe Centre hired additional extra staff, who may not have had to pulp and reprint all the programmes, but one by one, day and night for the next forty-eight hours before the play's opening premiere, they ripped out 79,000 copies of the photograph of Elizabeth Taylor and Richard Burton.

There is a famous Broadway story of a distinguished and much-loved actor who goes to visit a psychoanalyst. When the psychoanalyst asks him what he can do for him, the actor explains that in recent months he has found it impossible to learn his lines, that he feels a deadly sense of depression, that his skin comes out in ugly blotches, that he has an allergy to wearing make-up, that he is moody and restless with his fellow actors, that he has fired his agent, and that he is wanting to divorce his latest wife, and he is incapable of understanding what on earth is the matter with him. The psychoanalyst listens very patiently, and says finally: 'My dear sir, it's perfectly obvious what is the matter with you. You are terribly agitated by the prospect of acting, your profession has driven you into a nervous breakdown, you are clearly at the end of your tether, and my advice is very straightforward. You must give up acting.'

'What do you mean give up acting?' said the distinguished patient, 'I'm a star.'

Or, alternatively there is the story of the little boy who tells his father he is going to be an actor when he grows up. 'You can't do both, son,' replies Dad.

When finally Rex and I caught up with Richard Burton, it was at the Uris State Theatre in New York, on his tumultuous last night in *Camelot*. One of the last performances he was ever to give on the stage. Objectively speaking, it must be admitted most of the show was rather terrible (it's a terrible show anyway), and much of the time Richard Burton seemed to stand rooted to the spot centre stage, not giving away much energy, neither singing nor dancing with any particular distinction or involvement. And, yes, there *was* something the matter with his arm. But in the last scene he was magically and unbelievably moving in the speech of the once-and-future King to the little boy, and that high trumpet Welsh tone rang out as if blazoning his troops to scale the Heights of Mount Abraham. It was a truly electrifying and glorious demonstration, and those ten minutes at the end somehow made up for everything, and reverberate in my memory as freshly today as they did then. Richard Burton gave a very moving farewell speech, and with the tender grace which in his finest moments only he was capable of, he paid a generous tribute from the stage saying that as he lowered the standard of King Arthur and abandoned the stage of the Uris State Theatre where he had been so happy for so long, 'I now make way for the Incomparable Rex'. The entire audience rose to its feet and stood and cheered the two great veterans of the eloquent school of English acting to the rafters. I, on my feet beside them, felt very privileged to be Richard Burton's friend.

Oh, there was one tiny incident after the performance, a coda worth remembering. Rex and Richard met and embraced, and gossiped away with affectionate enthusiasm in Burton's dressing-room.

'You should have been here the other night,' said Burton, 'darling Johnny Gielgud came round after the show. I wasn't sure whether he'd met Suzy before so I introduced her.'

'Have you met my wife, Johnny?'

'Oh yes,' said John Gielgud, 'but not for a long time. Why Sybil, you've changed the colour of your hair, since I saw you last.'

Richard and Sybil Burton (his first wife) had been married about twenty-five years, and three divorces, earlier.

Chapter 11

HURRICANE ALAN

In August, I heard Alan J. Lerner was back in London, bruised and unwell from his searing experience with *1600 Pennsylvania Avenue*. This was intended to have been a great tribute to the history of the White House, but in spite of a staggering score and some impressive lyrics, it never succeeded in focusing itself, and sprawled like the carcass of an ungainly whale stranded on a beach. Besides, it was interminable. When it opened in Philadelphia the curtain went down at twelve midnight and the audience were sent home with the Second Act still incomplete. Seduced by an eloquent largely black ensemble, Leonard Bernstein and Alan Lerner, where they should have cut ruthlessly, equally ruthlessly added, and wrote more and more swooning chorales for the cast. This gave rise to the legend back in New York that Alan Lerner and Lenny Bernstein had returned from Philadelphia having freed the slaves.

One of the finest things in the show (and it *is* most impressive) was the song Patricia Routledge sang, as Abigail, the wife of President John Adams to a diminutive black page. It was called 'Take Care Of This House' and is the best piece salvaged from a wreckage as monumental as the Titanic. Ignorant of American history, I referred to it as *1300 Pennsylvania Avenue* in a letter to the famous agent Robbie Lantz. He wrote back 'There were a lot of things wrong with Lennie Bernstein's musical, but getting the address of the White House incorrect wasn't one of them.' Patricia Routledge told me she saw Leonard Bernstein one day at the back of the stalls at a run-through, weeping into his coat-sleeve. With some concern she ran up to him:

'Lenny, what is it? What's the matter?'

'It's my music,' he answered, through his sobs, 'it's *so* beautiful.'

Alan was always a turbulent presence at rehearsal, however, and throughout *Camelot* there were frequent rows between him and the director, Frank Dunlop, if and when he interfered.

'Watch out fellows, here's Hurricane Alan! Gale Force 180!' warned Bud Whitney. And with good reason. When he advised one of the actors to 'do it like so-and-so, in the original production, he used to bring the house down', the producer Don Gregory had had enough. 'Alan,' he said, gently advising him to quit his own show, 'you are proving to be counter-productive.'

His final show, *Will You Dance a Little Closer*, had many beauties to admire, but it just couldn't work, and was popularly known in the musical world as *Will You Close a Little Faster*. Which it did, opening and closing the same night, in May 1983, the last show Alan J. Lerner ever wrote.

Returning then to London, back from a holiday in the West Indies, tanned and glistening with health, Alan waved down a taxi with a frenzied kind of tribal dance. As the taxi-driver drew up to the diminutive half-blind figure on the pavement, after a long hard look at him, he answered: 'Blimey guv'nor, for one moment there, I thought you was Sammy Davis Junior.' He was always so frenetic and anxious and ill at ease, biting down his nails to their quicks. But I loved the man. He was so fascinating in his infinite knowledge of theatre, such a vivid storyteller, lover of women, and so unusually naive and romantic amid his worldly and professional life. In August I visited him, and, with news of *Camelot* and *My Fair Lady* and Bud and Rex, cheered him up, I think. His work was firing on, in spite of his absence on the other side of the Atlantic ocean.

'I sit here alone all day, and see only shadows,' he said in a faltering voice.

Alan told Mike Merrick that after Rex won the Oscar for his role of Professor Higgins, in the film of *My Fair Lady* – in which George Cukor collected the statue for Best Director and Jack L. Warner, for Best Picture – he was uncharacteristically and selflessly determined that Alan should have an Oscar too, even retrospectively. In fact, to Alan's acute discomfort, he was on the warpath about it, and determined to create a scandal. 'This is ridiculous, Alan, it's absurd that the director and producer pick up an Oscar, and the true creators, you and dear old Fritz, get fuck all! It's not right and I'm not going to stand for it.' It was discernible, Rex was less enthusiastic that the Eliza might have picked up an Oscar as well, but he never rated Audrey Hepburn's performance as noteworthy of any credit at all; besides, she didn't even sing it herself. It was 'a voice in the wings' as he put it. Alan thought this was simply a passing phase on Rex's part, an altruistic inconsistency which would soon drift away; but to his surprise, this time it didn't, and Rex seemed to be determined to drum up support among the Academy, to award Lerner and Loewe some kind of honorary Oscar. 'It's going very well, Alan, I've got several hundred people all ready to sign their names to a petition – this is an extreme injustice, on the part of the Academy, which has got to be rectified. I insist upon it! Had I known you were going to be left out, I'd have made a scene at the ceremony on the night, and refused to accept my Oscar.' As much as Alan Lerner genuinely tried to put Rex off the scent, he stubbornly went on insisting. One evening, during his campaign to set right chivalrously what he esteemed to be a wretched wrong, Rex drove home to Alan's apartment in New York, where he was living at the time. Following Alan up the stairs, into his book-lined study, for a chat and a bottle of wine, Rex suddenly observed, standing somewhat like a line of sentries, the three Oscars Alan Lerner had formerly won, two for *Gigi* (out of nine!) Best Screenplay and Best Song, and Best Screenplay for *An American in Paris*. Rex stared at the golden statuettes in a kind of anguished horror.

'What are these, Alan? Are they *real*?'

'Sure, of course they're real. They're my three Oscars.'

'Then what the fuck are you complaining about, Alan!' spluttered the indignant Rex, and that was the last time the subject of the elusive Oscar for *My Fair Lady* was ever heard of.

In January 1981, one evening I went to talk to Alan, presumably about the troubles we were finding or not finding with Eliza, and the difficulties we were also discovering with Rex's total resistance to reality, and found him in sombre mood.

'You've got to get the girl who can hit the top G, at the end of "Dance All Night",' Alan said to me. It was proving difficult to find an English Eliza, and Rex was implacably opposed to an American one. 'Oh, the music,' he burst out, 'for Christ's sake you're talking about the music! I've never listened to that. That's something that goes on behind my back, when I'm on my way to my dressing-room to change into my Ascot togs.' Which reminded me of the occasion when Jack Gwillim, who played Colonel Pickering to perfection, said for him, 'singing was a side activity'.

'Got it in one,' smiled Rex, '*My Fair Lady*, or "Fuck the Music".'

Sadly, I explained to Alan that Rex was singularly ungiving at this stage, isolated in his selfishness, arrogance, and unreasonableness.

'I know it,' said Alan, picking fiercely at the quicks of his nails, 'Rex is so cruel and horrible to me these days. He rang my secretary last month, and asked her sharply: "Where's your boss?" When she replied: "On safari," he snapped: "Well, I hope he meets a hungry lion."'

Chapter 12

SUMMERTIME, AND THE SINGING
IS EXTREMELY DIFFICULT

THE LONG THREE-YEAR experience (and never a moment wasted) of *My Fair Lady* second time round, took off in late March 1980, in a set of impersonal rehearsal rooms fifty floors up a Times Square skyscraper. Musical auditions, open to everyone, a sort of 'cattle-call.'

It had been schizophrenic weather in New York all winter, and March was no exception. 'The City's weather needs to go into therapy,' said the stage manager, gazing up at the alternating snowstorms and spring sunshine, 'March needs analysis.' We were sitting around in Julie's casting-office, schmoozing. I never quite discovered what 'schmoozing' consists of, it has a sexual ring to it, but that was apparently what we were doing. Talking back and forth, really.

Julie's office eighty-five stories up, towers above the City. Drizzle up high as this freezes into heavy snowflakes dripping out of the cloud, but lower down, at street-level it melts into cold rain. Puddles and lakes of slush splash out from passing taxis. A transit strike adds to our difficulties. All within is warm, friendly, competitive. In the cinema nearby I see billed 'The World's Worst Film Festival'. Everything in New York, even catastrophe, is excessive. We are studying last year's posters for the New York Metropolitan opera programme.

Bob Kriese, the deputy Musical Director, says: 'I had a girl-friend in the Meistersinger ballet, at the Met, and I'd ask her, "Who conducted you this evening?" And she'd say, "I don't know – I never looked – it's so long, we all hate it, we just want to go home."' We sympathize over our cardboard coffee cups.

Crandall Diehl, the choreographer, usually referred to dispar-

54

agingly by Rex as 'the Number One Boy' (which he had been twenty-five years ago in the original production as a teenager) is telling us about some of the shortened touring versions of *MFL* he experienced: 'Henry Higgins used to *speak*: "Why can't a woman be more like a man?", then *cut* the rest of the scene.'

First it is pre-production, then auditions, and looking for Eliza, then rehearsals, and finally the tour. Broadway is rather like an alluring island far off in the distant ocean.

For the singing auditions, for the first time I meet the conductor of *My Fair Lady*, *Camelot*, and *Gigi*, first time round – and guest baton at the Vienna State Philharmonic, Franz Allers. White-haired, characteristically Viennese, later I discover he was born Czechoslovakian, talks and behaves like a German, and is an American citizen. His first comment at auditions is endearing, when he sees an attractive Jewish girl, who gives a respectable version of a Leonard Bernstein aria from *Candide*: speaking in a bold stage-whisper intended only for our ears, he declares: 'Another one of my race, I see. I'm completely anti-Semitic, just as much as I'm anti-German. I only like music.'

The first afternoon is unsatisfactory for all of us. The coffee cups accumulate, the choreographer dozes, Franz grumbles: 'We seem to have been subjected to a plethora of bad sounds.' Around 4 p.m., after a resolutely plain mezzo-soprano has impressed him, Franz announces: 'Mezzo-sopranos of this quality don't grow on trees, so we can be a little tolerant towards ugliness: however, ugliness by itself is not recommendation enough.' I discover how soon Franz gets irritable with those who insist on singing for too long. 'Please send out the word,' he orders the assistant, 'we want sixteen bars *only*, not thirty-two. We are quite adamant about that. We will stop them in the middle of a note, if need be.' One girl comes in and sings only six words: 'Summertime, and the living is easy . . .', before Franz stops her: 'Summertime, and the living may be easy, but the singing, unfortunately is extremely difficult – next lady, please!' Then, turning to me, he whispers, none too quietly: 'You know my middle initial is B, and it stands for Brutality. Franz Brutality Allers.'

Another girl comes in, and we study her résumé. She has

written: 'My roles are on my CV, but irrespective of what they express, I am pretty happy with myself'. Bob Kriese says: 'This girl has an attitude problem.' Later still, a black girl comes in and sings exquisitely something from *Porgy*. She is a delectably pretty girl, but after a quick glance to Crandall Diehl, to see if she will do, he gives a sad shake of his head. 'She's pretty, she sings well but I just can't see her in the Ascot Enclosure in 1910,' I say.

'You English are so racist,' grumbles Franz. 'In Vienna once, I had a black Desdemona and a white Othello. And I remember also in Bayreuth once seeing a black Brunnhilde, who was superb. But Wieland Wagner's production was so dark, that nobody noticed.'

Bud Whitney and Frank Dunlop come in to join us, greet Franz, and then sit around discussing musical problems about *Camelot*. In a kind of gruesome free-for-all, they begin setting about our auditions, and make nearly-overheard wisecracks behind our backs. It would be irritating, were it not so damn funny. And accurate. Discussing a rival no-hope musical about to open, Bud Whitney says: 'I hear the box-office is pretty quiet.' Bob answers: 'Quiet? It's fucking taciturnity out there.' An old lady with pretensions comes in, claiming, poignantly, that this is her first 'Chorus Call' (presumably 'an actress'). Franz explains she is auditioning for the part of the old lady Rex wants as the housekeeper. To which Bud replies, not over-quietly: 'Or the mother of the old lady . . .'

By the second day, our uncleaned rehearsal-room takes on the shape of the morning after the night before of a teenager's prom party.

The rehearsal pianist tries to make the occasion an acceptable one by playing with sensitivity and imagination for each auditionee, often signalling to us, by his expression and eyebrows, either his approval, or indeed, disapproval. A male singer, about to sing the solo from *Carousel* for the twentieth time ('When you walk through the streets, with your head up high'), adds: 'I guess you've already heard this from the man before . . .' 'Well,' says Franz, 'if you can sing it in tune, you're in with a chance.' A blind girl sings for us. It is such courage. Franz is moved. Bob has seen her before. She is well known to turn up to audition for big shows, like ours, which she knows she cannot get into, but with what bravery and determination. The pianist bursts into tears, and *he* is the one who needs cheering up. Still they pour in, one after the other, 'Hi, how're you doing?', sixteen bars, 'Thank you, have a nice day,' and on to the next. It seems clinical or bloodless, it appears superficial, but the truth must be acknowledged, Franz Allers is so accurate, so quick, so precise, he only needs to hear sixteen bars for his decision, sometimes, I suspect, not even that. After an edgy soprano had left the room, he says: 'That's what is called the celebrated rusty razor-blade sound. Diction you can teach, and interpretation, phrasing, breathing, volume, even the quality of the tone. But you cannot teach Ears. Next lady.' I have no doubt in my mind, hearing Franz say that, I will be quoting him in twenty years' time.

This has been my first real taste in New York of a style of musical competitiveness which has never existed in England. It is typical Broadway brutality, carrying on imperturbably through the lunch-break ('So, who brings in the hamburgers?') and reeling away dizzily at the end of the day with an auditions-hangover. Tables are littered with horrid half-consumed plastic plates of ersatz food, empty cans of Coca-Cola, pickled cucumbers, plastic forks, bottles of mineral water, soaked sachets of sweeteners, cardboard cups of cold coffee. And Franz, his cropped white head, and beaked nose, sits unwearily, sizing up, condemning, criticizing, complaining, congratulating, judging. We exchange eyebrows of rejection or acceptance. Not always with perfect patience. When somebody politely wishes us goodbye, Franz interrupts: 'All right, no farewells – next lady!'

Near the end of the day, our grip slackens, and we begin perceptibly to lose ground, and overrun. The head spins, the same songs reverberate, all sense of distinction collapses. Even more singers are queuing up – none of us dare venture out of the room, not even for a cigarette, or a phone-call, or a pee; we are holed up, besieged by hundreds of unknown people who keep threatening to sing to us. It's like Hollywood – everybody auditions for you.

You want a cup of coffee, they audition. The stage manager says: 'How about we audition them, ten at a time.' Just to make some impact on the overwhelming numbers. It strikes a nerve of compassion even in Franz: 'Oh, no, that would be intolerable to us, and inhuman to them. We are cruel enough as it is.'

Earlier on, over the hamburgers hastily stuffed, during a snatched 'no-show', the talk gets round once more to the last musical Alan Lerner had written with Leonard Bernstein, *1600 Pennsylvania Avenue*, Arthur Schwartz had gone on record, prophesying it would be a disaster because, 'on the road, when a show is in *big* trouble, you can make it better – you can never make it good.' Or as Richard Rodgers used to say: 'When the book isn't right, the scenery doesn't fit in Philadelphia.'

We weaken under the weight of countless 'Old Man River's, and 'Over The Rainbow's. I look forward eagerly to the wistful poetry and worldliness of Stephen Sondheim. 'A pity we called all the girls in the morning,' said Bob, 'with only men in the afternoon, there's nothing left for us to look forward to.' A moment of theatrical magic takes place when a girl – rather an aggressive girl, actually – transposed up an octave the melody of Richard Rodgers' hit song, 'You'll Never Walk Alone'. Franz said sternly: 'The great man didn't like it when anybody recomposed his songs – not one bit.' 'Perhaps he would have liked it, if he'd heard my top note,' argued the girl. This angered Franz. 'No, he would not. He was much ruder than me. He would chuck anybody out, if they altered his song. After all, Beethoven wrote: "da-da-da-Daah!" in his Fifth Symphony, not "da-da-da-Deeh"!'

At the exhausted end of the auditions, I go back to my hotel on 57th Street, the Salisbury, and collapse into a lukewarm bath – Franz flies off to Miami, Crandall to Las Vegas to choreograph a show for Siegfried and Roy, the incredible Illusionists. Bob packs his case, saying: 'That's quite enough day for me!'

After three days and two hundred singers auditioning, I realize, without my notes, I can barely remember a solitary one of them, what they sang or what they sounded like. That night, I dream countless songs by Gershwin, Porter, Rodgers, Hart, Loewe, Sondheim, Lloyd-Webber, being sung over and over by the front-desk receptionists at the Hotel Salisbury. Wystan Auden's lines 'On the Circuit' bleed into my brain:

> *Though warm my welcome everywhere,*
> *I shift so frequently, so fast,*
> *I cannot now say where I was*
> *The evening before last,*
>
> *Unless some singular event*
> *Should intervene to save the place,*
> *A truly asinine remark,*
> *A soul-bewitching face.*

And all the time, Rex Harrison's unbidden disapproval thunders across the Atlantic as we vainly searched for an Eliza from New York. What none of us realized was that Rex was essentially uninterested in a perfect Eliza. As André Previn observed about casting the 1963 film, 'Did Rex Harrison want Julie Andrews or Audrey Hepburn for the movie? He didn't want *anybody*. Whatever fuss was made about Miss Doolittle was pointless, because nobody was interested in the girl. They were only interested in *him*.'

Chapter 13

STYLE – PUTTING ON THE RITZ

WHILE WE WERE sweating through the rank and file chorus, where was Rex all this time? Now March had grudgingly yielded to a more genial April. The geyser spouts of boiling steam which gushed out of the manholes of New York's crumbling streets were less extreme. Figures appeared on roller-skates, wearing Sony Walkmans like diminutive ear-muffs. Children patrolled the streets on the upper East Side beside the Park, holding balloons in their hands on long strings. I left New York with a lingering look backwards at the sun setting behind the Queensboro' Bridge, and returned to London.

'Memsahib and I are staying at the Ritz,' said Rex airily referring to Mrs Harrison number six. 'Last time it was the Savoy, but it all seemed a bit far away.' I had asked him once before, which was his preferred hotel, when staying in London.

'I think I like the Ritz, although the Savoy always looks after me very well. The grub's good, but they've changed the Grill Room around, when I last went there, it was all in the wrong place, and there was nowhere for me to put my hat! But everything's such a long way away.'

The reason he enjoyed the Ritz, was, he said, because it was so handy. 'I can walk to my tailors in Jermyn Street, get my shirts from Turnbull & Asser, Lobbs for my boots, Locks for my hats, Wiltons for a little fish, Berry Bros. for the booze, Hatchards for books, and George Trumper for my hair. It's all just round the corner.' His litany of West End pleasures continued after a few moments further consideration:

'In fact the Ritz is handier altogether. After the show, I can slip into the Mirabelle, where they keep a special table for me, there's Fortnums up the road, just a stone's throw, if Mercia wants to go shopping, and there's Moyses Stevens for my flowers, in Berkeley Square.' He might also have mentioned his clubs nearby, the Garrick and the Beefsteak, and his preferred theatre, like Sir Ralph Richardson's, was always the Theatre Royal, in the Haymarket. In a way Rex was the perfect Regency West End man. I could imagine him in the early 1800s, walking confidently down St James's, looking up at George Brummell on the balcony of Boodles, seeking approval for his necktie, or the cut of his coat, and probably finding it.

When I was in the army, stationed with a Royal Horse Artillery regiment in, of all unexpected places, Southend-on-Sea, there was an historic figure, a mere two-stripe man, called Bombardier Partner. He was notorious, as much as the Gunner, the celebrated Beecroft, who introduced himself to the Queen at a horse-show where the RHA were participating. Recognizing the familiar cavalry uniform, as she walked through the tents, the Queen exclaimed to one of her aides-de-camps: 'Oh, King's Troop.' The scruffy Gunner drew himself to attention and threw up a salute, as if addressed personally: 'Yes, ma'am,' he replied, introducing himself, 'Beecroft, ma'am.' Obviously Gunner Beecroft had class. But even more so, in his manner, had Bombardier Partner. Although to the world at large a mere Corporal in rank, every Friday night, he would strip off his khaki, and dress himself in a smart rat-catcher suit, throw on a cream riding-mac, tuck a copy of *The Times* under his arm, stick a cheesecutter on his head, and swagger confidently into the foyer of the local flea pit. As the Manager of the cinema fawningly approached, Bombardier Partner, every inch a Regular Lieutenant in mufti would say: 'Good evening to you. Just seeing how the lads are getting on.' And the Manager, deeply impressed, would show him personally to a comfortable seat in the back stalls. This simple action of confidence and illusion was successfully carried out by Bombardier Partner throughout his year as a National Service Bombardier.

If Beecroft had a sort of class, Bombardier Partner undoubtedly showed he had Style. It is in this way I have frequently thought of and admired Rex. Perhaps this is what Noël Coward was referring to when he told Harrison, after some rage or other: 'If you weren't the second-best high comedian in the country, you'd be selling second-hand cars in Park Lane.' Himself being the best, I suppose.

This takes us into the shady area of deception and illusion – as in a story I once heard from the Governor of Oxford jail. He told me one of the most worrying tragedies he had ever had to deal with was of a confidence trickster, an embezzler of sorts, who despaired and hanged himself with his Old Etonian tie. Only it turned out, upon examination, the man never went to Eton. True to style, however. But Rex Harrison must not be confused with a con-man, even if his persona was to a certain extent self-invented. Rex was an actor. If he appeared the epitome of the traditional English gentleman as well, this was because he acted the part, not because he looked for the social advantages of the English gent.

It was well attested, when Rex first came to Hollywood in the late forties, those legendary stars, Gary Cooper, Clark Gable, and Jimmy Stewart, all accepted him admiringly as the epitome of the English gentleman. In fact, endearingly, when Elizabeth Harrison recently married to him was showing him round the beautiful mansion, Beauchamp in St Jean-Cap Ferrat, fit for 'un milord anglais', Rex suddenly exclaimed: 'I can't possibly live here, Elizabeth, I'm only an actor.'

Another illustration of style which had formerly caught my fancy, was told me by the legendary Madame Prunier of the famous St James's restaurant. When she was regaling myself and some other friends of hers over a particularly ghostly turbot soufflé, which with an exemplary Pouilly Fumé represented one of the most delicate meals I've ever had the privilege of tasting, of some of the distinguished visitors to her restaurant, among them General de Gaulle and Maurice Chevalier, naturally; I was somewhat surprised, however, to hear that the Cardinal Archbishop of Paris had a room set aside for him by Madame Prunier in the Paris restaurant, so 'the Cardinal Archbishop could visit the restaurant privately', said Madame Prunier politely, 'in order to celebrate his Easter fast. Oh, he was a man of great delicacy,' said Madame Prunier wistfully, 'he was always most discreet, retiring to a private room at Prunier's to celebrate "ses petits riens".' Evidently, a Cardinal Archbishop of some character and style.

One evening, when I was watching *My Fair Lady*, standing next to him in the wings (a romantic 'Degas-eye view' of the performance captured poetically in a refracted light), I heard Rex quietly and persistently clearing his throat. 'Hmmm! Hmmm . . . !' It was a very muted, confidential sound, much like the surprisingly modest 'ahem' made by the silver-back gorillas.

'Have you got a bit of throat-trouble, Rex?'

'No,' he replied, 'just doing my voice exercises. Hmmm . . . hmmm!'

The wisest and wittiest of that great age of Hollywood agents, of the *ancien régime*, frequently refugees from Hitler's Berlin, Robbie Lantz, told me once of a magical evening he had spent with Rex and Mercia and a small but glittering group of friends at La Colombe d'Or, in St Paul de Vence; he remembers that for much of the evening, Rex was talking with extreme passion and lucidity about the glories of *À la recherche du temps perdu*. But could Rex have ever read Proust? I doubt it, somehow; but that would not deter him from talking eloquently on the subject of the Duchesse de Guermantes, Albertine, and the Baron de Charlus. It's difficult to describe, taking place in a kind of heavenly dumb-show (something from a Jacques Tati film) but I also witnessed Rex one day at Nice airport, working through an entire wine-list, with a waiter who not only spoke nothing but French, but assumed Rex was speaking French also.

The only way Rex could be remotely persuaded – many months later, on tour in Boston – to agree to a change of cast from the ailing English Eliza, was for him to see the American understudy, Nancy Ringham, during a matinée, and that meant, formally, for Rex to be 'off'. He was always, what is virtually a theatrical cliché, 'a consummate professional', and missed very few performances for a man of his age considering the demands of the role and his seventy-five years. The contemporary comedian who dashes off-stage from fright, unhappy notices, and other whey-faced timidities, was not in Mr Harrison's calendar. But, after many blandishments and guileful plaudits on our part, with great reluctance, Rex did finally agree to watch from the auditorium *one* matinée performance. And, it was made a stern condition, only if he was so thoroughly disguised, 'the customers' (as he called the public) could not possibly recognize him. This was agreed, and once accepted, became something of a schoolboy charade, and hence rather fun. Rex took the disguise as seriously as he took everything else, and was determined to make a professional job of things; needless to say, at great expense, an entire suit of tailor-made clothes was hired from Brooks Brothers in New York, and there was the usual business of the handmade shirts. Even more elaborate was the make-up, the hair-piece, and the beard. By this time, Rex was intrigued by the idea of this extra-mural perform-ance as a simple member of the audience, or General Public, and a great deal of preparation was devoted to it. Should he wear a full wig, and beard, should he have sideburns, should it be a moustache, white or brown, to match his hair? Should he wear make-up, or should he, as he said, 'aim for a Royal Court effect and not wear make-up at all?' Mistakenly, I proposed a flattering five-and-nine with blue eye-shadow, in the style of one of his spectacular bêtes noires, and the threatening forefinger lifted in my direction: 'I don't want to look a c**t, Patrick.'

Finally, he decided on a full wavy, white wig, which gave him some of the distinction of Paul Scofield as Salieri, and a white waxed moustache, and ministerial beard. He rejected the mous-tache pure and simple, as he felt 'it makes me look like that terrible Kentucky Fried Chicken arsehole . . .', and a generous spade-white beaver made him look like Clemenceau. We attempted the Edward VII look, which was almost too much 'the loveable old buffer' (not a role he craved), and our other efforts resulted in him complaining he looked like 'one of those low-comedy men from the RSC', which was possibly his most ferocious term of abuse. But when we stood away from him at his mirror – in attendance, his valet Walter, the wig-lady, two producers, the director, the dance-captain, the conductor, his lawyer, and I imagine the press-officer, Rex announced that he was highly delighted with the result. I fear that not one of us had paid anywhere near the same attention to the nervous understudy, just about to play Eliza, trembling no doubt in the Number Two dressing-room. But, that would have been the way Rex wanted it. In Number One, however, all was confident, relieved, even gratified. Standing his full six foot two or three, wearing a curiously old-fangled suit of traditional Brooks Brothers herringbone tweeds, almost like a caricature of an elderly senator in a Lubitsch comedy, or, even more, like any scene with Sir Cedric Hardwicke in it, Rex surveyed himself in the cheval-glass, as we admiringly hovered around:

'I look like one of those wonderfully well-preserved old-fashioned Savannah queens!' he announced delightedly. Certainly he was unrecognizable as Professor Henry Higgins.

The plan was for all of us, as a protective shield, to surround Rex on his circuitous way backstage, up and over galleries, fly-bridges, corridors, side-exits, and pass-doors, with the surreptitious shuffling of presidential assassins. We slipped, as unostentatiously as possible, into a cosy corner of the balcony stalls, three stories up – even a side-box would be too conspicuous it was felt – and it was pre-arranged none of the party would take their seats before the orchestra was well into the overture, and the audience's attention focused firmly in the direction of the stage. The usherette, at our signal, pulled back the curtain – we slunk in as a furtive group, and shovelled Rex into his seat in the midst of us. As we did so – it was an afternoon performance, you must remember – an outer door, beyond the curtain which led into the auditorium, opened at the same time, and one simple shaft of clear white light, momen-tarily, no longer than the opening and shutting of a door, fell comfortingly on Rex, in all his Colonel Saunders finery: 'Oh, look honey,' said one of the customers, right behind us in a loud stage-whisper, 'there's Rex Harrison!'

Thinking of Rex, I have often been reminded of those lines of, inevitably, Oscar Wilde's – they seem so appropriate: 'In matter of grave importance, *style* not sincerity, is the most important thing.'

Chapter 14

ANTECEDENTS

So, WHEN JACK MINSTER, long dead now but an urbane director
of social comedies said of his first job in *French Without Tears*, that
he wondered – as he stood on the balcony of the Liverpool
Playhouse after the dazzling first night in 1936 – whether life
would ever be as sweet again, there was some truth in it. 'Mind
you,' he went on, 'it was a pretty sensational cast. The up and
coming Trevor Howard, Roly Culver as the juvenile, the young
Katy Hammond, the emerging Jessica Tandy, and of course not
forgetting a spotty-faced butcher's son from Liverpool, who was a
high comedian of genius called Reginald Harrison.'

Rex liked to correct this impression by making it clear he
came from Huyton, not Liverpool; this substantial genteel suburb
which is to the big seaport what Edgbaston is to Birmingham. And
this was long before Harold Wilson put Huyton on the political
map, by choosing to represent it as his constituency in Parliament
in the 1950s. According to Rex, and more significantly, his sister
Sylvia, Countess de la Warr, his antecedents were virtually aristocratic. A romantic mist obscured the origins of the family fortune
in the late eighteenth and early nineteenth century, hinting darkly
at the Liverpool slave trade, but by his grandfather's time the
family lived in some provincial style. Then, probably in the
twenties the fortune foundered, and money declined during the
gradual laying off of merchant fleets. But it was always established
that Rex's grandfather did fall on hard times and that his father,
William, somehow or other lost hold of the family fortune, and
was declared bankrupt. It was even rumoured that Belle Vale was
turned into a jam factory and finally knocked down to make way
for a housing-estate.

William, his father, possessed the traditional family charm which Rex in later years inherited, perhaps from birth, and drifted through life with a singular nonchalance, a certain arrogance, combined with an indifference to work. Not unlike the curious father of Beatrix Potter at almost the same period, who trained as a barrister, but through a similar indifference to any form of industry, never practised the law, and spent his life mainly in his clubs or visiting friends. For William Harrison, perhaps it may be said, life to him was always associated with play. Later Rex informed me he was brought up with his two sisters at Derry House, Tarbock Road, Huyton, a characteristic suburban house with a large front lawn and laburnum tree shading the front gate. So where therefore did this rumour about Rex being the son of a butcher in Liverpool spring from? It's difficult to tell. Which is fiction?

In the short biographical film I made with Rex the year before he died, he trotted out the familiar story of his grandmother cruising the cascading lawns of Belle Vale Hall in her electric wheelchair, complaining of a sudden and catastrophic loss of funds. A Dickensian image of genteel poverty emerged, and maybe that is the correct one. However on our film, we had the services of the finest research assistant ITV could buy, and purely for the fun of it, I sent her up to Huyton to prowl around and find, if she could, old photographs of Belle Vale Hall, and if we were lucky Derry House. All these English cities have great pride in their heritage, and in the city councils generally files can be found containing visual evidence of Victorian and Edwardian suburbs. I can only report that this exemplary research assistant returned without any evidence that she could discover of Tarbock Road, Derry House or Belle Vale Hall. This is not to say that Rex was inventing his background and indeed much of the detail of those times came from his impeccable sister, Sylvia, Lady de la Warr, whose word was above reproach. Perhaps it was a family myth, reflecting an affluence and indifference to the realities of life which had been passed down through recent generations. Perhaps it wasn't a myth at all. I could find no evidence of Rex being the son of a butcher either, but Jack Minster's report was not the only one I heard of his original background. And finally, does it possibly matter? Not at all, there are important precedents for such an inheritance, especially that of Cardinal Wolsey, who was also a butcher's son, though not I believe from Huyton; but it does explain I think that Rex Harrison's early years were transformed and romanticized. What is worth mentioning about that period of his life, and is reported without dispute, is that from his fairly early years, Rex was very keen in putting on his own one-man productions. In fact, the very first performance he gave was around the age of eight or nine, intoxicated from the result of seeing pantomime in the Hippodrome in Liverpool, when he returned home and in front of the audience of his parents and sisters placed a couple of chairs between the curtains of a bay window and presented his performance. With an originality, and it has to be admitted, a confidence that informed his entire life, this first performance consisted of no performance at all other than the repeated taking of bows to the adulation and applause of his family. It can be fairly said that the taste Rex acquired for star billing began at an early age.

Chapter 15

PREMIER CRU

FAY WELDON WRITES: 'Disgraceful people often develop very rare and precise skills, so that others will be obliged to put up with them.' Quite right too, in my opinion (possibly not in hers), but certainly this was true of Mr Harrison. High-comedy acting was one of his rare and precise skills, and an apparent magisterial knowledge of wine was another. Not being there, and how much I wish I had, on the occasion of Rex holding forth on Marcel Proust, and the Guermantes in La Colombe d'Or and invariably, the conundrum of time-passing, I cannot say how convincing he was; but I expect he was pretty good. Many times I had been with him to observe his mastery of that elaborate art of selecting the right wine with the right dish. He seemed most at home, as I've said before, among the Premier Cru white burgundies, but I never saw him ill at ease within the complicated pages of a wine-list. Once at an elegant Italian 'dive', as Rex called it, on the upper East Side, despite all my frenetic nose-wrigglings, eyebrow-squirmings, hiccups and foot-nudgings, I was unable to prevent our two friendly producers, considerately they thought, handing over the wine-list to Rex in order for him to choose the wines. The dinner passed off most agreeably, the burgundy pronounced so admirable as to be ordered a second time, and even a third, but when the account arrived, I saw our two friends blanch the colour of their napkins. Rex had casually ordered the top of the list, and the bill for the wine came to $480.

'Never, ever ask Rex again to choose the wines,' I warned.

'There's no chance of that,' said Don, 'he's just used up the contingencies of the entire *My Fair Lady* budget!'

The astonishing thing was, according to Rex's great friend,

John Standing, the son of his famous co-star in *French Without Tears*, Kay Hammond, Rex knew nothing whatsoever about wine. But he always behaved as if he did. Furthermore, with the authority of André Simon or George Saintsbury. The wines at various dining-tables would ricochet back and forth with the speed of an artillery barrage, as bordeaux and burgundies, riojas and rieslings, *maître d's* and vinologists bustled about with bewildering rapidity. Wine waiters in England, when they ask whether the wine is acceptable, always make use of the 'nonne' interrogative, and are halfway through filling the first guest's glass, before an occasional wine-bibber might timidly volunteer: 'No, I think it could be a little cooler.' In Rex's case, the habitual response was: 'Christ! The bugger's corked,' and before the supercilious, and astounded waiter could regain his nerve, there would be an irritable summons: 'Fetch me the sommelier, *now*.'

I dreaded these occasions, although a number of them ended in rather cheerful relations, once due fuss had been made by the aforementioned sommelier, especially if he was in full-dress uni-form, *tastevin* on its silver chain in evidence, and a great deal of cork sniffing, and tasting and spitting and swizzling around the cheeks had gone on. John Standing assured me he had heard Rex send back a perfectly drinkable Chablis because 'the grapes were grown on the wrong side of the hill.' In other words, beneath the authority, the esoteric jargon, all of which had been admirably learnt and absorbed (like an actor assuming a role, dare I say) there was no knowledge, absolutely no education in viniculture *at all*. He had some excellent phrases, some of them, I believe, picked up and consigned to memory, from George Saintsbury's enchant-ing work: *Notes from a Cellar Book*. Smarting his lips over an unripe claret, he'd say: 'This is a bit boot-strappy,' or, more compassion-ately: 'It's all right on the nose, but I feel a little too much sun on it in September.' And woe betide a wine waiter who dared attempt to argue. For my part, however, I don't believe that Rex in all his 'performance' over the quality of a certain wine, should be thought more reprehensible than the score of experts we read today warbling and chirruping the most awful rubbish about vintages in their jubilant columns. Besides 'grapes grown on the wrong side of the hill', has a wistful poetry about it, a quality of 'où sont les neiges d'antan?', unless of course, you're a wine waiter.

His greatest triumph however, I believe, took place under John Standing's eager eye, one summer's evening in Rex's elegant Edwardian house, Beauchamp under the pines of Golfe Saint Jean. This was a frivolous weekend of celebration, storytelling, expeditions for good food and drink, and above everything else, to commemorate the ritual preparing, caressing, uncorking, inhaling, savouring and ultimately *drinking*, of a magnum of Château La Mission Haut-Brion, 1943, when the harvest was of great opulence and renown. A small group of theatrical 'chums' were invited to stay the weekend at Beauchamp, among them two particularly close friends, John Standing, and Jimmy Villiers, a colleague from the production of *Enrico Quattro* of Pirandello (and by tormented genealogy, one hundred and twenty third in direct line to the throne of England). All weekend, as the atmosphere of pine-scented, lavender tinged, Golfe Saint Jean permeated their senses, the robust, full-fruited wines of the Southern Rhône were dutifully despatched, and their appetites were constantly tempted and teased by Rex's anticipation of the celebrated Haut-Brion, 1943 – 'Premier Cru, from the monastery of the Lazarites, with a Médocain character, a majestic wine, of great style and class', as Christie's catalogued it. Rex admitted he had purchased it some years before at a Christie's 'wine-job', and bid several hundred pounds for the privilege. This was in the mid-1960s, and hence, a lot of money. The magnum had rested comfortably in the wine-cellar beneath the house at Beauchamp ever since – living, breathing, maturing, whatever clarets do, ripening – now was the day of its passionate harvest. With great ceremony, first the seal was carefully drawn away, then the cork was decorously drawn, and handed round to be 'nosed'. Rex bent his head over the graceful neck and shoulders of the precious Haut-Brion, 1943. He inhaled deeply. There was an expectant silence and a sudden, shattering retort: 'Christ! The bugger's corked!' and with the climax of the Beauchamp weekend shattered irreparably, the ambience collapsing around them, Rex stamped off to his bedroom in a rage, from where he could be heard shouting, swearing, and banging doors about.

'So what did you all do?' I asked.

'Well, we thought it was probably too good to waste, so we drank it,' said John Standing.

'And *was* it corked?'

'No, of course it wasn't. There was nothing wrong with it. Rex didn't have the first idea about it. If I had to speak the absolute truth, I suppose that bottle of La Mission Haut-Brion, 1943, was probably the most heavenly wine I have ever tasted in the whole of my life.' And what glittering style! Premier Cru!

I was reminded a little of the exchange in *Cyrano de Bergerac*, when the starving Cyrano eats a solitary grape, and drinks a thimbleful of water in order not to show his stark condition to his enemies.

'What insanity,' says an onlooker. 'Yes,' says his trusted friend, 'but what a magnificent gesture.'

Chapter 16

REX IN THE PIAZZA

IT WAS ON a warm September day in 1979 that I first walked with
Rex around Covent Garden in the middle of the afternoon,
cobbled and deserted, to have a look at the Piazza, and the
colonnade of the famous Inigo Jones church, standing literally
under the pillars where Henry Higgins first meets Eliza Doolittle.
The afternoon sun was warm and beguiling, and I felt that Rex
was very aware of the occasion, and gloried in it; perhaps that was
the first moment I recognized that Rex really *is* Henry Higgins.
Bernard Shaw's original, played the way the author would like it
to be played, is rather a spinsterish, arrogant Dr Dry-as-Dust, but
I have always felt that Rex's great contribution has been to add to
this complicated, and possibly autobiographical figure, a strong
dash of romantic sex. It is this extraordinary quality, which is
unique to Rex, that has made *My Fair Lady* both on the stage and
on the screen the universal phenomenon that it is. It is the actor's
privilege to inject something entirely original into a character,
which the author has left out. As we walked around the deserted
Piazza, Rex began to ruminate about his fellow colleagues and
collaborators with whom it must be acknowledged he has always
had an uneasy relationship. Whenever I saw them together Alan J.
Lerner and Rex fell upon one another's necks like long-lost lovers,
but taken on their own each seemed to delight in hurling spiteful
invective at the other, and in spite of the benevolence of the
afternoon, this was no exception. 'Now Alan – what would you say
about him?' pondered Rex. 'How would you describe him? An
unreliable dwarf . . . ? Would that be right?' And then later over a
glass of wine, and still in the half-deserted square Rex spoke a little
more fondly about Fritz Loewe, the composer, whom he had seen

73

not long before at a press conference in New York: 'Poor old Fritz seems to be getting rather forgetful. He was asked by one of the press where he was living, and he seemed to find great difficulty in remembering. "Yes, I live now in . . . in . . . in . . . in Palm Beach? Palm Heights? Palm somewhere . . ." "Springs?" suggested the press man. "Yes, that's it. Palm Springs." Poor old bugger,' concluded Rex, 'he couldn't remember where he lived.' But in a warmer vein Rex delighted in telling me how in the early days Fritz so enjoyed the prodigious success of *My Fair Lady*, with the endless parties, and celebrities, and the champagne, and chorus girls, and used to delight in turning up at five o'clock in the morning to join the queue which was already round the back of the Mark Hellinger Theatre, introducing himself to those already in line, and sharing with them his flask of coffee or champagne.

On another occasion, when *My Fair Lady* was out of town and on the road during its original production, Fritz Loewe, joyfully intoxicated on champagne and still hitting the high spots, noticing an adorably beautiful girl perched on a bar stool in a rather sophisticated night-club at two in the morning, enquired: 'Now, what's a beautiful, enchanting, delectable girl like you doing in Boston at this hour of the morning?'

The girl replied charmingly: 'I guess it's because I'm playing the leading chorus girl in your show, Mr Loewe.'

But then, as Rex said rather drily, 'Fritz enjoyed his success a little too much, and had a heart attack.' Of course it was at one of these savage pre-production meetings with Alan J. Lerner, Fritz Loewe, and the legendary director, Moss Hart, that an infernal row broke out among themselves, Fritz took on the role of peacemaker. 'Listen, my dear friends, we have all worked together for so long on this show, and we still have a great deal of work to do, and it is ridiculous and undignified that we should all fall out simply because of this arsehole, Rex Harrison. For God's sake, in a hundred years from now, all of us shall be dead . . .'

'Yeah,' said Moss Hart, 'except Rex Harrison.'

And on a more serious note, it has to be acknowledged that by 1985 Fritz, Alan and Moss were all dead, and Rex alone among them was very much alive. It had been said of him on one occasion, when he erupted into one of his violent rages, that he would injure himself one day and have a heart attack. 'I don't have heart attacks,' shouted Rex, 'I give them to other people.'

As September blended into October with no deterioration in the weather these autumnal days were full of affection, strolling in parks, reminiscing, and lazy hours. The air around Cadogan Square thickened, leaves spiralled slowly down, but it was still warm for the time of year. Rex used to come out and join me in the tidy gardens, while we watched the last tennis players in the court, and on one occasion a curious eccentric, fly-fishing all by himself with a tall rod and line in the middle of the square. In my flat which faced the afternoon light, powerful sun burst through the window of the drawing room, lighting the books in the library brown and green and gold.

Rex told me about Coral Browne, whom he had seen not long before, *très grande dame* in Los Angeles with up-swept and stylish grey hair. He told me he remembered her in earlier days, and of one glorious occasion when he was on stage, and casually looking into the wings – Coral was probably in her early twenties at that time – and to his astonishment she caught his eye from the wings, lifted up her pullover to reveal the most glorious pair of breasts he thought he had ever seen, and without a smile, or a wink, or the merest gesture, delicately restored her pullover to its rightful place. Rex admitted to me that it was with great difficulty he continued the rest of the scene.

Later, they had a short romance, which profoundly offended and infuriated Michael Hordern, who was enjoying a youthful success in the same play, at the same time as having a passionate affair with Coral Browne. The stories about Coral are innumerable, and like those attributed to John Gielgud or Robert Atkins or Ralph Richardson, invariably of the same quality and texture. Coral, surprisingly perhaps, was a devout Roman Catholic, and was one day coming out of Brompton Oratory where she had just attended High Mass. From the corner of her eye, she espied her great friend, Charles Gray, advancing up the steps of Brompton Oratory with the gleam of gossip in his eye. From the corner of her mouth, Coral hissed: 'Fuck off, Charles, I'm in a state of grace.'

One evening Rex and I had supper together downstairs at the Mirabelle, over his favourite Bordeaux, and we talked endlessly about plans for the show, the ideal casting we would wish, of the original play, *Pygmalion*, of his experiences with the wonderful director Moss Hart, and later, of love. He spoke fondly of his great friend, and indeed mine, John Standing who had just gone through a dreadful and hurtful divorce and was embarking on marriage yet again; and this, I believe, reminded him of his own frequent marriages, and he spoke about enduring these great shipwrecks and voyages in life, of the essential truth of letting things go, enduring them, surviving them, and re-beginning. A look of unutterable weariness crept across his face, and the lines at the side of his mouth deepened as he spoke of so much sadness among us, so many rotten, and cruel, and horrible things. And then, more cheerfully he spoke about his happy life with his new wife, Mercia, and how together they cosseted one another's insecurities. He spoke about the book of poems, *If Love Be Love*, they had selected together, which had great charm, and poignancy within its pages, and a very beautiful, perceptive Indian poem she had included. 'I dedicate this anthology to my beloved wife, Mercia, from whom I have learnt the art of living and loving at long last (1979).' But this sentiment was not to survive. The poem 'Bhatmari' – is enchanting – translated from the Sanskrit:

> *In former days we'd both agree*
> *That you were me and I was you.*
> *What has happened between us two*
> *That you are you, and I am me?*

Rex was always *me*, in most wives' view!

Mercia had been brought up by Anglican nuns as a child in Calcutta and was the daughter of a mixed marriage; in beauty, she resembled Merle Oberon, but with a striking allure of her own, and an extremely well-read intelligence and political perception. I recall a complete run of signed first editions by Graham Greene, who was a friend from Antibes. I never felt she was entirely contented, even in their happiest days, when Rex persistently

76

referred to her as 'Mem' (presumably, a shortened version of Mem-sahib), nor was Mercia particularly amused when Rex would sometimes interrupt her conversation, whenever she touched on an anti-British note, by gently reminding her: 'Always remember, Mercia, you are *half* English.' Rex was always aware of his status.

It had been John Standing who told me that when Rex was wooed by Sir Peter Hall to go to the National Theatre, the experience was not a happy one. Rex had no resistance to some of the plays that were mentioned but he did object violently to the policy of egalitarianism which prevailed at the National Theatre then, and he was particularly put out that there were no star dressing-rooms and everything to do with the billing was based on alphabetical order. However he did propose an interesting solution, and told John that he had suggested to Peter Hall that if he dropped the 'H' at the beginning of his name he would be able to kill two birds with one stone: 'I told Hall, my name's 'Arrison, and I'll take top billing and dressing-room Number One, please!'

Chapter 17

LONDON JOURNAL

2 October, 1979

ENDLESSLY PURSUING ELIZAS.

Rex and I went along to see John Barton's *The Merchant of Venice* at the Donmar Rehearsal Rooms. It was principally to watch Lisa Harrow who was so beautiful and clear-eyed, and had given a wonderful interpretation of Eliza when she auditioned earlier in the week. In the small space of the Donmar Theatre, her unblinking, forthright Portia was remarkable. Rex also liked Patrick Stewart as Shylock, a splendid blend of unctuous distastefulness and tragic humiliation. There is something so utterly detestable about Shylock, and in equal parts, the revenge the Christians take is so brutal, even taking from him his religion. When we were having supper together later on, Lisa said that she thought that Shylock was a survivor, I commented I did *not* think so, or if he was, what a terrible price he had to pay for that survival. The traditional ghetto mentality, aping and mimicking the gentiles, even to the point of having to laugh at the humiliation which they offer him. *The Merchant* is a cruel and endlessly relevant play. As dinner progressed, and we blossomed from the excellent wine, so did Lisa wax forth hotly about the wonder of Shakespeare's women, and how they educated and enlightened the men who fall in love with them. To express her argument, she referred to Rosalind who educates Orlando in love, Viola who educates Orsino, and Beatrice who educates Benedick. I was tremendously convinced by everything Lisa had to say which she expressed with exuberance, and energy, and a genuine innocence, although, out of the corner of my eye I began to realize that my distinguished friend was by no means as won-over as I was. After Lisa had finished her little dissertation about Rosalind and Viola and Beatrice, and for all I know Imogen and Cleopatra, Rex's eyes narrowed to slits. Rachel Roberts said his eyes were like embrasures in a medieval fortress behind which archers fired arrows and poured boiling oil. 'But not Eliza, however, to Higgins,' he warned.

'No,' countered Lisa, faltering in her stride, 'I suppose it might be said she learns from him.'

'Yes, she does,' said Rex, 'and, I hope, VERY SLOWLY OVER THREE ACTS! There's none of your Shakespearean nonsense with Shaw,' he snapped. 'He teaches her!'

I arrived home at one thirty in the morning, and unable to sleep, partly trying to cast Eliza (has Lisa a top G, I wonder?), and remembering her romantic performance and clear-eyed beauty, listened to Frank Bridge's Piano Sonata, which fitted the splashing of rain on the leaves of the large lime trees outside in Cadogan Square.

8 October

Lulu arrived, very pretty, vivacious, wearing a cute black hat. Something rather raunchy about her, which I could see Rex found very attractive. He was elegantly dressed, but somehow wearing the wrong clothes for the part, as he was in pyjamas, and an elegant dressing gown naturally, sharing with us his smoked salmon and champagne. I realize how much of a true gentleman Rex is when I notice he never seems to wear a wrist watch. I ask him what time it is, and he never knows. Wonderfully nonchalant.

Ned Sherrin has an ingenious theory about Rex, and the curious way he seems to be behaving at this early stage in proceedings. His unending exploration of Eliza, and rejecting dozens of potential Elizas, in pursuit of an imaginary Eliza who exists inside his head (and once there, we hope, finds herself able to sing), the choreography that he keeps churning over in his mind and rejecting, are all devices for *him* to recreate the part of Henry Higgins, and in pursuit of some original way of performing it, to end up, ultimately doing it exactly as he did it years before. But he

79

requires to go through all this laborious probing to reach the freshness, and the novelty, that he is looking for.

Insofar as actors genuinely adopt the mannerisms and attitudes of the characters they perform, it is my bad luck to be so closely involved with an actor whose role depends largely on outrageous behaviour, and thoroughly bad temper. Comedy, says Victor Pritchett somewhere, has a militant, tragic edge – or, in Rex's characteristic phrase: 'Unless I can add something new, and find something authentic which I can bring to the production, I don't want to do the fucking thing.' And perceptively, about Eliza, whom he feels is almost always wrongly played by being an upper-class girl struggling to speak stage-cockney, instead of being a cockney girl struggling to break into middle-class speech, he nags away at the same theory: 'Eliza is the same girl, right the way through, she is the same character, the same spirit, in the first scene in Covent Garden, as she is in the last scene with Henry's mother. And that streak of coarseness, and that note of danger, that at any moment she is about to fall off the high wire and make an absolute ass of herself, is exactly what Henry Higgins, namely Bernard Shaw, falls in love with. That's why his own mother disapproves of him as much as anyone else does.'

Chapter 18

AMERICAN JOURNAL

14 October, 1979 – 46th Street

IT'S ABSURD, REALLY. You travel all that way, cross the Atlantic ocean on a jumbo jet, and then end up just as I was at home, back in London, sitting inside a darkened theatre, looking at an unlit stage with imprecise shapes on it, clutching a cardboard cup of coffee, and there are voices struggling at cockney accents, and singing that they 'could have danced all night', or that they want a room somewhere. When I was travelling on the plane, first class, for me something of a luxury as well as a novelty, I could not help but overhear an extremely chic literary conversation about Iris Murdoch from the seats in front of me: 'The last time I saw Iris,' said an unmistakably Harvard voice, 'she was being interviewed in an idiotic room on an incredibly horrid white sofa. The typical Oxford don. Was she at Oxford with you, by the way?' I didn't hear the reply, and the Harvard voice started again: 'You know, I have this theory, supported by several others, that Iris Murdoch originally started writing aged fourteen, and so by the time she was publishing those novels like *The Bell*, and *Under the Net* (which are actually quite good, or at least quite readable) they are really her approximately forty-fifth, or forty-sixth novel, and the present ones (which quite frankly I find extremely dense) are working backwards to her juvenilia.'

But here we are sitting in the crumpled auditorium which still smells faintly of the evening before, staring at an appalling set for *Peter Pan, the Musical!* And a crude tinsel star suspended from the vacant flies. And, rather like a sinister structure belonging to an itinerant torturer, Peter Pan's harness swinging at the side of the stage. Don Gregory, one of the producers, says: 'At least, looking at the set, means I never have to go and see the show.'

'I'm astonished that *Peter Pan* is on at all on Broadway,' I say. 'Do you mean to tell me that they still manage to believe in fairies in New York?' I ask.

'Particularly in New York,' came the cryptic reply.

Our casting directors Barry and Julie organized the auditions. Naturally, just as I suspected, not one of the American girls who came to see us could *not* sing, some of them effortlessly, a C over the G. But the cockney eluded them totally, and at best they managed to make Eliza seem as if she came from Sydney Harbour. We had great hopes of a sweet-faced, soul-bewitching beauty, who sang divinely, and looked exquisite, but when she opened her mouth she spoke with a lisp. Blushingly, when we said goodbye, she said of the Eliza scene she had just completed: 'It'th tho beautifully written . . .' There was a middle-aged woman who came in make-up and costume, with one of those terrible battered straw hats that Rex so disliked, which embarrassed us all. Some spoke in a kind of make-believe cockney, which was so ferociously wrong, they were incomprehensible in any language. During the afternoon we enjoyed the audition of the runner-up to Miss America, who could not sing, alas. How we all wished she could.

The next day's auditions took place in a studio overlooking Times Square, and we struggled in a bare rehearsal room looking at our reflections in the mirror glass all round, while the noises of *West Side Story* (which was auditioning in the room above) came thundering through. 'Is Jerry Robbins there?' I enquired. 'Surely.' And the chorus boys all got extremely excited when out of the blue Baryshnikov turned up at the rehearsal rooms to look for him.

I suggested at the end of the day as the Americans all seemed able to sing it, but could not handle the dialect, the best plan was to cast an American girl in the part, and have Twiggy dub the dialogue from off-stage.

When I spoke to the casting director about the problem of the high G in 'I Could Have Danced All Night' he replied: 'It's the same problem when we were casting *West Side Story* – any of the girls who sang "I Feel Pretty" weren't right and we automatically looked elsewhere.'

At midday a rather good-looking man gave quite a good impression of Freddy, Eliza's would-be admirer, but he didn't seem right somehow. 'You don't like him?' asked Barry. 'What a pity – a friend of mine's having an affair with his wife, and we wanted him out of town for the day, so we were hoping on a re-call.'

All this time I had been rather impressed by Rex Harrison's understudy, who had made a very good job of reading Higgins spontaneously and well, but when I commented on the fact to the producer, Don Gregory said: 'Listen, Higgins is cast – we are not looking to cast Professor Higgins.'

Frequently I observed an endearing cultural difference over the reading of Mrs Higgins's reaction to Colonel Pickering's comment about 'the flower girl who now lives with Henry'. When Mrs Higgins answers 'Is it a love affair?' I noticed this was always interpreted with hope and expectation by the Americans, and it had always been greeted with withering contempt by the British.

The music director said of an attractive girl auditioning: 'My dear, you don't really sing well enough for the chorus, you'll have to be a star!'

Chapter 19

REX AT THE SHERRY

15 October, 1979

WE GATHERED IN Rex's apartment in the Sherry-Netherland Hotel overlooking Central Park. Rex had arrived, characteristically, on Concorde, and had already occupied his spacious apartment overlooking the lake, in the mirror of which the Fall leaves were subtly turning. Miles below, it seemed, as at the foothills of a tall mountain, an ethnic display of Hispanic peoples was taking place. An adventurous walk out on to his easy balcony gave me vertigo looking both upward and down. Re-entering his opulent suite, I saw an attractive bottle of Dom Perignon, already open on the table, two flutes, and the British Sunday papers – a welcome sight. We ate a supper of sole fillets, with an exquisite Pouilly-Fuissé. Rex, I notice, insists on calling our two producers from now on 'The Bus and Truck Merchants'; ever since the episode with Richard Burton as a rival attraction, the relationship seems to have deteriorated.

Many of the delicate problems appear to have been soothed and sorted out in casting, the design, and choreography. Rex was rather buoyant about having just completed the Parkinson Show in London, just before he set out for New York: 'Poor old Parkinson got himself off to a very unsteady start – the first question he asked me was "Would you call yourself high class?"

' "No. Why? Should I?"

' "Well, you play high-class parts."

' "Would you say that the Pope, Henry VIII, and General Burgoyne are high class?" – Parky seemed a bit nonplussed, so to help him out, I said, "Perhaps you mean to say that my acting is

High Comedy."' Rex paused and smiled enthusiastically to himself. 'At least I didn't ask him if he was lower-middle class!'

It was Parky, however, who told *me* a story Wilder told *him*, which reminded me acutely of Rex, his gift, his danger, his indisputable place.

Billy Wilder worked with Marilyn Monroe on two movies. She was extremely difficult, never knew her lines, was frequently late, drove everybody mad with her problems, but, agreed Billy: 'On the other hand, I have a cousin Mabel, who lives in New York. She is a kind woman, is always on time, always polite, and makes the best apple-strudel I've ever tasted. The problem is, no one pays to see her movies.'

The next day's auditions were as exhausting as ever, but when we spoke on the telephone before dinner, I was able to tell him 'I feel much better now, Rex; I must say, I did feel tired, but I went back to the hotel, and took a bath, and had a glass of champagne, and now I feel fine. How about you, Rex?'

Rex answered me: 'Well, I went to my hotel, and I took a bath, and I had a bottle of champagne, and now *I* feel fine.'

We dined at Trader Vic's, a short stroll from Rex's hotel. I was not without misgivings, because as we were choosing from the menu Rex muttered to me: 'Take it easy, if I were you, on the spare ribs – they poisoned Yul Brynner, and he took two million dollars off them.' At the end the kindly Chinese waiter said, bowing low: 'Thanks to Mr Fair Lady.'

Our pursuit of Eliza is frustrating and unrewarding. The difficulty of finding anybody, of any nationality to play the part is that she herself is a series of contradictions, musically – a belter with an infuriating, operatic top G to find – dramatically – a cockney sparrow who passes herself off for a Duchess – and psychologically – as a young woman who falls in love with her dominating teacher, and tries to find her own independence. Of course all these anomalies are also part of her great attraction. I was reminded of something Sir John Gielgud told me ages ago when we were working together on my first production of Alan Bennett's *Forty*

Years On. As a child he had seen Mrs Patrick Campbell play the original Eliza, and even then – perhaps as an up-and-coming contemporary actor – he had not been greatly impressed. 'It would never do today, what she was doing on the stage of Her Majesty's Theatre, and I thought it was all very improbable and inauthentic. She was nearly fifty years old for a start. She spoke cockney in a laborious lah-di-dah way, ponderously, "loike that", with very patronizing old-fangled pronunciation which she imagined was meant to be cockney. No wonder Shaw found her so infuriating, as much as he was madly in love with her. I thought it was totally unrealistic, and completely unconvincing.'

In the room above the rehearsal room at Times Square there's the extraordinary spectacle of several pairs of crutches. The choreographer of *West Side Story*, Jerry Robbins, in order to bring the cast to life, is playing games to antagonize the Jets and the Sharks. '"Anybody's" has a bloody nose in the punch up,' says my assistant director, 'the kids are limping out one by one, like walking wounded coming away from the Battle of Gettysburg.'

Chapter 20

THE LITTLE CHURCH AROUND THE CORNER

SOON AFTER I arrived in New York I felt an overwhelming urge to visit my favourite Church of the Transfiguration, popularly called 'The Little Church Around the Corner', and based at the junction of 29th Street and Madison. In 1850 the story goes, Joseph Jefferson, while trying to arrange a dignified funeral service for his actor friend George Holland, was rejected by a Pharisaical establishment uptown. 'There is a little church right around the corner,' explained a condescending verger, 'where you will find they might do that sort of thing.'

'Then God Bless the Little Church around the Corner!' replied Mr Jefferson, and thus began the affectionate relationship between this episcopal church and the American theatre. In style it is designed eclectically, rather like a fourteenth-century royal chapel, full of shadowy nooks and crannies, not unlike an ornate illustration from a classical Book of Hours. In fact it always appears a little over-dressed for the plain piety of the episcopalian religion in New York. Something of Ninian Comper about it, and the English Arts and Crafts movement. For me it was always a small oasis of calm Anglicanism, amidst a desert of deranged evangelicals who thunder from the television screens with barely disguised hysteria. Recently prominent sex scandals had emptied the pews in the electronic churches, and no less an oracle than the *New York Times* itself pronounced that most of the big evangelical names are in eclipse, or exile, or prison, with their ratings slumped down as low as *Dynasty*. Gone are the Sundays when 6,000 people attended Jim and Tammy Bakker's 2,300 acre Theme Park. Other 'Heaven's My Destination' Evangelicals, Jerry Fallwell of the Moral Majority and Jimmy Swaggart, who was recently dismissed from the Assembly of God, and the unhappily named Oral Roberts, have all fallen madly from their spheres; the latter claimed in 1986, if he couldn't raise four and a half million, he'd lose his life. He didn't raise four and a half million nor did he lose his life.

In peaceful resolution these days the Sunday morning service at 'The Little Church Around the Corner' floated out of New York's dizzy traffic 'downward to darkness on extended wings'. I enjoyed spending my Sunday mornings there, and it reminded me very much of the sort of church where in the twenties and thirties Wallace Stephens would have quietly worshipped. Other famous American actors are buried here. Rex Harrison, when we were rehearsing, not infrequently came to read the lesson from time to time, and here he was married to his wife, Mercia, and here, in 1990, on a June morning the actors held his memorial service.

The priest in charge of The Little Church was Father Norman Catur, who was very close to Rex and to Mercia. One day he told me he had been invited to see Rex in *The Kingfisher*, who promised him a specially reserved seat; unable to find a taxi, he had walked hurriedly from 29th Street, which is fairly far downtown, to the mid-40s where the theatre was situated, but he arrived ten minutes late all the same, in something of a sweat. To his horror he discovered that Rex had held the curtain for him. As he entered the auditorium sixteen hundred pairs of eyes turned to him in total silence, transfixed him with a hostile stare and followed him as he walked gingerly down the carpeted aisle to take his seat in the fifth row of the stalls. As he settled in comfortably those on either side of him sat down again with icy glares, and only then did the House Manager give the sign backstage to the stage management and the house lights slowly dimmed and the curtain gently rose. Father Catur said it had to be the most humiliating evening of his life, although in his heart he was deeply touched by Rex's grace and kindness in holding the curtain for him, because as Rex explained afterwards, 'he knew that something must have gone wrong with the arrangements, and that he had no intention of letting the play begin until his friend Norman Catur was comfortably sitting in his stall.'

Chapter 21

STOPOVER IN TINSELTOWN

18 October, 1979

Rex went on to Chicago to continue his tour of *The Kingfisher*. I
had my first meeting with the legendary designer Oliver Smith,
who was also credited with the original *Fair Lady* settings, in a hotel
dining room at the Drake Hotel. We very swiftly became excellent
friends. When I informed him that one of our dates was the Fisher
Theatre, Detroit, he asked me if I had ever been there. 'No,' I told
him, 'I had not had the pleasure of entertaining the people of
Detroit, nor was I familiar with the theatre.'

'You haven't missed a great deal,' replied Oliver, 'to know
the Fisher Theatre is to loathe it.'

We made a great number of decisions to change everything;
we wanted to change the settings, we wanted to make the production move more lightly, more swiftly, be more on the balls of the
feet as it were, by using back projection, and not have to weigh
ourselves down by insuperable realistic reconstructions of the
market at Covent Garden.

My friend Derek Jennings arrived in New York, for the first
time, somewhat overwhelmed by the rapacity of the great city, and
announced rather naively, I thought, that he found it all so foreign.
'Sure,' smiled Oliver, 'it's America, first of all, which is always
foreign, and second, New York is a foreign city in the centre of the
United States.' Walking down Madison Avenue in warm October
air, Derek said to me that he felt on reflection New York was a
little too much like Woody Allen's films: 'It seems to be composed
of two kinds of people. Jews, and neurotic Jews.' He had seen a
line of graffiti on a bare wall downtown which he thought summed

up the city to perfection: 'Too much ain't enough.' In thorough-fares not far away from us the whirr and wow of fire engines of such echoing intensity captured within the narrow confines of the Avenues reverberating upwards and around the skyscrapers like a great whirlwind, one anticipated the dread of a Martian invasion.

On the evening of the 18th of October I returned to Los Angeles to continue some editing I was doing on a film called *The Cay*, which starred James Earl Jones, and had been filmed in British Honduras. While I was in Kennedy Airport a man whose head emerged, curiously enough, bobbing intermittently above the top of the door in the gentlemen's lavatories in the First Class Sky-Club was, it turned out, actually practising his jogging.

I went out to dinner at Chasens with my great friend Frank O'Connor, the producer from Universal Studios. He is always a magnificent mine of Hollywood gossip, neurosis, anecdote, and history. He told me one of the stock jokes going around the Hollywood studios: 'Do you know the story of the Polish actress, who, to advance her career, fucked a writer?' Typical Tinseltown.

I was staying in Jenny Agutter's apartment in Laurel Canyon. There is a consolation, whenever one stays in Hollywood, in looking out at distant and glittering objects. Late at night from this wide window of Jenny's house, I get great pleasure standing quietly – rather like a figure silhouetted in a 1930s movie – staring at downtown Los Angeles glinting far beneath me like a southern constellation. Jenny's old-fashioned house feels good to be in, as well as comfortable, and never lonely whenever I've been alone in it. She has two charming cats which either fluster about in their imaginary pursuits, or lie peacefully asleep on cushions. Her house was built limpingly in the 1920s on one side on the edge of a hill. The fires last summer came quite close by above the Canyon and rained hot ash down on the roof. The garden contains exotic Mediterranean plants, eucalyptus, bougainvillaea and avocado trees. She has a brick-paved garden with an empty fountain which gives a sense of faded grandeur. The view from these windows faces the legendary Château Marmont and at a distance I can see people walking out on to their terraces without any clothes on. It is the haunt of visiting rock stars and visiting British, reminiscent of faded hotels I have been to in Mussoori or Darjeeling, and it is typical of the British contingent to relish its peeling shabby hauteur. Sometimes animals descend from the Canyons – racoons invade the gardens and swimming pools; even coyotes have been known to rummage and forage the dustbins, kill the domestic cats, and once I saw a huge bird of prey.

'Probably a buzzard,' said Jenny, 'and waiting for somebody dead to be thrown out of the Château Marmont. And as it's above Sunset Boulevard, it wouldn't be merely wheeling, but dealing as well.'

Frank O'Connor told me about a man he knew, married to a new wife who wanted to set the record straight from the start.

'Honey, I'm a golf-freak. I want you to know that, I don't want any secrets from you, and I don't want you to have any unpleasant surprises. Every Saturday and Sunday without fail, I go down to the golf links, and married or not, rain or shine, nothing is ever going to stop me.'

'Well,' answered his wife, 'I'd better get the record straight too. I'm a hooker.'

'Well, Honey, maybe you've got your left hand too low down on the golf club . . .'

Jenny told me that the fabulously wealthy wine alcoholics in Beverly Hills all congregate together on what is called 'Skid Drive'. There's a large, successful English movie colony in Los Angeles, who meet socially, play cricket, meet for brunch, bagels and the *Sunday Times*.

Bob Hope said, apparently: 'There'll always be an England. Even if it's only in Hollywood.' Apropos of Bob Hope, Dulcie Gray told me she toured round the US airforce bases with him during the early months of the war. He confessed to her he had fallen deeply in love with Rex Harrison's first wife, Colette, and wanted desparately to marry her. As she was divorced from Rex by this time there was no obstacle, but, said Dulcie, she refused him, 'because she always hoped Rex would return to her.'

Chapter 22

LUIGI'S

28 October, 1979

FLEW BACK TO England, unable to shake off the cough that I seemed to have picked up in New York and Los Angeles.

On arrival find that the English *Fair Lady* has opened to rave reviews in London; I think Rex felt disgruntled, as it had been his ambition to bring our production over eventually. Alan J. Lerner himself takes over direction, making a great deal of difference to the show, hauling the original back into shape reducing the over-acting and pulling Eliza (whom he has fallen in love with) into a sympathetic role. All of this, according to Rex. I went along to see it after the first week, and the reception on the first Monday was ecstatic. A great ovation from the audience, and expressions of radiant joy on the faces of the cast, almost in disbelief, as the curtains rose and fell on their success.

After the performance I had dinner at Luigi's with Alan J. Lerner. As we entered the head waiter said to Alan: 'Good evening, young man. Nice to see you for the next two years.' Alan was in excellent form, buoyed up by the success to which he had greatly contributed. It's been a long time since he has enjoyed success as a musical creator, and it clearly benefits him as it does anybody. Frustrated in his original musicals, it has been happy for him to return to the scene of a former indisputable triumph. Peter Baylis who plays Alfred Doolittle put an arm about him, and whispered in his ear: 'My dear Alan, you are Christmas on my shoulder.' He assures me we will have no trouble with getting an English Eliza into the United States: 'If I have to ask the President I won't hesitate to do so – and I'll have you know that the President of the

United States is a very good friend of mine.' He told me about Katharine Hepburn, who was enduring terrible disruption from the noise the workmen were making, busily tearing down the skyscraper outside her theatre during matinées of *Coco*, a failed musical about Mme. Chanel. The grinding and crashing and shrieking and scraping proved unendurable. Nobody was able to make any headway officially, and so Katy Hepburn went outside to visit them in person, put on one of their hard hats, and sitting gracefully across a vast iron girder shared champagne and beer with them, explained the predicament, appealed to their sense of New York solidarity, and effortlessly won them over to her side so that matinées were performed in future in perfect peace. A typical Broadway story.

A few evenings later, Alan J. Lerner, still flushed with pride and success over the triumph of his production, arrived at Luigi's to join myself and the producer Don Gregory and his new wife, Kaye, an exquisitely beautiful girl with a face like a portrait by Memling. Alan is always the best of company, rich in anecdote, and musical comedy folklore. On this occasion however, he made us all a little nervous as he drank, first, some soda water, then a glass of white wine, lit several cigarettes, which he equally feverishly extinguished, he then ordered a plate of antipasti, which he ate while smoking and drinking wine literally at the same time, and sometimes muddling himself up whether he was eating, smoking, or drinking. In the confusion, he forgot to bite his nails. Suddenly he decided to disappear – he told us 'for a smart date'. As he left the restaurant Don Gregory raised an eyebrow: 'Is Mrs Alan J. Lerner number nine in the offing?'

Don said that he had been talking to the New York agent, Robbie Lantz, and that we were speaking to Cathleen Nesbitt concerning the part of Mrs Higgins.

'And did she answer?' asked Robbie.

Years later Robbie Lantz represented me in New York and I relished his glorious much-spoken-of wit as much as his brilliance in negotiating my contracts. When I told him that I was working with a Hungarian designer, he said: 'If ever you meet a Hungarian in the street, slap him soundly on the cheek. *He* will know the reason why.'

Chapter 23

NEW YORK DIARY

4 January, 1980

REX AND I, back in New York, went out that evening to Charlies' Restaurant on 48th Street, and the night after that to the Montparnasse-style café the Museum, where I ate a fine dish of boiled scrod. Rex tackled a plate of small fry, and a delectable Sancerre. I was reminded of Jonathan Miller's remark that North American fish are very well bred and wear Brooks Brothers' herringboned suits, like mackerel, and they have good masculine Yankee East Coast names like bleak, whiting, sprats, and scrod. None of your frivolous pansy Californian angel-fish. Walking back from the Museum our attention was caught by a high-walled red-bricked church. Across the door a sign was pasted: 'We Regret The Appearance Of Our Building, Due To Vandalism Beyond Our Control'. The debate still rages on the streets about the American hostages in Tehran.

I went out to one of the Times Square dime stores and bought myself a special 'Fuck Iran' badge. Another one with a caricature of the Ayatollah had scrawled across it 'Khomeini Sucks'. Back in the hotel, on my way to the lift, I could not help but hear a girl's voice up-raised in the corridor shattering the calm, penetrating the walls of her hotel bedroom with its urgency and passion, as well as its sheer volume:

'Do not tell me I'm *irrational*! Do not tell me I'm *sick*! Do not tell me I'm *unworthy*! Do not judge me! Do not judge *me*!'

Over and over again the same passionate distressed litany, and another voice, or voices – husband? lover? parent? – so subdued, patient, tolerant, attempting to ameliorate, to pacify.

What suppressed domestic distress did this hideous outburst conceal, I wonder?

In the early hours of the morning snow fell heavily, thickening the ledge on my window of the forty-fourth floor and carpeting the neatly mowed lawn on the summer extension of the Equity Offices twenty floors below.

5 January

Went to the theatre and saw Lillian Hellman in person at the opening of her play *Watch on the Rhine*, old, unnecessarily fragile, and endearingly eccentric. When she took her call on stage she wore a curious plastic gas-mask for her emphysema, and in her left hand carried a burning cigarette. After the first curtain she was helped across the road by two men, one at each arm, to Charlies' for a drink and missed the middle act – out of frailty, I believe, not disgust at the performance. But the distinction of her presence did not save the show – Broadway (in spite of the Iran crisis, and the parallel of heroic ideas expressed in the play for Americans to stand firm) is nevertheless Broadway, and the show folds at the end of the week. As Sam Goldwyn used to say, 'If the public won't go to the box-office, there ain't nothing you can do to stop them.'

Jimmy Nederlander, the theatre-owner, argued passionately with Don and Mike, The Flying Wallendas, that they were being foolhardy with their budgets on the show. 'What are you spending all this money on *My Fair Lady* for? Two and a half million dollars, for God's sake! *The Music Man* with Dick Van Dyke only cost $340,000 and it looks great.'

'But,' reasoned Mike, 'did you ever see it, Jimmy?'

'Sure I did, I saw it.'

'Well, what did you think of it?'

'Well, I guess it looked pretty tacky.'

Rex confided in me that he had been in touch with his former wife Rachel Roberts, albeit somewhat reluctantly: 'She's rather sad, poor thing – but it's the bitch in her that gets on to me. The Soviets invade Afghanistan, but it's those bitch-wives who invade me.' This could be troublesome, were Mrs Rex Harrison VI to find out.

Downtown Radio City announces its Christmas Show: 'The Living Nativity – A Magnificent Spectacular Presentation!' The snow blizzard came early to New York on Sunday morning, provoking every kind of eccentric gear. I am romantic enough to be moved when I see New Yorkers skating over the ice to work.

Chapter 24

HAUTE COUTURE

IN THE LATE 1950s I spent some of my Christmas vacation at
Jacqmars, then based in Bond Street, selling yards of silk to the
affluent. One of the delights of this part-time job, apart from
countless attractive girls, was the personality of a decidedly individual salesman, called Percy Brocksbank, whose name implies that
he was the junior scion, of a very distinguished family, but fallen
on hard times. In fact, he was the traditional black sheep of the
family, and having got through a large inheritance, devoted himself
regularly to what he euphemistically used to call 'demon', namely
vast nocturnal consumptions of alcohol. Every morning he would
come in, ravaged from the night before, and pausing at the large
mirror used to mumble: 'Good gracious me, don't I look plain!
Older than Time, and Tide, and Petra . . .' He had a tart approach
to many of his *nouveau riche* clients, whom he served with fastidious
politeness, but secretly despised, and when one of them once
questioned whether Jacqmars was truly haute couture, he
answered: 'Oh, certainly, dear madam, how haute can you get?'

This is not quite as irrelevant as it sounds, because anyone
involved in directing Rex Harrison in a show when it came to
costumes, would find himself deeply involved in the world not of
theatrical costumier but of haute couture. Both in London and
New York long hours were spent at the tailors and they were
extremely dramatic and full of tension.

I remember vividly the day, and it *was* an entire day, we spent
in Jermyn Street at Hawes and Curtis for his suits, and shirts, all
of which were to be tailored for the show. The original cutter had
been flown out to Cap Ferrat, to wait on him personally, had then
returned to London, and we were now to try on the first set of

97

clothes. When we arrived breezily in the morning, a sense of anticipation and delight was in the air and we were greeted by an effusive tailor, and the original cutter who had visited the South of France. I can only conclude, however, that by the time we ended there were in attendance the managing director, a member of the board, one master tailor, three junior cutters, a designer, the stage designer, and countless assistants exhausted and virtually on their knees. At one time Rex had regarded himself in the mirror looking with mischievous horror at the apparition which confronted him in the glass, and gesturing to it exclaimed to the heavens: 'For God's sake! This is fucking ridiculous!' And on a second occasion went so far as to rip from top to bottom all the stitches out of an entire suit of tails. The master tailor had tears in his eyes, but Rex was relentless. 'Well, this won't do at all, you'll simply have to start from scratch!' Tea, coffee, smoked salmon sandwiches, wine all came and went throughout the day but Rex was indefatigable in his pursuit of perfection for his sartorial appearance, and it must be said that he could be sometimes as complimentary towards something he liked as he could be destructive towards something he hated.

He sailed out of the shop I remember, briskly into Jermyn Street and the car where his chauffeur waited, leaving behind this carnage of tailors and cutters, weak-kneed and exhausted on the floor; Rex turned and with debonair charm exclaimed to the room: 'Thank you very much, gentlemen, not a bad day at all – now I'm going back to the Ritz to freshen myself up with a little champagne and a new set of togs, then the theatre and then I'm going to take Memsahib dancing at Annabels – so I look forward to seeing you all tomorrow morning at 9 a.m.,' breaking off with a triumphant cry, 'FOR THE *HATS*.' Later on Don Gregory told me that twenty-six hand-made shirts were all sent out for Rex's approval with an attendant tailor in tow to Beauchamp, and were approved, worn through the twelve months of the tour, and ended up there at the end of the run for the personal use of the star.

It was virtually the same in New York. We took a break for rehearsals and I accompanied him to Brooks Brothers where he was being fitted for the second time for his tail-coat.

It was now the end of June, events were moving forward, time passing, deadlines approaching. The news out of New York was that *Camelot* was not enjoying a very successful tour. Bob Kriese and Franz Allers who had seen it were both critical: 'Too much interference. Too much interference.' Stage Manager, Marshall, informed us that the Trafalgar Theatre was now somewhat unheroically named 'The David C. Neiderlander'. And Rex had asked for air conditioning to be installed in his dressing-room, a refrigerator, and something called a 'contour chair'. I thought Rex sounded quite happy for the time of year even though I hadn't seen him for a few days.

'Well, he should be happy,' replied Marshall, 'he's just bought two pairs of shoes and shoe trees for $1300.' When I saw Rex later on at Brooks Brothers, he was in a fairly contentious mood.

'The Boys won't tell me anything about *Camelot*: they refuse to be drawn, they won't mention it at all, and I long to hear their positively doom-laden stories.' I asked him how the fitting was getting along.

'Clothes are not what I'd hoped. Herbert Johnson's are not what they used to be – the hats are not very good. The suits are quite good. There's a trim dressing-gown which I wear in the Second Act, but Mr Johnson can't cut a tail-coat. Nobody can. It's a lost art, I think. Luckily I've got a couple of mine.'

In fact Rex was not called upon to provide his own tail-coat for the show but did bring in one of his own which they copied rather skilfully. He was admiring himself in front of the mirror, considerably cheered up, later in the afternoon when I walked through the door. Unfortunately my presence dispersed some of the optimism when I brought up the awkward subject, which I confess I had kept back for as long as I could, of where he was going to hide the battery of his radio-mike. In the original production, at the small Mark Hellinger Theatre, there was no such thing as radio-mikes, and apart from a set of fairly crude foot-mikes which served to assist the hearing of those unlucky enough to sit in the rear stalls, the notion of balanced sound was unheard of. At first Rex expressed his determination to work without one: 'After all,' he grumbled, 'I never needed one at the Mark Hellinger, and nobody ever complained about audibility then!' But we were performing on tour in old movie theatres like the Pantages in Los Angeles, or worse, in Chicago, the Arie Crown, which had something like three and a half thousand seats, so to perform any kind of musical, or indeed play without radio-mikes was unthinkable. Even the City Opera performed with microphones in Chicago. Rex's main concern, clearly, was not so much whether he was audible or not, because I think at this stage even he *recognized* that at some point he would have to wear some form of assistance with the vocal projection, but how ugly it would make the cut of his tail-coat. When I suggested that his radio-mike would be artfully concealed in the second button of his dress shirt, he responded with a wail of indignation and despair.

'In that case, Patrick, if I'm wearing one of those things I shall look like a c**t,' but I pointed out to him that in these large theatres if he didn't wear a radio-mike he would be completely inaudible. My argument proved not to be very persuasive.

'It seems to me, Mr Director,' he said in that tone of voice which I recognized only too well when he was angry with me, 'that either you want me to look like a c**t, or sound like one.'

Some time later when we were moving into the New York theatre, as we were assembled for our band call, Mickey Rooney who was in a neighbouring theatre came in personally to greet Rex. It was marvellous seeing these two great stars together, one so tall and slender, the other so minute and robust, and they fell upon one another's necks as best they were able to with a great show of affection, and nostalgia, and fun. I was very happy to meet Mickey Rooney, and thanked him, which I genuinely meant, for being so courteous to our company as we arrived. Mickey Rooney was almost indignant: 'What? Have Rex Harrison arrive on the stage of a Broadway theatre, and I'm playing just opposite him with *Sugar Babies*, and not be there when he arrives to welcome such a great figure on the Broadway stage! Why, it's unthinkable!'

A little later, when we were actually in preview, there was congestion of the airwaves, and something did go wrong with all the radio-mikes, which needless to say infuriated Mr Harrison, who summoned me, the Sound Supervisor, the assistants, the producers, and anybody else within earshot, in order to express his rage and impatience. We all attempted rather feebly to provide an explanation. One of the things that was clearly going wrong was that the airwaves were picking up the lines and song and dance numbers from *Sugar Babies*, Mickey Rooney's show just across the way. And fun though it was as a great burlesque show, Rex was less than delighted to hear screams and whoops and shrieks of jubilation from *Sugar Babies* breaking into Bernard Shaw's timeless prose. I attempted to explain haltingly: 'You see, Rex, there's something wrong with the sound waves, and it seems that our radio-mikes are picking up dialogue from the radio-mikes of *Sugar Babies* over the road.' Rex was not to be pacified so easily.

'What do you mean *Sugar Babies*!' he snarled.

'Well, Rex,' I stammered, 'it's Mickey Rooney's burlesque show in the theatre on the other side of the street, and their radio-mikes are interfering with ours.'

'I thought,' said Rex, 'the little shit had so much energy, he wouldn't have needed radio-mikes!'

I have to say on that occasion we all thought his reply was so funny, and in a ghastly way so truthful, especially when we remembered how loving the two egomaniacs had been to one another earlier in the week, that everyone in the Number One dressing-room collapsed with laughter. And so, it must be admitted, did Rex.

Chapter 25

THE LAST OF THE HIGH COMEDIANS

The Art of the Haiku

First you have to learn the form – next you have to master the form –

When you have accomplished both of these important things, then, and then alone, you have the freedom to create.

from *The Master of Haiku*, MA-CHU

ONE DAY (IN THE 1970S), a group of us were sitting around in the old H. M. Tennent offices, where 'Binkie' Beaumont once held absolute power over the West End theatre, a sort of Metternich-figure. We were talking of autobiography.

'So, you're writing your Memoirs, are you Lindsay?' asked Arthur Cantor, an American producer involved with the New York end of *The Kingfisher*, a gossamer vehicle currently starring Rex Harrison and Claudette Colbert, under Lindsay Anderson's direction. Lindsay reflected for a moment before replying in his customarily sardonic voice.

'Yes, Arthur, I am, but I've not got very far, I'm afraid.'

'May I enquire *how* far?' he said.

'Well, not at all far, to be honest. In fact I've only got as far as the title.'

'May I be so presumptuous, Lindsay, to ask what that title might be?'

'Yes,' said Lindsay, 'I'm going to call it "Surrounded by Idiots".'

This led us on to other titles, and I mentioned the imaginary title for the memoirs of a rather overlooked (but deeply admired in the profession) character man, called Ken Wynne: 'They Never Came Around'.

Alan Bates said that sometimes press-notices for a play depressed him so much, he couldn't bear to read them. He had

102

been in a new play by David Storey, which had attracted fairly hostile notices, and so upset him, that when he came to the sentence which began: 'And as for Alan Bates . . .' he couldn't bring himself to read further.

'There's the title for your autobiography' said Lindsay enthusiastically, ' "As for Alan Bates".'

'What about you, Patrick?' asked Arthur Cantor, 'are you writing your memoirs yet? "The Years of Chichester" would make a good read.'

'I'm not interested in writing about myself, Arthur,' I replied, 'but I am writing a book about Rex.'

'About *Rex*?' said Lindsay. 'What an extraordinary thing to want to write about.'

'I don't see why.'

'Well, is anybody going to bother to buy a book about them?'

'Them?'

'Other than sailors and light-house keepers . . .'

I said, 'I'm talking about Rex as in Harrison.'

'Oh,' said Lindsay, 'I thought you meant *wrecks*.'

Once that was cleared up, I told them that the title of my book about Rex would have to refer to his unique achievement as virtually the survivor of the 'High Comedy' players of the pre-war era. Something like 'The Last of the High Comedians'.

In the gap between auditions, and the unending, almost fruitless pursuit of an English Eliza, and the tour Rex was making of *The Kingfisher*, we lunched occasionally at the Garrick Club, and on one heavenly afternoon, when all the members had gone, we studied the Zoffanys, Reynolds, and Mathews, and deciphered among our old legends of past footlights and scrubbed floorboards, those who could be called 'high' comedians, some one would call 'light', and those who were irrevocably and irretrievably 'low'. Life has not changed through the centuries – the same standards apply. Forbes-Robertson, and Irving, looked in their portraits unquestionably grave and dignified, so did Mrs Siddons, and Garrick. Kean appeared wild and revolutionary (perhaps like the magnificent O'Toole at Stratford in the 1960s), Dorothy Jordan resembled Maggie Smith, we thought, a mixture of brittle wit, and profound vulnerability, and it was interesting to see what a dignified figure Charles Dickens's great friend, Grimaldi, cut, in his blue velvet-collared coat, once out of the motley.

Rex was absolutely right. You could see they were not the breed of actors to strain the effect, or angle for cheap laughs by indulging in stagey business with their lacy cuffs, walking-canes, and snuff-boxes. But others there were – it was unmistakable – with exaggerated costumes, trying to provoke laughter by comical clothes and props, and promiscuous gesture and flamboyant face-pulling.

'You can see, Patrick,' said Rex as we scrutinized these eighteenth and nineteenth-century players, 'how some of them are just as desperate to get a reaction from the customers as the present-day crowd of shouters. Look at him, over there' he said, pointing to a wildly overdressed clown, pulling the face in a crude check top-coat, with slightly crossed-eyes for comic effect, 'I mean, really, imagine having to share the stage with a c**t like that?'

The name Jack Minster is largely forgotten today, but in the 1950s, he was a highly respected director of comedy. He merits, in my view, a permanent place in the *Oxford Book of Quotations* (or, Oxford Book of Theatrical Know-how, perhaps) for one simple comment of absolute insight. In answer to a comedian indignantly defending (as so often) an instance of coarse acting, trouser-dropping, face-pulling, eye-bulging, by the riposte – 'Oh, well, old boy, it gets a good laugh from the audience' – Minster replied: 'You should see the faces of the people who aren't laughing.' This is a sentiment with which Rex would passionately agree.

Alan Bates is right when he says you can't actually talk *about* acting, you can only talk around it – what better example than Ralph Richardson, when he declared mysteriously: 'I always aim to be a little wide of the mark'. In contemporary times, Victoria Wood has expressed the same ambiguity, and supports the intuitive approach. 'As soon as you try to talk about comedy,' she has explained recently, 'it disappears in front of your eyes. It's all about the moment. Somebody says something, somebody else laughs, that's all there is, really . . .' Rex would lift his glass to that, with the one addition, I think: Somebody says something, somebody reacts, and then there's the laugh. He was also a superb *listener*. Like Spencer Tracy on screen, when he listened, he was listening for the first time. Frequently, he could provoke a laugh by *not* reacting.

Rex, when he stayed in England, and wasn't putting up at the Ritz, lived in Mayfair, and had the lease of a grand house in Wilton Crescent for some years, but I always thought he was most at home around the green and leafy Squares of Lord Cadogan's estate, between Knightsbridge and Sloane Square. At night, in my Cadogan Square apartment, the street lights reflected upwards through the castles of lime branches so that the high-ceilinged rooms were illuminated with a mysterious green glow. In between auditions, in our frustrating pursuit of the evasive Eliza, we enjoyed walking together around the Gardens and Squares and Mansions, and it was during these genial excursions he would disclose some of the mysteries of the art of High Comedy.

'When I was first up in London from Huyton, I used to go to the gallery night after night. I was a great lover of the matinée idols of the time. I looked for work during the day, and I watched these actors at night. Ronnie Squire, Gerald du Maurier, Charles Hawtrey, Seymour Hicks. My goodness,' he said, 'I was lucky to have the chance to see them in full flight, all at their peak, working with all their talents, and this extraordinary elegance – elegance of dress, elegance of gesture – and highly wrought fabric of art, and this extraordinary *concealment* of art. To me, and my fellow-actors, we were utterly unable to emulate them. What they *didn't* do, what they didn't display, was so remote to everything we thought acting was, and what we had been taught in repertory. They didn't look a) as if they were acting, and b) they were trying to be funny, ever. They played their comedy, I can only say, on the balls of their feet. I remember to this day, their alert posture, well-balanced, but pitched slightly forward, attentive and yet relaxed. Producing gold cigarette cases out of inside pockets, with a kind of magician's sleight of hand, removing, opening, closing, concealing the case again, and then flicking up the cigarette from finger into mouth with the same effortless dexterity, and then lighting it as if from a hidden flame, and jigging, perhaps, the silver lighter for a few seconds from hand to hand, before mysteriously trousering it, without pausing in the conversation. They were marvellous! And what it was, I think, really what it was, was a great inner energy. You see, by definition, an actor can't get up on the stage and do nothing. That isn't acting. But equally, he shouldn't be *seen* to be acting. I can only compare their quality, their technique – if you have ever seen film of him, and if not, I urge you to do so – to the great pre-war Spanish bullfighter, Manolete. Everything he does is imbued with a kind of silence, and choreography and a sense of grace. The true comedian, like the true bullfighter, should affect to do nothing. I learnt that much later, but as a youngster, I was just enthralled watching them. I was like one of those shadowy characters you can see up in the galleries of Walter Sickert's music-hall paintings. Chin in hand, neck resting on the velvet counterpane, under the brass railing of the balcony. Would have waited outside, in the rain probably, for hours, rushed up the stone steps, to secure a place in the very front row; looking down, I couldn't take my eyes off them.' We circled round the rose pergolas, and watched a quartet of women helplessly playing pat-ball, and then, continued our stroll, in the area reserved for nannies and their young charges. The air was perfumed, the noise of passing cars, remote.

'It's a shame that the young actors of today don't have the example I had when I was young, coming up to London, being able to see these men in different plays. I used to go three, six, seven times, just to watch what they did. But I couldn't make it out.'

Our favourite garden was the rather obscure Hans Place, for which I obtained a private key. It was like a secret garden on the way to Harrods, full of old-fashioned trees, a wilderness of shrubs and in midsummer the centre was completely obscured, as the willow-branches hung right down, and no children ever seemed to play there, no tennis-players intruded, no sunbathers proffered their impudent breasts, or dogs ran wildly round. It was a corner of Victorian London abandoned in the twentieth century. The sunshine which bathed the pavements and windows of the Crescent round about, or reflected the shining bonnets of parked Mercedes, scarcely penetrated the plane trees, the oak elms, and sycamores of our leafy oasis. An old sign by the gates warned no ball games should be played, no dogs left unleashed, and, curiously, no servants were to be admitted. I could never work out whether this sign was genuine, left over from before the war, or was some kind of obscure joke from the Residents' Committee. I felt certain, unlike the other Private Gardens, Hans Place was a last remaining wilderness of the original park land of the great seventeenth-century House, which must have once existed in its magnificence at the north corner of Cadogan Square, long before Pont Street, and the Victorian baronial of the Cadogan Hotel was even dreamt of.

In the beautiful narrow lawns behind Cadogan Gardens, one of the old fellows who lived there showed me a crippled mulberry tree, which had, he said, been planted by King Charles II. One warm September evening, Rex and I sat in Hans Place, in the overgrown summer house, just catching the shimmer of a setting sun behind the yellowing leaves of the lime-trees, and he told me the impression Hawtrey and du Maurier gave on stage, as if they had somehow lost their way, en route to their Club.

'It was the total concealment of the fact they were acting, that did the trick. I know by now enough about it, they were all working very hard. It's very difficult,' he said, 'to conceal what you are doing. American film-stars are very good at it, Cooper, Gable, Fonda, Tracy, and when he dances, what better example could there be than Fred Astaire. And it was very conversational also, du Maurier had an uncanny way of coming on to the stage, and somehow seemed to be directly addressing you individually, wherever you happened to be seated in the stalls. Almost like ventriloquism. Just talking to you, individually, and nobody else. You see, the problem is, some of the younger actors think it can do the trick by coming on, and raising their voices. And of course, it doesn't.'

We watched a hesitant squirrel worry away at some fugitive spoils under the leaves; the light was falling unevenly now; we were in the shadows, 'You see, the easiest thing to do in acting, is come on the stage and rave and rant. There is nothing easier. And over-project. It's easy to do, and it makes acting easy to do. It was terribly difficult to do what those gentlemen did. People dismiss it these days, never having witnessed it, and say: 'Oh, that was merely technical virtuosity,' but it wasn't. It wasn't acting, it was *thinking*. Stripping off layers, reducing the whole thing to its spare essentials. You should look at Manolete, you should look at the tennis playing of Suzanne Lenglen, you should watch old footage of Walter Hammond at Lords. It's the same sort of thing. I suppose that's what I tried to do with my acting.'

'Holding,' I said, as Prince Hamlet says to the Player King, 'a mirror up to Nature.'

'Exactly. I mean, I could hardly have invented this, coming as I did from little Huyton in Lancashire. If I hadn't seen those marvellous people like Hawtrey, and du Maurier and Squire, I wouldn't have known anything about it. I always remember Garrick's advice to some impatient young member of his company, who wanted to progress to Tragedy the next year, when he warned him, 'Any fool can play Tragedy, but Comedy, sir, Comedy is a damned serious business.'

Remembering the conversation about appropriate titles for an autobiography, I thought, perhaps, that would be ideal for Rex's memoirs, which, at that time, he was contemplating writing: 'A Damned Serious Business'. And for once, Rex actually accepted my advice.

Chapter 26

VILLA SAN GENESIO

IT COULD WELL be said that in his way, although it had existed
for hundreds of years as prettily and tucked away as ever, Rex
Harrison 'discovered' Portofino for the world, or at least, he
invented it, in the same way the Scott Fitzgeralds invented the
Riviera. 'I was having a little rest in the Italian Riviera on a yacht,
and we sheltered in a harbour just to the north of Santa Margherita. It was almost landlocked, a little bay dominated by a fourteenth-century castle, overlooking a port. I looked around, and
thought to myself, my God, I've never seen anything so beautiful
as this.'

We were sitting in the hills above Vence one evening in
October, which was as warm as a midsummer's day. Racks of
lamb were slowly turning on the spit above faggots of rosemary, in
the open air; Rex, his sixth and final wife, Mercia, and myself were
sinking into the second bottle of Provençal wine, coarse, full-
bodied, the colour of setting sun. We were looking out to the
French Riviera, while Rex remembered eloquently his first expo-
sure to the Italian coastline, only a hundred or so miles southwards
down the map.

'Quite by myself, I walked through the old port, up an old
mule track, up and up, right on through a couple of iron gates,
and sometimes no gates at all, ruined bedsteads, and fences
strangled in thorn, right to the very top of the hill. There I sat
down, under the shade of an ancient olive tree, and looked around,
and listened to the cicadas, and it was absolutely magical. Not only
could I look down into the old port, but I was able to see the entire
bend in the coastline of Italy, along the Apennines, down to Santa
Margherita, I could see as far as the Cinque Terre, the Five Lands,

each of them topped by a castle, sometimes in ruins, and I thought to myself, this is Fairyland . . .'

The rack of lamb, perfumed with rosemary and sweetened with myrtle, pink at its centre, dark at its extremities, lay before us now, a large bowl of salt-sprinkled dry frites in the centre, and salad of tomato, onion, and heavenly basil on our left hand; the patron joined us, in his white apron and cap, and shared the rapture summoned up by Rex, as he remembered the golden years at Portofino.

In tribute to the excellence and simplicity of his cuisine, Rex patted the upturned head of the patron, tenderly, like a girl. For a little while, we ate in wondering silence, as the sun's great arc, half-blurred in heat-haze, descended into the sea. The candles, crazily scattered around, assumed their own flickering power; we ate in silence and in darkness.

'C'est bon?' enquired the patron, after a respectable time for appreciation had elapsed. We shook our heads from side to side, the way Indians do, when they mean 'yes'.

'I sat there, and rested,' continued Rex, 'under the olive tree, and a few mules tottered by. A small boy passed, carrying a lamb, I remember, and wearing an odd straw hat, I sat there and rested, and then I decided to walk down again, back to the boat. It was very, very quiet, all the trees were lichen covered, there was a mixed perfume of every kind of herb' and gesturing to the table, 'rosemary, fennel, tarragon, basil, and slowly, slowly, I descended the mule-track, back to the picturesque little harbour, and as I walked, I thought to myself, 'I wonder if there's any possibility in the world that land might be for sale . . .'

The patron served us with the best – that is to say, the least fierce – Corsican wine, 'un très bon vin de Patrimonio,' the flower of the island. We looked at Rex, swirling the dark glass stem in the candlelight. Nobody spoke. He nodded his approval, and wrinkled his basilisk eyes. The wine was poured evenly around.

'I got back to the hotel, the Splendido, rather a large, broken-down old pub, this was in the summer of 1949, I think, not really that long after the war. There was no such thing as a Marina, or a boutique, or even a trendy restaurant, just little fishermen's shacks around the port. Mercifully, Gucci was not even invented in those days, and the Splendido wasn't splendid at all. So, I went into the hotel, and spoke to the old concierge, and asked him if he thought there might be a chance of buying some land on the top of the hill. "Oh, just a minute," he said, pottered off to make a telephone call, and he came back to say: "Well, as a matter of fact, some of that land is for sale. I have spoken to the proprietor, the Contessa Besozzi, and she will meet with you tomorrow morning, at 11 o'clock, at the top of the hill." So I went back on the yacht to Santa Margherita, and in the morning, I came back, and there, standing in the centre of the very piece of land that I had been sitting on was this elderly Italian lady, the Contessa Besozzi, who was very anxious to sell the land. Can you believe it, three acres on top of the hill were for sale. I was on my way to Rome to make a terrible film, with my wife, Lilli, and together we worked on almost anything, just in order to pay for it, so I took old Contessa Besozzi with me, in order to meet the producers. I had the producers in one room, the Contessa in the other, the film was paid up in front in lire, and I bought the land. Can you believe it? God must have been sitting on my shoulder.'

The last flare of the red sun had been immersed in the red stain of the sea. Candles shook and danced like fireflies; our faces were shaded from one another by now. Light fell on large painted dishes of green figs, sprawled among their leaves, and goats' cheese, pungent, piquant, and overripe.

'Un fromage comme ça,' laughed the patron with mock severity, 'Ah! Il faut le respecter . . . Lui, c'est sérieux!'

'It's a fairy story,' said Rex, speaking out of the shadows by now. 'It was incredible. I built my house, and lived there for twenty-five years. Whenever I wasn't working, I made straight for San Genesio. Some of the happiest and unhappiest days of my life were spent at San Genesio. Max Beerbohm, who lived down the road in Rapallo, he gave me the idea of the name of the house. In Italy, San Genesio is the Patron Saint of Actors, so it was a wonderful haven for me throughout my restless years, a godsend. The three things I loved most were acting, primarily, and wine and the Italian Riviera. But with San Genesio, I got both the wine and the Italian Riviera.'

Of course it was at San Genesio, in July 1961, after a longish spell of unwelcome idleness, away from the film-studios, that Rex received his best break so far, since the film of *My Fair Lady*. This was the role of Caesar in what later proved to be the notorious romantic picture, inextricably tied in with their private passion, off-screen, the Burton–Taylor *Cleopatra*. It was touch and go Rex would be offered the part, for which he was desperate, in order to revive a flagging movie career. There were several other candidates, just as there had been for Higgins. The director, Joseph Mankiewicz, an old friend of his, was rooting for Rex. Finally, he got his man accepted and telephoned Rex, excitedly, at his home in Portofino, where Rex had studiously stayed away from the firing-line (a typical ploy, by the way).

'Rex, I've got you the part,' said Joseph Mankiewicz, almost shouting his excitement down the phone from Hollywood. 'The part of Julius Caesar is yours. But, to be honest, I truly had to fight for it. The studios came up with all sorts of names, but I held out, and finally, I told them to fuck themselves, and that if they wouldn't accept you in the part, they should start finding themselves a new director. I put myself on the line for you, Rex, old boy, and they finally gave in. Isn't that great news! See you in Rome, old boy!'

Rex had been seated in his large picture window, overlooking the sea. Beside him, sat his great friend and manager, the legendary Laurie Evans, agent to the stars and all the crowned heads of the English Theatre, Olivier, Richardson, Edith Evans etc. Just as Mankiewicz rang off, and Rex was still in the action of replacing the receiver in its cradle, he turned to Laurie Evans, and said: 'You know, Lol, I'm wondering whether Joe Mankiewicz is the right director for *Cleopatra*.'

Perhaps twenty-five years, and say, three marriages and divorces is long enough to live in any foreign country, however magical, however romantic; but after this time, and due to the breakdown of all the domestic relationships with his Italian staff, and the election of a local Communist Mayor (a somewhat Don Camillo situation), Rex grew increasingly disaffected with San Genesio. The roads were barred to him, traps were extended, his former butler tried to blast him with his shotgun, his jeep was sabotaged, and finally Rex sold the place, or, so he told me, gave it back to the Italians, with some bitterness. It was all rather tragical-farcical, with right and wrong on both sides. 'You've no idea,' screamed Rachel Roberts at him, during one of their fights, 'how the people *hate* you!. They haaaate you!' Around this time, the dog days in Portofino, his former press officer from *Anne of a Thousand Days*, Arthur Cantor, came to stay. He was forced to walk down and back again, up the no-longer romantic, pastoral mule-track, carrying the champagne from the old port, in an ice-bag, which had melted by the time he got there – the Communist servants were all on strike, and when Rex tried to break through to meet his guests in his jeep, the gardener blazed away with his shotgun. The poetry, alas, had evaporated.

There is a curious anomaly in the history of San Genesio, about which Rex was completely unaware. The story of the original Genesio, before sanctification came his way, concerns an actor, who was converted to Christianity, naturally, and crucified for his beliefs. Rather an unactorish thing, it must be admitted. The story captured the imagination of several people, including some playwrights, Plautus among them, I think, and Lope de Vega. It's surprising that Shakespeare, with his unerring gift for the metaphor of the theatre, passed it by. The contemporary playwright, Peter Barnes, had a shot at it, and came up with this rather effective scenario. After his conversion, and arrest, the original Genesio, apparently, and his company of actors were summoned by the Emperor, and told that, because of their artistic gifts, they would be offered a choice. Either they would be made to tour the provinces, or they would be crucified. Most of them chose to be crucified, Genesio among them. As that is undoubtedly the choice Rex Harrison would have made, it seems worth mentioning here, even as an afterthought.

Chapter 27

REHEARSALS APPROACHING

27 July, 1980 – New York

As WINTER GAVE way to spring in Manhattan, and then summer, Rex finished his tour of *The Kingfisher* with relief, and our rehearsals approached. The return from Santa Fe where I had been directing a centenary D. H. Lawrence Festival proved to be punishing in ways that the journey out was not. On my return, the unending build up of fatigue, the accumulated jetlag broke into one of the most terrible sensations of lassitude I had ever felt, which itself turned into bronchitis and then worst of all an abscess on my back upper molar which necessitated an extraction of my wisdom teeth. An unhappy sense of being reduced. I felt as if I was falling apart or decomposing in a rather unexpected and terrible way, reminding me that I was not as young as I once was, or thought that I was, and that it was like my deteriorating reaction to alcohol. In my glorious youth I used to get drunk, now I merely get hangovers. Jetlag sometimes feels to me like a terrible medieval punishment, as if one has stored up divine retribution.

When I came back to New York for *My Fair Lady*, there was a sense of expectation in the air. Formerly it had been a pleasure, sometimes a luxury, frequently a relaxation. This time we were truthfully in earnest. There were only forty-five days to curtain-up, we were to be performing in New Orleans on 16 September, which did not seem suddenly very far away. New York was shimmering and vibrating in a haze of dust at 3 p.m. as I drove in against the sun in a temperature of eighty-eight degrees. I collapsed in the coolness of my friend Harold DeFelice's Montparnasse-style apartment, on West 69th Street falling heavily asleep to the sound

114

of distant police sirens, and from somewhere remote, half from upstairs rooms of the same apartment the pulsing beat of a jazz combination. Harold reminded me of a Hollywood executive, who found to his astonishment he was always on intimate terms with the Top Ten, although he claimed not only to despise rock music, he was never aware of having ever listened to it. It emerged, he was sleeping above a disco and the music had subtly entered his subconscious. New York in the torpor and the taxi-drivers were impatient in the heat, driving as they do in Israel in summer, holding their doors ajar.

The next day I met with the team – Crandall Diehl, the choreographer and Bob Kriese, the Assistant Music Director, and Marshall, company manager, who had the air about him of a planter from one of Hemingway's Key West stories, always wearing pale linen suits, and faded straw Panamas. Crandall asked: 'How's the wig situation?'

Marshall replied: 'Well, the requirements say, forty-two chorus wigs, nine switches, twelve moustaches, three side-burns, two Harrison toupees, four Eliza wigs, two Mrs Higgins wigs, one Mrs Pearce wig, and one Mrs Eynsford-Hill wig. All of which, if you are ready for this, comes to $26,000 on hair alone. Oh, and the hairdresser wants an assistant also.'

I was rather alarmed at this sudden escalation of forces. 'My God, at this rate we'll end up with more assistants than people on the stage.'

Crandall answered me: 'Well, it did prove necessary in the last *Camelot* production. We drafted in somebody from the chorus, but as her tour progressed, the girl spent more time in the dressing-room with wigs than on the stage. Eventually she ended up opening a hairdressing salon in dressing-room 12, and to be quite frank she made quite a profitable business out of it, although contributed little to the show.'

Rex rang me later in the day, rather concerned, because he had had a conversation with Wilfred Hyde-White, and Wilfred was insistent that we ran the race at Ascot correctly. 'Tell your Director,' apparently Wilfred Hyde-White had said, 'that the horses must run from right to left, and not the other way around as they did in the original production. It always offended me every night I went on stage that although the audience never seemed to notice, or if they did, didn't seem to care, that the Ascot race was always run the wrong way round!'

That night I was at dinner with some very rich and smart friends of my wife, Alexandra, Lydia and Arthur Emil. They have a very beautiful house out on the Bay and spend their weekends in their country home in Rye, Westchester. One of their close neighbours and friends is Vera Stravinsky, widow of the great composer, and one evening when they were having dinner, al fresco, the evening looked as if it might be ruined by the intrusion of Arthur and Lydia's adolescent children, who were playing Rolling Stones rock music very loudly. When they apologized to Vera Stravinsky, she very gracefully said: 'No, do let them carry on, it's the same sort of noisy music my husband used to write.'

Happily, it was around this time, a young woman with a natural cockney lilt to her voice, as well as a poignant beauty, fitting for a Duchess, sang a little song: 'Colour me Blue', and succeeded in winning Rex's artistic heart. She played the all-important comedy scenes to perfection, neither strained nor arti-ficial, and appeared to fit the clothes and character of Eliza Doolittle. Her name was Cheryl Kennedy, and she was ultimately to play a dramatic and critical role in all our lives. As well as the mixture of commonplace and classical every Eliza needs, the comedic gift for Rex, the top G for Alan Lerner, her reticent vulnerability impressed me. I dislike a ballsy Eliza as much as I do a dry-as-dust Higgins, or Rex, a vulgarian Alfred Doolittle. But it was a vulnerability which was to affect all our lives eight months later on, in a way we had none of us anticipated.

At an early age, the infant Reginald put on a stage performance for his parents and sisters, although his act consisted entirely of himself taking a curtain call.

THE GENTLEMAN-ACTOR, *circa* 1930.
Not unlike his theatrical heroes, Hawtrey and du Maurier, who were, he thought, captured on stage as it were 'en route to their club'.

Rex as Platonov, one of his truly great characterizations, on the first day of rehearsal at the Royal Court, with two of his Russian 'wives', Elvi Hale (left), and – the very morning he met her – Rachel Roberts. Frank Finlay, who was in the company, describes how they fell immediately in love, the moment George Devine introduced them.

Disguised behind his beard, for Captain Shotover, around the same time Laurence Olivier failed to recognize him. Here chatting to Douglas Fairbanks Jr.

As Pirandello's deranged Enrico IV, after Professor Higgins, his indisputably finest role in the theatre.

An unusual reunion between Rex, as dapper as ever, and Alan Lerner and Fritz Loewe at Sardi's Restaurant, to launch the 1981 revival of *My Fair Lady*.

As Professor Higgins in the 1981 revival, which I directed on tour and on Broadway.

Rex and Memsahib (Mercia, the sixth and final Mrs Harrison)
on their wedding day in New York.

SIR REX HARRISON,
the morning he was
presented with his
knighthood, when to his
dismay he found 'the Queen
was not properly briefed'.
© Courtesy Solo Syndication.

The Incomparable Rex in his final year.

Photo by Kay Towner, © Courtesy Solo Syndication.

Chapter 28

FINAL DAYS AT THE AMSTERDAM ROOM

SO, WE ARE to open in New Orleans, hotter and muggier than New York, it is threatened, on 16 September, at the Saenger Theatre, an old presentation theatre. On Basin Street, for heaven's sake.

Talk centred around the disastrous opening of *Camelot* in Toronto: the girl was fired who originally played Guinevere, and they took in someone else from another show. Crandall said: 'They found a way that was *almost* legal to get the girl out of *Oklahoma*.' During the final auditions at the Trafalgar, a rather abrasive woman said sternly to me: 'I can't sing.'

'Neither can I,' said Rex, shortly and to the point.

During discussions over the sets with Oliver Smith, who appeared languid and articulate as ever, Bob said, regarding the scale of a newly demanded Cabman's Shelter: 'It sounds to me like it's $400 long by $300 wide.' I suggested jokily that we could fill out the number 'The Street Where I Live' with a few prostitutes strolling by, and Don Gregory, who like all producers was guarding against rising costs, said: 'At least I know how much *they* will cost – $100 maximum.'

August weather in New York is unkind to insomniacs. I stay up reading as late as I can at night longing for the temperature to drop, but it doesn't lessen or lower; the television weatherman jokily forecasts 'Thowers and Therms', and one bathes in perspiration. At midnight, sitting in one of Harold's cool armchairs enjoying the chill of the leather against my bare back, and listening quietly to a late performance of 'Siegfried Idyll', suddenly I hear a terrible savage shrieking row breaking out from an open window somewhere, unidentified in the darkness. It is a horrendous Hispanic argument accompanied by screams, breaking glass, and smashed windows. What Terry Southern, in one of his novels, calls 'an insane faggot hassle'. To the distant sound of approaching police car sirens, overwhelmed by heat, and the exhaustion of the day, I sink into an uneasy and unsettled sleep.

My dream is personal and precise. I am sitting half-way down the stalls, by the directors' table, technical supervisors, assistants on each side. A run-through has broken down, and the actors down-stage are appealing for guidance. Somehow, I am fast asleep. My first assistant is gently nudging me, but someone else (the choreographer?) is explaining: 'We're trying to contact Patrick, but he's asleep and at home in bed.' I find myself grateful for the morning.

The last days at our rehearsal space are spent on final preparations and final auditions. With Eliza cast, Pickering, and the chorus, now we are auditioning the understudies, and the stand-bys, there is no turning back. We found a splendid character man for Karpathy, a good cheerful soul for Mrs Pearce, an excellent quartet of servants, and a truly superb and inventive cover for Doolittle, who thrilled us and delighted us all. Called Ben Turpin, he had a Victorian white-haired Dickensian look, an Englishman stranded in the United States for something like forty years after World War II, and a quality not at all unlike the legendary Max Wall. He suited the music-hall element which of course Stanley Holloway always brought to the role, with a wonderful rubber-legged walk, allied to a melancholic countenance. Almost as if Don Quixote was playing the part, which was unlikely to be Shaw's idea of Mr Doolittle, but gave it an eccentric and original colour.

So now we are to begin rehearsals at the Trafalgar, Ray Cooney's short-lived attempt at an Anglo-American theatre, which stands on the seedier side of 41st Street. I shall miss the New Amsterdam Room, but not in the evaporating humidity, I admit, of the last few weeks. Rex said to me that he'd miss the nostalgia of the New Amsterdam Room, and the many memories he had of what he called 'those old white-tie days', but not as much as he would miss the proximity of porno houses on 42nd Street. A new version, I observed, in a lewd cinema next door, of *The Blue Lagoon* is called 'Disney Porn'. I wonder what the rather strait-laced puritanical Walt thinks about that.

Behind the Trafalgar alleyway is a nice old-fangled bar called the Writers and Artists Club on 40th Street with a private room to which we can withdraw. Interestingly enough, it was in this very room, that Andrew Lloyd-Webber, on a fleeting visit button-holed me to enquire if I might be available to direct his new musical based on T. S. Eliot's *Old Possum's Book of Practical Cats*. It struck me as an unlikely idea at the time, but an original one, and I said I would love to be considered, provided it could be staged on the splendid thrust stage of the Chichester Festival Theatre, to which joyful enterprise I had recently been appointed Artistic Director. Andrew had the, I thought, not very wise idea of adapting the New London Theatre, which nobody ever went to, and which was regarded as a vast white elephant, for an appropriate and permanent stage. He said that he wanted to originate his musical in this particular theatre, and that he believed instinctively in its future, however unlikely it may sound. I think that it must be admitted, now that *Cats* is twenty years and several hundred million pounds further on from this conversation, that his instinct was probably right.

Chapter 29

REHEARSING AT THE DAVID C. NIEDERLANDER

30 July, 1980

EVENTS MOVED FORWARD. Time passes. Deadlines approach irrevocably. The news coming out of New York is that *Camelot*, truly, is not very good. Richard Burton apparently has a strange illness called bursitis, and not long ago the stage manager was forced to bring the curtain down as he staggered and slewed around on stage.

Rex telephoned me, incapable of concealing a note of glee in his voice at the demise of our sister-show and therefore rival: 'The Boys won't tell me anything about *Camelot*: they refuse to be drawn, they won't mention it at all.'

Our stage manager, Marshall, tells me that now we are beginning rehearsals there, the Trafalgar Theatre has changed its name, and now on the Marquee is the unheroic title of its new owner: 'The David C. Niederlander'.

'We seem,' sniffed Rex, 'to have lost our formerly aristocratic flavour – I always felt "The Trafalgar" had class, even though it was a dump!'

1 August

Sitting in the middle of a tropical rain storm, soaking with perspiration, barely lifting a finger, attempting to find a draught. Even Harold's spacious and reposeful flat is like a perpetual sauna, the humidity is unrelenting, even as late as midnight, which it is now. The company manager, Marshall, telephones me to assure me: 'All our little chickens are safely in their hutches. Cheryl

Kennedy (Eliza) and Cathleen Nesbitt (Mrs Higgins) have arrived today, and are at the Mayflower Hotel. Cathleen was met politely by our producer, Don, and is dreadfully deaf. He said to me the first time he ever met her in London he should have been a little more cautious. When he asked her how her hearing was, she answered: 'What?' It isn't just a matter of raising your voice to her, it's a matter of shouting at the top of one's lungs and even then only getting a half-hearted reaction. In addition if she has asked me Marshall's name once, she has asked me a hundred times. I begin to anticipate an element of recklessness in hiring a 92-year-old, but I suspect Rex was determined the Boys would not cast, in the role of his mother, anyone younger than himself.

2 August

The next morning I go to see Cheryl and Cathleen at the Mayflower. We all had tea together with John Ridge, the sensitive designer of the Cecil Beaton wardrobe. Cheryl was looking most attractive, wide-eyed, bare-shouldered: in mid-town New York she looked, as indeed we all hoped she would, the epitome of English beauty, soft skin, light fair hair, dove-breasted, full-lipped. She has bought two pink mice for company, and keeps them in a cage. Cathleen three times her age looked like a little pink sugar mouse, diminutive, carefully made-up, equally pretty wearing a round pink hat. The three of us looked, I thought, like characters out of an early play by Somerset Maugham, in the middle of a New York delicatessen. Cathleen became quite animated on the subject of *Hedda Gabler* which Cheryl's former boyfriend, an Irish actor called Frank Grimes, was performing with Jenny Agutter at the moment in London. 'The last play of Ibsen's I was in was *The Cherry Orchard*,' she said, 'or was that by Strindberg?'
    'Chekhov actually . . .'
    'Oh, of course.'
    Cathleen ordered a child's ice cream. While she devoured it eagerly, she told me about former visits she had made to the United States in her lengthy past.
    'The first time I went across the Atlantic was in the old *Queen*

Mary. I was in a play by Lady Gregory and travelled with the Abbey Theatre Company from Dublin. It was my first job and I went over as an understudy. The leading lady was a marvellous woman, *très grande dame*, but for all that she got dreadfully seasick, and I heard her say: "Captain, make the ship stop this minute and let me off." ' It turned out that the dear leading actor, a distinguished Irish player, who was green, grey and white, alternately, as the ship lurched up and down, spread all his press notices in front of him on the floor, and was praying loudly: 'Oh dear God, now don't drown a great actor.' And to reassure himself he read aloud his notices: 'Now, God, listen to this. You can't possibly kill me, a famous actor, with press notices like that.' Interestingly, she reminded me, that when they got to New York, the Irish troubles plagued them even then, and as they disembarked there were protesters with banners on the docks, held back by New York cops behind the barricades. The slogans inveighed against an Irish company (Yeats and Lady Gregory) coming over under the protection of the British flag. This was before World War I.

That night I had dinner with Rex at Le Périgord. It was still suffocating. Cheryl joined us and we had a lovely dinner, although I couldn't help but notice that it cost $290. We devoured two excellent bottles of Montrachet 1976. I was delighted to discover that Rex took a real shine to Cheryl in the course of the evening, and gave her the benefit of his excellent and tasteful personal advice, that she should use her own hair swept up for the ballroom scene, and perhaps should think of a cloth cap for the Covent Garden scene and not the rather cutesy black straw hat of traditional usage favoured by Julie and Audrey. As we left the restaurant a police car came alongside with the top down. The shirt-suited traffic cop leant out and said genially: 'Hi, Rex, how ya doing?'

3 August

A valuable meeting on their own with Rex and the choreographer, Crandall Diehl. We talked about the posh version of Ascot, and changes that we hoped to make in 'Get Me To The Church On Time', and sorted out the 'uh' sound, imposed by Franz Allers, referred to in a rather unhelpful way by Rex as 'that c**t in the pit'. We altered theoretically 'The Rain In Spain', and took some of the vulgarity out of the cockney dances. Rex and I walked back together to the Drake, where we were staying, for our Sunday papers, and Rex spoke about seeing his neighbour, Greta Garbo, in the St Regis Hotel.

'She's an awful old grouse, really. Years ago under the influence of two whopping great vodkas she could be a lot of fun, but now she is a colossal bore. When somebody recognized her in the lobby of the hotel and asked: "It's Greta Garbo, isn't it?" she replied: "Some of the time."

'Which may be true,' said Rex, 'but is fucking boring.'

He dropped several hints that his wife Mercia, who was away at the time in Switzerland, was too bossy. 'I had a really frightful summer in Switzerland.' Do I detect the minutest of storm clouds? My God, I hope not. Is it even possible that Cheryl is in his eye as the seventh Mrs Harrison? We already seem to have a ninth Mrs Alan Lerner back in England. What a coup if Rex, as well as Alan, marries his Eliza! No, it's unthinkable.

4 August

Rex is certainly intent on Cheryl, and behaves most protectively towards her, and played the scenes we rehearsed *to* her with his familiar concentration. Long may it last. On the other hand, although we have most dinners together in the evening and Rex clearly enjoys her presence, and her rather dainty femininity, I think that he is always attentive to any attractive woman who is around, and always courteous, but that it means little more than that. And in addition, besides, he's on his own, and whenever he feels lonely on account of one woman, he will automatically turn to another. When I was talking to the producer, Mike Merrick, I wondered whether Rex was actually jealous of Burton, or whether he found any other star performer working in the same stable, as Burton obviously was in *Camelot*, an instrument of jealousy. Mike Merrick said that Richard Burton always maintained that John Gielgud enjoyed reading bad notices as he found it stimulating. 'Balls,' snorted Rex, 'no actor enjoys bad notices *ever* – it's simply a ridiculous Burtonism.'

Back in my cooler, but certainly not cool, room, I turned on the television and caught a few moments of Truman Capote, being interviewed, and speaking in his lazy, lisping drawl, like an iguana stupefied by the heat: 'I don't think tolerance will ever alter the attitude towards homosexuals. It's the instinct alone that can alter that, and it's one hell of a job to alter that.' I heard news concerning Alan Lerner in London, and that his cataract operation had been unsuccessful. Apparently he woke up and thought himself blind, and descended straight into symptoms of hysteria. He is now totally dependent on the kindness of his girlfriend, Liz Robertson, who takes him each evening to the theatre where he sits in her dressing-room all night, sightless, until the curtain. For once, I must say, Rex was extremely sympathetic, suffering himself from sightlessness in one eye, on account of a very early childhood attack of measles. Edward Fox told me, when Rex was rehearsing his role as the barrister-father, in John Mortimer's television version of *Voyage Round My Father*, that he refused to play the blindness. A somewhat crucial part of the character.

First there was the hand on the shoulder, next, the white stick, then even the challenge of the seeing-eye dog. None of these proved effective, and after a few days more, Rex enquired: 'I was wondering, John, if I could try perhaps a mote in the left eye?'

Shortly afterwards the production ran short of funds and was aborted, but Edward didn't think it looked particularly optimistic anyway.

5 August – First Attempts

First read-through and it went very well. Milo O'Shea (Doolittle), was very good and straightforward and played his shots down the middle of the wicket. Plays the cockney dustman Irish, but why not? The old lady was frail, but precise, and there was an impeccable Pickering from Jack Gwillim (the role is generally actor-proof). Rex was full of strength and vigour and humour and enjoyed himself, trim in look and charming. Cheryl Kennedy held her own and played the scenes very neatly. We only paddled around the edges of the songs as very few of them are learnt, but it was good to hear them. Rex made an excellent opening speech to the ensemble, and spoke effortlessly and without notes for several minutes about the history of the show and his involvement with the original. He said that the company should look upon him as a sort of 'father figure' and feel free to 'drop in on him'. I wondered, if, in the course of our long adventure, the rehearsal period, the tour, the New York run, any of those ingenuous and eager faces would actually have the courage to knock on his dressing-room door and take him at his word. While Rex made his paterfamilias declaration, the producers and I resolutely refused to catch one another's eye.

6–10 August

Every day slow determined plodding through the scenes, groping to remember what was good originally in the past production, and reform and revise what is either stale or perhaps not so good in any case. Rex demanded some authentic cockney dancing, and not the awful choreographic version of it, as of cheerful boys and girls dressed as Pearly Kings and Queens, sticking their thumbs in their braces, yelling out 'Oi! London . . .' and doing a kind of giddy knees-up.

Even so he was bothered by Nick Wyman, who plays Freddie, simply because he is so tall, and has difficulty with a natural English voice, and troubled by Mrs Higgins's understudy as Cathleen isn't very well. When I explained to him that this is unlikely to be the woman who will end up playing the part on stage, Rex retorted: 'Cathleen, who was totally disoriented when she arrived, still had authenticity and a sense of correctness.' I hope authenticity will not be our knell, as the worry always is with Rex that it is *My Fair Lady* we are performing and not Bernard Shaw's *Pygmalion*. Franz enlightened me into the artistry of what he calls the 'Luft-pause'. It is a peculiarly Viennese thing, something almost instinctive and most gracious, which he is able to introduce into the largely waltz rhythms of Fritz Loewe. It gives that fractional uplift in the middle of the waltz and introduces a delicious feeling of lightness, a minuscule caesura, far removed from the plodding *one*-two-three, *one*-two-three, of the Anglo-American version.

On arrival home, sitting by the window, gasping for fresh air, as darkness descended along the street, one had the impression of naked bodies emerging sensuously behind the slats of the blinds in the houses and apartments opposite. I recall a description given by Vladimir Nabokov in *Lolita* of Humbert Humbert on a similar occasion staring across the street and imagining he saw a comely nymphet with no clothes on in the room opposite, only to discover that he was looking at an old man reading a newspaper in an armchair.

12 August

Before rehearsal I was watching morning television and experienced a poignant reminder of the past, watching a repeat of Dick Cavett's interview with an alarmingly skeletal Kenneth Tynan. He was describing a visit to England in the previous summer, which he called 'a nation of good television and Indian food'; but this is a different summer, and there was no visit to England. Curious to observe his stammer, that small and characteristic flaw, now he is dead. A long time ago when I was at Oxford, he was terribly kind to me, and encouraging, and I remembered staying with him at his apartment in London, which felt to me the height of glamour. He was eloquent and tragically asthmatic in the television interview, and longing for cigarettes, upon which Cavett rightly commented. Tynan spoke of trying to give them up, and how there was an organization which offered your money back if their cure didn't work within a week. He got his money back. He said that he only smoked when he was under complete stress, which was, he admitted, most of the time.

At rehearsal it was another hard day, to be expected at this period in the schedule. It's difficult to set scene one, the Covent Garden scene, on its feet. Even in *Pygmalion*, it's always difficult, it's a prologue rather than part of the play. There seem to be too many opera-goers and too many cockneys in the same scene to allow a flow, and it's important not to over distract. The real problem is every time Franz enters, the rehearsals, even when they're going well, seem to grind to a grudging standstill as music takes over. Rex gets angry with him:

'I'm not going to hurry the tempo along just to win a few hands in New Orleans, and limp around the stage looking like a c**t.'

Cathleen Nesbitt is still ill, having only attended the first read-through, and my confidence is hardly encouraged, as whenever I go to visit her she doesn't remember me!

'Who are *you*, dear?' she says, or, 'Do I know you, dear?'

In the same scene I have always been impressed by Alan Lerner's impeccable timing in introducing the vital introductory book-number 'Why Can't The English Teach Their Children How To Speak?' which exactly reflects the opening line of Shaw's prologue to his stage play: 'Every time an Englishman opens his mouth, another Englishman despises him.' Although, Rex pointed out at the time that Alan didn't always get it right himself, when in the line 'He should be taken out and hung, for the cold-blooded murder of the English tongue', Rex observed the proper word should be 'hanged' and not 'hung'. Sometimes in performance he used to stop the number to point out this grammatical error to the audience.

13 August – Rehearsals move to the Trafalgar Theatre

Streets full of Democrats all bearing badges. An hour of magic on stage as Rex sang 'Accustomed To Her Face' in front of an empty auditorium to perfection. It was the first time he'd been through it with the pianist. The silent row of servants in the Higgins household watched spellbound from the rear of the stage and applauded when he finished. Throughout morning rehearsals I had noticed the curious presence of an entire bourgeois family, sitting in the stalls, father and mother, and three children, who shared innocently this moment of history. At first, I thought they were backers, or even technical staff. But I can only assume they must have wandered off the streets through the open doors of the theatre to get out of the heat of 42nd Street.

The producer David Merrick is postponing *42nd Street* for technical reasons. My assistant, Harold, who delights in news of any form of disaster, told me the celebrated Express train got completely out of control, and propelled itself firmly towards the orchestra pit. Tap dancing girls jumped off it in all directions left and right, musicians leapt out of the pit into the auditorium, they just about managed to bring the curtain down, but the nose of the train ripped right through it and stuck out into the auditorium at a lurching angle. I asked: 'Will the show run do you think?'

'Run – it won't even crawl.' Harold answered.

I can see why this hostility rises between the book people, like Rex and myself, and most of the actors, on one side, and the orchestra people, whenever a musical is being rehearsed. It still infuriates me that whenever Franz Allers emerges, my rehearsals grind to a terrible standstill, and somehow nothing gets done. Rational thought goes on hold, and gives place to the abstraction of sound. It reminds me of the famous anecdote about John Gielgud who was directing Berlioz's opera *The Trojans* at Covent Garden, in final dress rehearsal when the on-stage chorus arrived at a point in the Storm Music which Gielgud had either forgotten to, or failed to, direct. Being singers, and not being actors, instead of improvising their way through it, the chorus stopped everything dead and just stood there, and Gielgud's voice – totally audible to the director, conductor, and most of the management of the Royal Opera House – was heard wailing above the orchestra: 'Oh, for God's sake, can't somebody stop that terrible terrible music.'

In my absence, while I was directing the ensemble, a furious row broke out between Franz and Rex. Rex, lifting the well-known forefinger, stormed: 'I always knew he was a c**t, and this merely confirms it.'

For all his faults, Franz was much more of a peace-maker, and all he said was: 'Rex was wonderfully rude to me this morning, but then so he was twenty-five years ago.'

On this occasion I managed to resolve it diplomatically and could not help but feel rather pleased with myself. The problem is that there's a cut in the music of 'Get Me To The Church On Time'. Franz was insisting on a *different* cut, even the restoration of the cut. I make it clear that that is out and, rather to my surprise, Franz capitulates quite easily and changes the music. All ends well. As the choreographer, Crandall, says: 'This cut in the cockney dance is a *condition* of Rex's acceptance of the part, not a caprice; and it protects us (or should do) from even more brutal cuts. For once Franz was amused at the deceit. Ever a man for Machiavellian subtleties, Franz reminded me of a story of how a famous aria got into the last act of *Die Fledermaus*. The diva, an intensely egocentric woman, no less than Rex Harrison, was carefully manoeuvred by the producers into a very complicated costume change in her dressing-room, and, being off stage at the time, never knew that another show-stopping aria to be sung by somebody else had been inserted.

The rest of the day progressed splendidly. Rex truly is in superb elegant form, knows all his lines, and his songs far better than anyone else. I realize that they are deeply buried in his subconscious even from twenty-five years ago. The three principals Doolittle, Eliza, and Pickering played up well.

Franz may be obstinate musically, but he is an intensely cultivated man, and was most complimentary after he had watched a little of the rehearsal, commenting to me that there was nothing funnier in the world than elegant English high comedy playing, although – a considered and awkward reservation – he queried seriously whether the audiences we were playing to in America were going to be intelligent enough to appreciate it. Rex has now all his numbers staged, and knows his words within them impeccably, apart from 'I'm An Ordinary Man', in which he's in great danger of repeating 'I'm a very gentle man' in place of 'I'm a quiet living man', thus sending us and the orchestra back to the very beginning of the number all over again. Rex enjoys his fellow artists, especially Milo and Cheryl, and has established quite a close friendship with Jack Gwillim as Higgins and Pickering should. He said to me this morning in a short break: 'I don't know that Jack will make all his points as Colonel Pickering; still, probably no bad thing.' He does however have an awkward tendency to treat the *actors* playing Professor Higgins's servants as *his* servants.

He can't be counted upon always to be so engaging to his fellow artists. At a first reading of a play by Freddy Lonsdale, nodding his head in the direction of a very respectable character actor, he grumbled to the director: 'Who's that bastard over there?' and, worse, at the beginning of a television play he asked the script editor: 'Who on earth is that woman, who looks like a prostitute?' Unfortunately, it was the script editor's wife. He's taken a great shine to Judith, the delightful girl who plays the modest part of the Cook, he likes to call her Cookie. This morning she came to work rather fetchingly in a striped leotard, which emphasized to the full her curvaceous form: 'Why doesn't Cookie play the part like that?' said Rex, 'The customers would love it.'

14 August – The Democratic Convention arrives

To the strains of a brass band playing 'Happy Days Are Here Again', we had the nominations and acceptance by Jimmy Carter and Fritz Mondale for the leadership of the Democratic Party; but in spite of the jubilation there seemed little conviction, no confidence, and empty liberal rhetoric. It reminded me of the Labour Party Conferences back in England, and the May Day parades, choking, well-meant, Liberal cant: 'Strong and Compassionate Government', when was it ever otherwise? But essentially it has been a one-plank platform preoccupied in keeping Ronald Reagan out rather than forcing Jimmy Carter in, who looks pretty much of a non-entity at best. As a commentator in the hall volunteered on the performance of Carter: 'He inspired as much love as City Hall.' In the middle of a windy speech by Mondale, a lone dissenter in the braying hall held up a placard: 'Surely You Jest'. Its Liberal blandness hit a particular, and not unobserved low, by totally failing to refer to the US hostages, now in their 250th day in Tehran. The four main newscasters wear as a badge of office and affectation, head-phones with mouth-pieces and aerials which are the fashion of the year, rather like leg-warmers on the chorus boys, but make them look rather like underwater divers with snorkels, faintly ludicrous and idiotic. As a more waspish commentator observed: 'All that unifies the Democrats is November.'

At the end of rehearsals I thought to myself, great heavens we are only one month away, and building up to next Thursday's run through. It's good to see how we are getting on. Back to work now and seemingly recovered, Cathleen is rather effective in a qualified way; marvellous in atmosphere, like a dear little sparrow, her spindly legs in their white stockings, her neat pressed clothes – over-dressed we would say – always wearing a smart hat, but absentmindedly forgetting her deaf-aid, and with a lovable smile failing to understand a word I, or Rex, or anybody else says. She *seems* to know her lines. Rex goes from strength to strength, really putting the performance together.

Drinks at the Barrymore with Franz and Bob Kriese after rehearsal, and relished our talk of operatic music and the symphonies of Mahler and Bruckner, rather refreshing to get away from the world of musical comedy. Franz was most sensitive to Rex's lack of enthusiasm or even interest in the problems of the musical element. 'He wants me to conduct by magic,' complained Franz, 'I don't mind taking the beat from him, or following him, provided he gives me at least an indication of what it is he wants me to follow.' This was a rather inhibiting interpretation of Rex's famous retort: 'I don't follow the conductor. The conductor follows me.' Out of the blue, Bob asked me: 'Why did God create the Goyim?' I said I didn't know. 'Someone had to buy retail.' Speaking of the early days of the show, when it began under the impressive leadership of Moss Hart, a Broadway legend, Franz told me that quite a lot of the material was changed on its original tour. Rex once performed a number called 'Dressing Eliza', and that was cut in New Haven. Also the waltz, later incorporated into the Ballroom scene, called 'Lovely Liza', of which Rex so disapproved when he was first involved. Franz was deeply impressed by the quality of Rex's high-comedy skills. He described him perfectly: 'He has the precision, the industry, and the obsessiveness of a vaudevillian.' – the highest praise. Rex used to complain that the very name 'Eliza', fell spontaneously into three-four time.

15 August

Collecting Rex from his beautiful East Side apartment overlooking the river began in comedic terms as a curious *opéra bouffe* took place between Rex and his housekeeper, Angèle, who speaks no English in exactly the same way that Rex speaks no French. Both of them totally failed to communicate with one another. Angèle, to her great credit, being elderly, and French, and a housekeeper, and having nothing to do with the insane world of the theatre, holds her ground splendidly, and expresses just as much impatience with Rex's incapacity to understand her, as her incapacity to understand him. I suspect she thinks of him as a 'con'.

A slug of a day, ironically, when the weather switched round, and light winds cornered in all directions, setting the intersection traffic lights swinging haphazardly back and forth. The unusually eloquent taxi-driver described the sky 'with its beautiful Turner-esque-cloud patterns'. At least he spoke English, thank God, or American anyway. Usually it's an inarticulate Hispanic, which I find deeply alien to the New York I know and love.

Whereas some things are avowedly simpler for me in the blocking, the scenes involving Rex and Colonel Pickering and Eliza and Mrs Pearce for example, other aspects are harder. As I'm not working from my own plan, but from undependable scripts, handed down, full of other versions added, Pygmalion apocrypha, if you like; it gives me a very easy idea of why there are so many irregularities in Shakespeare's Folios and Quartos. This show is after all only twenty-five years old and there seem to be all sorts of textual ambiguities. The day was exceptionally difficult, though, because of Cathleen, and this time I feel I have encountered an obstacle which is going to be insuperable. The poor old lady neither remembers, nor hears; she sent back to the hotel for her hearing aid which she had left there, but when she found it she couldn't adjust it properly. She can't hear without it, she doesn't know how to manipulate it, and she usually forgets where she's mislaid it. Marshall, more than ever looking like a Caribbean planter in his straw hat, which he persistently wears inside as well as outside the theatre, tries to help her. Her sadly tormented arthritic fingers, twisted like plant roots, cannot feel to adjust the volume, which is either too silent, or on occasion hums very loudly. The morning seems to be interminable, and for me exhausting; I shout the instructions as politely as I can, but shouting raises one's emotional temperature, and everything gets worn away. My brain is mesmerized by the prospect of Cathleen, I'm unable to think of anything else. Freddie's size still intimidates Rex. And another row brews over the vexed question of the double-banked xylophone in the pit, which emerges as a terrible red rag to Rex. Perhaps Rex had good reason to be anxious. Most timpanists are slightly insane, and at Drury Lane some years ago, during the third or fourth year of the run of *No, No, Nanette*, the drummer – suddenly and without warning – stood up during a tender moment in the show, and struck his gong, announcing to the astonished audience: 'Ladies and Gentleman, dinner is now served.'

16 August

Today an extraordinary thing happened. In the morning Rex went to his tailors, Brooks Brothers, for a second fitting of his Ascot togs and the Embassy Ball clothes. So I was left with his stand-by, who regularly fills in for him, far more than an understudy, a dear fellow called Michael Allinson. On his own admission, he has made quite a career out of standing in for Rex in various productions, irrespective of whatever they may be, and not only *My Fair Lady*, all over the world. But as I advanced the rehearsal, thinking I would get a chance to concentrate on the other characters in the Higgins Study scenes, namely Mrs Pearce, Eliza of course, and Colonel Pickering, nothing seemed to be going right. Worse than that it was as if the elementary blocking which I had been working on painstakingly for about a fortnight would all have to be done again. Nothing of it seemed to make any sense, above all the focus was not in the right place. Shaping the scene, giving the moves, which Wendy Hiller (who played Eliza originally on screen to Leslie Howard's Professor Higgins) called 'the footwork', all of these things are merely the director's job in making sure the focus of the scene is in the right place; namely, that the audience are looking where they are meant to be looking, and listening to what they are meant to hear. This is the director's most important function, and in my case, in this particular play, it was not making sense, and I became more and more horribly aware of it. Above all Professor Higgins was, not only, *not* in the right place, but somehow he was not even in a logical position on stage, and I knew that Rex, when he returned, would query it, and demand the moves to be changed. So I began doing the thing that I most dislike doing, and which drains one's confidence like an emptying swimming pool, namely re-ordering the blocking. Old moves were rubbed out on the deputy stage manager's script, and my assistant was busy with his ruler and pencils re-marking mine.

Eventually I managed to bring some sort of coherence and sense into the scenes and by the time we broke for lunch, everybody seemed reasonably happy. Michael Allinson, the cover, was extremely cooperative, and said how he too had often noticed that the blocking needed to be altered when he took over the role because the sense of *command* which is absolutely vital, did not always seem to be in its proper place.

Rex returned in the afternoon, and somewhat timidly I began to introduce the changes that I'd made in the morning, somewhat intimidated, and certainly apprehensive of his sudden rages, aware that Rex was always very conservative and disliked any form of change. However, as he began to perform the scene, and as I'd already observed, was in many ways ahead of all the others, and

134

most secure on his lines, the moves which I had changed in the morning no longer seemed to be quite as essential as I had thought. In fact, Rex appeared positively jaunty, and bounced the lines back and forth with pleasure and with charm, and I found myself interrupting far less than I thought I was going to have to do; eventually it began to dawn on me that there was nothing wrong with the original blocking, and so long as Rex was on stage there was no need to alter anything because wherever he was, there the focus was. He could be behind the study chair, bent behind the globe, crouching over a gramophone, in a weak barely lit (although that was unlikely!) far corner of the stage, wherever he was the eye would automatically fall. It is saddening to have to admit, but such is the power of Rex's physical presence, that he could be anywhere he liked on stage and people would look for him; remove him from the scene and put in, dare I say it, an inferior, or less charismatic actor, and the eye immediately became restless in its intuitive search for harmony. This to me was as vivid an illustration of what is meant by that mysterious word 'star quality' than almost anything that I can think of.

One other example springs to mind. Several years earlier I had directed Ingrid Bergman in a rather charming English 1950s play called *The Waters Of The Moon* by N. C. Hunter. After it had been running for several months at the Haymarket Theatre, where it was extremely successful, some American friends of mine who were both very well known in the theatre, one a director, one an actress, went to see a matinée by themselves. When we met for tea afterwards, they were extravagant in their praise, joyful in their experience of the play, and to my personal delight, rather more complimentary about the direction than they needed to be. I genuinely expressed my gratitude but tipped my hat in the direction of the cast, I had after all Wendy Hiller as well as Derek Godfrey and Ingrid Bergman in the cast.

'No,' they persisted, 'you made some beautiful directorial choices, which were very discernible and greatly contributed to the harmony of the production.' Again, I suppose I must have replied to this with a shrug of so-called humility! 'For instance,' said my actress friend, 'it was a wonderful idea to have used a pin-spot just on Ingrid Bergman's face, following her around the stage, so that wherever she went, the eye of the audience was bound to follow. It gave a most wonderful sense of charisma and personal magic.'

'That personal charisma you speak of is the special allure which Ingrid Bergman bears with her wherever she goes on stage,' I said, 'because you have my word, that there was no pin-spot. It can only have seemed as if there was.'

But at the end of the day it was, I must admit, a great relief to me not to have to reblock the entire First Act. That evening I went out with Rex to a lovely North American fish restaurant, and we enjoyed a meal of bracing fresh Atlantic white fish. At the restaurant we seemed to strike unlucky with a daft or stupid manager, who made the great mistake of tempting Rex with wines, as if he was a schoolboy on an outing:

'A Pouilly, sure, we have a great Pouilly.'

'What year?'

'Oh, Mr Harrison, you'll love it, it's a great year!'

'I'll be the best judge of that,' snarled Rex.

As we had difficulty in getting the *maître d'hôtel* to understand our order, Rex thought that he was probably deaf.

'For one terrible moment, I began to think everybody connected with this production is deaf. Well, there's Jack Welles, the stage manager, and Cathleen, and Jack Gwillim doesn't hear too well.' In fact it was Jack who had said earlier to me that the long tour round America was probably like Napoleon's retreat from Moscow, and Cathleen Nesbitt would be the first to drop behind. In fact this was ominously correct.

There were no proper Grand Cru vintages on the menu, which infuriated Rex, and he seemed ill-tempered. The manager asked for his signature not once but twice, which Rex signed graciously but reluctantly, and then after a formidably expensive dinner when he asked for a taxi, the manager had the impertinence to say:

'They don't want to wait, sir. But if you go outside, make a left on 5th Avenue, there are plenty of taxis . . .'

Rex turned to stone and his eyes were hollow. 'Get me a taxi.

At once.' And as the man turned his back, in a loud voice sure to be overheard, he added sharply and firmly: 'C**t.'

17 August

A day off. Rex and I met for breakfast. He was in an excellent mood, and we had a recap on the journey we had already taken, how well we felt we might be placed, where the dangers and disadvantages were, where the weaknesses might be found.

'Patrick,' he said, 'you're doing this beautifully, infinitely better than I could have imagined.'

I expressed my surprise, but he seemed genuinely contented with the state of progress. Later on over the scrambled eggs and salmon, he said: 'In the 1950s, the angry young men adopted a certain pose, an attitude, and expressed a point of view, largely unpopular at the time . . . and in this mood of disapproval they became even more arrogant than before. I think our attitude on *Fair Lady* should be the same. We will do it as well as we can and the way we want it done. If the customers like it – grand. If they don't: fuck them.'

Later we walked down the thronged summer streets of the Upper 70s and Broadway, so reminiscent of Paris, and the pavement cafés on warm nights, into Bloomsday's, the all-night bookshop, to buy some W. H. Auden, and Scott Fitzgerald, and then into Food City – the exhilaration of the great supermarket and the highly charged poetry of miraculous and exotic packaged food. The fulfilment of the best food and cookery store in the Western world: Zabars.

Rest, Reading, my definition of R & R! To lunch at the Szechuan restaurant, an Hispanic Chinese place on the West Side. I took the exquisite, statuesque dancer from the ensemble, Elizabeth Worthington, popularly called by the rest of the gypsies in the show 'Wa Wa'. She had as easily caught my eye as well as Rex's, and she was soon to become his special favourite, until, that is, disaffection set in when we were at New Orleans. We went for a walk up the West Side of Central Park and she took me to a most extraordinary secret place, of which few people had ever heard, where in earlier days she used to go riding. These were riding stables, way up on 85th Street, in a huge Victorian warehouse, where the horses were stabled upstairs. The walls and ceilings were covered with cobwebs as thick as if artificially laid on at a movie studio. The horses were restless because outside in the streets reaching towards Harlem young kids were banging toy bombs. Elizabeth told me it had always been a livery stable, built as long ago as 1900. I asked her where she lived, and she replied: 'Where all the Show-Trash live, along the West 40s in Hell's Kitchen.'

18 August – Monday: The third week

With a kind of mercy, at long last cooler days arrive. The wind from both rivers circulates through the large spare rooms in Harold's Montparnasse-style apartment. But the work turned into rather a glum and rotten day. Cathleen is now physically a hundred per cent better, even perky, but she performs one hundred per cent worse. Before, she didn't remotely know her lines. Now she *nearly* knows them, and so there are tantalizing, agonizing lapses. Words and lines and moves suddenly and inexplicably vanish. There is a terrible tension throughout the entire company. At least I get through all of her scenes, but only just about to the end of them. A terrible incident took place yesterday, Sunday. The hotel called the third assistant at 9.30 a.m. to say Miss Nesbitt was all ready and waiting in the lobby. She had mistaken Sunday for Monday. During a break over a cup of tea she told me about the time she met Sarah Bernhardt: 'What was she playing?' I asked.

'It was what we call a flying matinée. She was in Dublin, and I met her in Belfast, she had come to a performance for the afternoon by train. She was then in her seventies.'

'Playing Phèdre?'

'I think it must have been. It was certainly a costume role, and she was wearing some sort of draperies. She remembered me from the time before.' And then Cathleen spoke in flawless French: 'Ah! c'est la petite fille adorable de mon capitaine aimable.' It was her father, the sea captain, who had allowed Madame Bernhardt to bring her animals with her of which she had quite a number: 'I don't remember what part she played,' said Cathleen, 'but I *do* remember the effect she had on the audience. We were all in floods of tears.'

Adorable though she was, and miraculous as a figure of history, at the end of the day we all met, Rex, whose unfortunate idea to cast the 92-year-old Cathleen Nesbitt as Mrs Higgins it had been in the first place, myself, the two producers Don Gregory and Mike Merrick. The unspoken reproach towards Rex was obviously that he wanted his mother to be played by somebody who could, authentically *be* his mother. So that if Rex was in his early seventies, it had by definition to be somebody in their early nineties. We knew it was fruitless to continue. We agreed we would stagger on until Thursday and the final dress rehearsal and invite Milton Goldman, her agent, so that he can see the performance, and find a way where she could be politely released. I think all the time of John Aubrey, when he remarks: 'Oh, the misery of old age. Surely the day of one's death should be counted among one's happiest.' As she made her way out of the theatre, out of the corner of my eye, I saw Cathleen struggling with her deaf-aid, and it fell on the floor, and her poor arthritic fingers struggling to pick it up, and to manipulate it. She had said to me earlier: 'I lost my sight ages ago, then I lost my hearing, and now I'm losing my memory. In a couple of years I shall be completely senile.' And of course, seeing her, I'm reminded of my own dear mother at home in Hampshire, and her receding senses, and the frustration and impotence of her memory, and how wonderful it used to be, and how forlorn she is now. She and Cathleen, sometimes, in an agony of frustration, resort to beating their foreheads with their knuckles, rather like an expressive mime in the Greek theatre. Just as I was leaving, I was a little cheered by exchanging a word or two with my friendly stage manager, Jack Welles. He had worked on the musical of *Irene* with Debbie Reynolds, which John Gielgud directed a few years before. He told me the curtain went up at the dress rehearsal, with the entire company on stage, and Sir John's voice was heard wailing from the back of the stalls: 'Will somebody please tell all those actors what to do!' I knew the feeling.

19 August

As Winston Churchill said about the origins of World War I, the terrible 'ifs' accumulate. Now Milo's ego is bruised and offended at the new conclusion of 'Get Me To The Church On Time'. He wants to restore the original far more vulgar ending. And what's more he has a point. As he explains to me: 'Why change something which has brought the house down for twenty-five years?' which is another way of saying what Alan Lerner firmly insisted to me back in London before we began. 'Never interfere with a hit.' But the vulgar ending of the number, when Mr Doolittle is carried off by his drunken cockney friends to the wedding, bearing a large and rather obscene lily, is exactly what Rex does not want. It has been an unfunny and grudging day. To everybody's dismay, Cathleen fell over on stage in the Ballroom scene, and then redeemed the whole episode by dropping a most beautiful, full curtsey, as the Queen of Transylvania passed by.

20 August – The First Stagger Through

Cathleen confounds us all! I suppose this is what is meant by Doctor Theatre, even if it arrives at a moment when none of us particularly wanted it. Apart from an awkward start: 'Oh dear, I thought it was a totally different scene . . .', at Ascot, she found her way through the play, miraculously, and flawlessly, not dropping a line, although a little underpowered. To our dismay and her agent's delight, who sat there enchanted, she even towards the end, played her scenes positively, and earned a genuine hand from the gypsies watching. So we are by contract *bound* to stumble on towards New Orleans. Nobody can deny that her courage is indomitable.

Her agent, the legendary Milton Goldman, is renowned for his astonishing memory, and the facility to introduce everybody, not only by name, but with their professional credits. Keith Baxter told me that Milton came round to his dressing-room one evening, after a performance of *Sleuth* in which Keith was starring, and introduced a series of people to him: 'This is Joe Tillinger, who is currently directing a new Neil Simon play on Broadway, this is Irene Cratchett, who is designing the revival of *Oklahoma*, this is Steve Golightly, who is just about to play the leading role in Woody Allen's latest film in New York, and...' Turning towards a last, anonymous, rather non-descript looking woman, he suddenly ran out of credits. 'And this,' said Milton triumphantly, 'is Mrs Hilary Wall, and she's a very devout Roman Catholic!'

Earlier, I had lunch with Cathleen at the Fashion Plate, on 42nd Street. She spoke of her life in Ireland as a child, and a young actress auditioning for the first time. It was there in Dublin that she first met the poet W. B. Yeats, and had innocently made the mistake of auditioning for him by reciting his famous poem 'The Lake Isle of Innisfree'. Cathleen told me that he was rather uncomfortable during her recital, and she wondered if she had spoken it incorrectly. 'Oh no, my dear,' replied the great poet to the young girl, 'you see when I wrote that poem, it appears I made something of a hit with it, but I'm so uncomfortable with its success that there are times when I wish I had never put pen to paper.' Later he told her that she read very well, but asked her: 'Now young lady, can you speak to me a few words in the brogue?' I'd held off all this time talking to her about Rupert Brooke, because I felt that she must be as fed up with hearing people ask her about her romance with Rupert Brooke as Yeats was in hearing his lines from 'The Lake Isle of Innisfree'. It was eerie hearing her call the long dead romantic poet, after all these years, simply, 'Rupert'. In fact, what she had to say was extremely interesting:

'I always think Rupert knew he already, so to speak, had written himself out by the time he left for the War. He wrote very well on the Elizabethans, and might have made something of a scholar. I believe he might have been an essayist, and he was planning a huge book on the History of England. He never really cared for the theatre, and frankly looked down on it. And certainly he disliked actresses! Rupert used to say to me, "you're really quite intelligent, you know, *some* of the time, for an actress...!" He wrote a play himself once, which I read, but it was a very dull, heavy piece, you know. It wasn't really playable. He was much more neurotic than people choose to remember, but not so neurotic as John Lehmann made him in his book.'

The stagger through went well beyond measure, apart from Cathleen's great comeback, everyone was off the book, the songs were well sung, the dances well danced, and everything seemed thoroughly rehearsed; apart from one or two tiny gaps, easily patched up, everybody involved with the show was highly pleased. As my colleague Michael Blakemore once said on what must have been a similar occasion, 'all grounds for confidence, but none for complacency'.

However Rex's attitude was very different from all of ours, that is the creative team, and his slit-eyes seemed to alight particularly on Milo as Doolittle and Cheryl as Eliza, whose splendid performance had created a little more reaction among her colleagues than I would have desired. The director's chief fear in any play or any show, is that the star's prodigious power will not shine by making the others dull. Cheryl had been a little too enthusiastically received by her fellow artists, who perhaps by then were rather used to Rex's performance, and had not seen much of hers. I pray that he will not try to undermine the effect of two performers, one of the front rank and the second whose scale is correctly judged for the large theatres in which we will be performing. I would not wish to see one iota of Milo O'Shea's exuberant, over-the-top performance reduced. After all *My Fair Lady* is not a string quartet, and our audiences will be in their thousands, not in their hundreds. It is a show, and indeed a character, which insists on fairly broad strokes.

As for Rex, he was impeccable. It is a special quality of grace on the stage, almost impossible to define, difficult to describe, and totally impossible to imitate. He has an utterly unique and fastidious style. 'Wrap her up, Mrs Pearce,' says Professor Higgins, as Rex lopes around the stage. He then sets out a brilliant and delicate mime of wrapping Eliza up in a brown paper parcel with string, knotting it eloquently, and tossing it on to the table. And all the time it's beautifully underplayed. Apparently there was a time when he was doing a film with another rather well-known English character actor, and after they'd read through the scene, and were about to shoot it, the second actor said to Rex, 'I thought I'd do nothing in this scene, if it's all right with you, old boy?'

'Don't you dare,' said Rex angrily, '*I'm* the one doing nothing.'

When he was in the film *The Agony And The Ecstasy* with Charlton Heston, which in his words to me, he said he thought was meant to be a film about one of the Borgia Popes and, in his own words, 'turned out to be some sort of melodrama about a roof-painter!' He was completing a scene with a splendid English character man called Richard Pearson, now retired, who played the Pope's Priest. When they had done a couple of rehearsals of it, and the scene consisted of a long tracking shot down the length of the Sistine Chapel, which had been reproduced in its entirety in a Hollywood studio, Rex announced to Richard Pearson that although he thought the scene had gone rather well, he felt himself aware that there was only one light on them. 'Well, that's what I thought,' said Richard Pearson, 'I got the impression that there was only one key-light on us.'

'Then for Christ's sake get *out* of it, Richard.'

21 August – Visit to Up-State New York

Events of the previous afternoon, and Rex's ambiguous attitude has made me very wary of the next few days. I truly hope that Rex's disapproval does not frown on Cheryl just at the moment as she's beginning to emerge as a successful and eloquent Eliza. *My Fair Lady* is not a one-man show, and of course I am now haunted by all the comments that Rex has made hitherto on his previous Elizas, none of them charitable, and on his disapproving comments about the many talented musical comedy ladies who auditioned for us. Is it rather that Higgins is jealous of Eliza or is it simply Rex not wishing to share the limelight? Either way is a disadvantage for myself and the balance of the show. There is nothing in the world I can actually do from now on to prevent Eliza being very good, nor will I. Cheryl Kennedy has tasted blood at exactly the right moment, and she can only get better and better. After all Rex selected her, with me, and indeed with Alan Lerner, and went to a great deal of trouble to do so, rejecting many others by the way. There is little now that anybody could do to prevent her being fabulous.

'I don't think I will ever trust that little girl again,' said Rex darkly, 'after what she did at the run-through.'

This is desperately unfair. Everybody *has* to change gear at some stage, it is axiomatic, otherwise the show simply remains in a rehearsal condition. Nothing, to my mind, is more ghastly than a modest or retiring actor. What you want is an actor with the killer instinct. Or, rather as Noël Coward commented once, 'inside the exquisite shape of an elegant and gifted actress you will usually find the twisted body of a horrible old man'. What Cheryl did, to quote Rex, 'was suddenly come forward and give a performance, which was (a) good and (b) threatened to dominate me.' My friend, the choreographer, Crandall fears that we should sacrifice all the musical comedy values. I see it will be uphill work from now on.

On a happier occasion Rex and I visited *Camelot* together, which has now reached New York. Richard Burton made an enchanting speech from the stage. He said that when he opened the show Rex had sent him a telegram, 'Are we both mad? Love Rex'. There were several celebrities in the audience, Farrah Fawcett and Ryan O'Neal and Tatum O'Neal. Rex received a standing ovation as he entered, after the entr'acte, and indeed as he left the theatre, typical of the generosity of American audiences. And then there is that strange easy-going intimacy. As members of the audience pass to and from their seats they say affectionately: 'Hi there, Rex.' I suppose it's true, they really are looking for some kind of royalty to admire, which is part of their intuitive generosity. Rex is puzzled and said to me once rather endearingly: 'Whenever I hear applause, I always assume it's because somebody else has entered the room.' Later, he began justifying his attitude towards Cheryl, or at least voicing his own deep unease. 'My instincts, naturally, are invariably right, and when I feel something's wrong I damn well know it *is* wrong. And I don't want to stand up there, looking like a c**t.' His customary refrain whenever he didn't feel entirely at ease.

144

26 August

August 26th began rather sensationally with the death announced on stage by its producer, David Merrick, of the choreographer and director Gower Champion, who was directing *42nd Street*. My assistant, Harold DeFelice, who was there said it was a grotesque experience, not unlike the end of *Pagliacci*, with the producer making a sentimental speech, which contributed obviously to the huge success of the show. There had been furious rows behind the scenes, which was an ironic counterpoint to the sentimental monologue played on stage on the opening night by Mr Merrick. The director had been fired, and all the producer would permit on the theatre-bills, where the director's credit would normally have been was: 'crossovers and lead-ins'. As Harold said: 'Why make a speech about it? Surely he didn't expect the public to turn up and say we must see *42nd Street*, that's the show that murdered the director.'

Although the front show-curtain is dreadful, the 'Street Where You Live' show-curtain is all right. Rex says it looks like Pittsburgh or Detroit today, and not London in 1912. 'It seems to be composed of industrial complexes, precincts, prisons and madhouses.' I rather agree with him. When Stephen Sondheim presented *Sweeney Todd – The Demon Barber of Fleet Street* under the direction of Hal Prince, they had gone to immense trouble, and almost illimitable expense to buy an original turn-of-the-century Industrial Complex from Up-State New York and erected it at even greater expense, on the stage. As the operetta is almost exclusively a chamber work, and most of it taking place in the Pie Shop, it seemed an extravagant waste of time and money to erect an intractable cast-iron building. Needless to say, all the stage needed to be restructured and strengthened in order to support its prodigious weight. And even if it hadn't been so expensive, and hadn't been so complicated to erect, and hadn't been so monumental, as my friend, the actor Keith Baxter said to Stephen Sondheim: 'But they didn't have industrial complexes in Fleet Street in the 1830s, Steve.' I don't think his comment went down very well.

'Another $9,000,' complained Don Gregory, 'and Rex asks me where the one and a half million has gone. I'll tell him where it's gone. On his constant trips on Concorde to and fro across the Atlantic, on his hotel suites, his costumes, his four pairs of shoes at $1300 each, his London tailors visiting him in his home in Cap Ferrat, his two tail-coats, his four suits of Harris tweed from Jermyn Street, his fancy Ascot hats, and do you know how many shirts? forty-eight, for God's sake! That's where our one and a half million has gone.'

But for all our complaints, the producers and the production team are acutely aware of Rex's sublimely elegant and reposeful performance. We've all witnessed the work that goes into it, and are profoundly admiring of the effortless relaxation with which it is performed. Everybody on stage and off burst into applause after his rendition of 'Accustomed To Her Face'. The faces of the gypsies, sat around on their haunches, in their leg-warmers, and head-scarves, was one of rapture. I saw Jack Gwillim chuckling away to himself after there had been a little cock-up at the opening of the Second Act. When there was a break, I couldn't resist asking Jack what it was that Rex had said to him, which had made his shoulders shake. 'Aah!' said Jack, 'an excellent piece of theatrical advice which I shall treasure for the remainder of my life. Rex said to me, "If Patrick has another go at the opening of that scene, Jack, would you try not to come on stage like an actor about to sing a song".'

The second run-through turned out to be a great improvement on the first. Although Cheryl complained to me that she found the tempo too driving from the 'Slippers' scene to 'Show Me'. I explained to her, if she ever found it comfortable, it could only mean it was too slow.

Today saw the return of the enervating and exhausting heatwave, and New York seemed to sag at the knees, especially around 42nd Street. There was a positive stink along the intersections between 8th and 9th Avenue.

To my dismay Rex's resistance to Cheryl came prominently forward yet again. Perhaps I'd hoped it might have evaporated in the night:

146

'No, I'll never quite trust that girl again,' he repeated to me when we were at the heliport, waiting to be flown to see how the sets were getting on in Up-State New York. To my astonishment he seems pointlessly envious at her effectiveness and power. I said that I felt she was not deliberately pushing, but keeping her energies in reserve – underacting, if you like.

'I'm the one who underacts,' said Rex testily. We spend the rest of the afternoon choosing expensive furniture at Newell's Treasure House, and Rex seemed to soften somewhat. Turning to the designer Oliver Smith, Rex said with delight:

'Oliver, this kidney-shaped desk is just perfect.'

Oliver replied: 'Well, let's get out of here, before you stop liking it so much.'

29 August

There are still two entire weeks to go in these rehearsal rooms at the Trafalgar, but the final few days have pulled everything together, and the entire show seems to be moving like a tidal wave, even allowing me evenings to myself. Isolated fragments of recollection: a delightful dinner at Brooklyn Heights with Oliver Smith. A glorious old-fashioned New York house, with a verandah, and slowly swinging fans; an old-fashioned garden, and an eloquent spiral staircase. Oliver has been here for decades. He told me, in the old days gone by, Tyrone Guthrie stayed there, often walking around the house naked: 'In fact,' said Oliver, 'I shall never forget the worms' eye-view of Tony Guthrie's testicles from the bottom of the staircase, looking up. Truman Capote spent hours of his time at the foot of the spiral staircase hoping to catch such a glimpse!' Oliver's close cropped hair, stately bearing, slight stoop of the shoulders (rather reminiscent of Harold Acton's, whom in a way he resembles) give him something of the air of a Chinese mandarin. He took me out to a lovely old-fashioned restaurant, where we ate lobster and drank an excellent Pouilly Fumé. I said to him how tense it always was dining out with Rex and how one's heart used to sink whenever an assiduous waiter approached. I always felt the waiter chosen to serve Rex had drawn the short straw. We got to talking of Coral Browne, with whom Rex had a swift affair back in the 1940s. I remembered the time when Coral in her maturity, was in a comedy with that enchanting Edwardian actor, Ernest Thesiger. Ernest was playing, as he often did in his later years, the butler. On this occasion at a certain point in the scene, Coral Browne was aware of some undetected distraction going on behind her, as she could not quite hold the attention of the audience. After the curtain calls, she asked Ernest to drop in to her dressing-room when he had changed, and have a gin and tonic with her. Dutifully he arrived, and Coral was unfailingly courteous to him, offering him drinks, and asking him to sit down. 'I wanted to have a chat with you, Ernest, because I've got to have a bit of medical treatment next week, and you might have to work with the understudy.' Ernest was immediately disturbed, and asked solicitously after her health. 'Oh it's nothing very much, Ernest, but I might have to go into hospital for a couple of days.' Ernest was appalled, he had no idea that she had been unwell at all. 'Well, it's nothing very much, but it might involve a tiny bit of surgery, Ernest.'

'May I be so bold, Coral, as to enquire what kind of surgery you might be having?' asked Ernest.

'Oh it's nothing very much,' said Coral, 'I'm just having my eyes sewn into the back of my fucking head!'

Much of the time's taken up in diplomacy, not wanting Alan Lerner or Fritz Loewe to interfere and check the flow. We drove over to Brooklyn to check the show curtains for the third or fourth time. I'm always quietly amused by the sudden electric click of the door as the chauffeur locks us in automatically as we pass 'a bad neighbourhood'. The scenery was set up in one of the old New York ice-rinks.

There was a line around the block at 42nd Street to see the new musical *Pirates of Penzance* in the Park. I went to see it with some friends on one of the most beautiful evenings in Central Park. George Rose and Patricia Routledge were quite magnificent in the patter songs and the whole show was exuberant, irreverent, and a great deal of fun. Kevin Kline, a new dynamic musical star. A heart-stopping moment as a yellow moon rose above the show, and the Park. The Dorset Hotel was hiding shyly behind.

We hear today that the advance in San Francisco has soared to break all box-office records in a single day, $76,000. Even our producers have a benign smile on their face as they walk in and out of rehearsals. Following a ferocious quarrel, I succeed in cutting a minute from 'Get Me To The Church On Time', and I've made a further snip from 'Ordinary Man'. The pressure is that we're in danger of yielding so much control to Rex that, Franz wisely says: 'The fun goes out of it.'

Franz Allers and Fritz Loewe pretend to be Viennese, and *speak* as if they are Viennese, but in reality they are both Czech. Cathleen Nesbitt makes another breakthrough; I fear for her, and admire profoundly her indomitable courage, enduring the last years of her life. The other day she wandered vaguely out into the street, and the third assistant saw her staggering bravely along 9th Avenue into the horror of 42nd Street, before he could rescue her.

When we took our downtown helicopter trip to Newburgh, to look at the sets we sailed over West Point. Don Gregory said: 'It's like being on a roller-coaster, which I hate for even three minutes, for three quarters of an hour.' Somebody asked: 'Where does the pilot land?' Don said: 'How on earth do I know?' It is almost like a Marx Brothers' situation, the two producers, the pilot, myself and Rex all of us helpless in this tiny helicopter cabin, none of us knowing where to land. We all hated it and Rex and I were content to return by limousine. Rex announced that he had the approval of the sets, and it was a deeply misplaced notion of the producers to invite him up to look at the sets when they were still capable of being changed. In their desire to please, they turned out to be ill-advised, because Rex on his return announced that he in fact *disapproved* of the sets. Cathleen continues to wander about New York rather lost, and has already mislaid her spectacles, her hearing aid, her handbag, her daughter's birthday present, her script, her credit cards and keys to her hotel, and, needless to say, Rupert Brooke's love letters.

One evening Rex and I went to see the well-received production of *The Man Who Came to Dinner* a good, dated play by

Kaufman and Hart. Rex and I both observed that there's a marked tendency in this country to admire as acting what we would call 'over-acting'. Rex says in the car, half despondently, half amused: 'Well, perhaps I should die quickly, or retire.' But a silence extends between us, because although we both laughed it off, equally we brooded on it, as it is a possibility that it is that extra degree of vulgarity which works, with the American public and neither of us could do anything about it, except forbid it. I had noticed exactly the same thing in another highly praised production, *Mornings At Seven*. It was full of what Rex and I consider 'acting-acting' – that is a form of showing off, of 'Mickey-Mousing', a kind of drawing attention to performance. Rather like a friend of mine, who somewhat disparagingly condemns the art of mime, because he insists that for him it is drawing attention to something that isn't there. When Rex last returned to London he was rather depressed by what he saw, and thought it was very different from the theatre of the Kenneth Tynan generation; again it seemed to be what people liked, namely over-acting. 'That didn't matter,' said Rex, 'but the theatre critics admired it as well, which was doubly depressing.' He came out of a revival of a traditional high comedy at the Haymarket one evening, sadly shaking his head:

'No good, Rex?' I asked him.

'I couldn't taste the champagne,' he replied.

It had been a good rehearsal day. Cathleen complained she'd been kept awake at night by people singing Negro spirituals outside her door, which seemed unlikely. The explanation was she had left the television on. She was sleepy and lacking in concentration, but can hardly be blamed if she imagined she'd been disturbed by the Kentucky Glee Club all night. I go to sleep concerned about the important run-through the next day and the disruptive return of Franz Allers from Vienna. Imminent collisions.

30 August – The Heat Wave

Ninety-six degrees mid-afternoon, too humid to work with any conviction, but it was an impressive run-through all the same before the Labor Day weekend. The final holidays of the summer and the New Yorkers stream out of the City, the gay crowd to Fire Island, the straight crowd to Jones Beach. Streets on the West Side crowded late into the night. Ice-cream parlours and pavement bookstores, and jazz concerts all teeming after midnight. The radio announces weather still 'hot and humid'. The headache is pollen and pollution, the air in downtown New York is thick as if penetrating a sandstorm. A matronly prostitute accosts me with the old-fashioned invitation: 'Hi there, do you want to make love?'

31 August – Sunday Off

A quiet walk by myself down to the river bank. The small houseboats bobbing on the Hudson, photographers weaving around looking for items to contribute to *Gay News* or the ominously titled *After Dark*. Handsome boys looking at themselves in mirrors, half dressed, sitting on the sidewalk fixing and spraying their hair. In spite of the heatwave a few brown leaves trickle tenderly down. Yesterday I struggled to protect Nick Wyman, whose solo song gets better and better. Cheryl sang 'Wouldn't It Be Luvverly' with her cage of mice in front of her. She likes them coming to the rehearsal. I thought it would be a nice touch for the scene. A hint of autumn. Perhaps a hint of boredom. We all begin to need the new disciplines, the sets, and costumes, in order to progress, 'the customers', as Rex calls them. Trunks begin to assemble at the Trafalgar, queuing up – like circus people – in the hallways and the dressing-rooms. Rex said to me that it reminded him of his early days when he used to tour round England, 'Actors and Fish'. Main show trunk is titled 'Rex Harrison in My Fair Lady Company – New Orleans – San Francisco – Los Angeles – New York!'

2 September – Suddenly We Have Enchantment

Autumn appears to have arrived while I have been spending my days in an air-conditioned darkened auditorium, almost as if unaware of it. Brown leaves lie beneath green trees. Suddenly, and it is sudden, unexpected, unlooked for, the end of the rehearsal

151

period looms towards me. This doesn't alarm me or trouble me from the show's point of view, but as it heralds the end of such a happy time in New York's Upper West Side, I must admit that it saddens me rather.

It has been a very contented period in my life, certain pavements have this effect, I shall miss this city and these broad dirty streets and its hot, lifeless weather, especially late at night. The part of New York in which I live is for me permanently reminiscent of the Paris I knew in the 1950s, the Place Contrescarpe and the Rue Mouffetard, the haunt of Rimbaud and Verlaine, Scott Fitzgerald and Hemingway at a later date. I feel unusually like an American in Paris, albeit a Limey in New York. Everything open until the early hours of the morning. As my West Side friend Marty Wallach used to say, 'The great joy of New York is if you wake up at three o'clock in the morning and you have a hankering to eat Hungarian Goulash, you will be sure to find a restaurant in New York which is open and ready to serve you. Should you be so deranged as to happen to want to eat Hungarian Goulash at three o'clock in the morning.' Their names reverberate in my memory like a litany, Food City, the Stage Deli, Amy's, Tony's Hawaiian, Mama Tin's Chinese Laundry, Manny Fine's Jewish, the (of all things) Hispanic-Szechuan restaurant, Marvin Gardens, Meat Market (singles), Teachers and the wonderful scented Zabars. I shall miss the Erotic Bakers from which I bought one afternoon Gingerbread Gays, and Tumescent Brownies. Even the weirdo churches proclaim themselves – '"God's Word" – Your Doorway to Adventure'.

I shall miss as well the soprano forever practising arias from Puccini and Rossini in the floor above me, and one evening from an open window, telephone bells colliding with radios, television sets, excitable newscasters or weathermen, distant fire trucks and paramedics, a woman waking me at midnight, shouting in her ecstasy, transfixed by some explosion of carnal love.

Over a couple of Budweisers after rehearsal at Charlie's Bar, Franz tells us that he feels Los Angeles is the city of Dolorous Troubles. He, Bob, and Jack (Company Manager) all swap Jewish stories, the best of which belonged to Franz: 'Did you hear the story of the Jew who wins first prize at the Synagogue? They tell him that the third prize is a Cadillac. The second prize is a chocolate cake. 'Hey,' says the Jew, 'what is this? The third prize is a Cadillac, and second is a chocolate cake, you're not serious.'

'You don't understand, it's baked by the Rabbi's wife.'

'Fuck the Rabbi's wife!'

'No, that's the first prize.'

The election still carries on. Nobody is particularly hopeful about the result, as Jimmy Carter represents a somewhat moth-headed candidate. The story going round the bars at the moment describes how President Giscard of France, and Herr Schmidt of Germany and President Carter of the United States are all standing blindfold in front of an execution squad. Each one of them is given the opportunity to say one word only which may extricate themselves from their desperate situation. President Giscard steps forward and shouts out: 'Earthquake!' President Schmidt steps forward and he shouts out: 'Hurricane!' Finally, Jimmy Carter steps forward, and he shouts out: 'Fire!'

Franz is bothered by a first trumpeter in *Camelot* whom he is unable to fire. Jack asks him how he's going to resolve the problem. Franz replies:

'The second trumpeter plays the first trumpet part, the first trumpeter plays the second trumpet part, and nobody's any the wiser, and so I save the show some money.'

Franz calls the trio of Doolittle, the Dustman, Jamie, and Harry, 'The Three Goyim!' (der drei Goyim). But none of this geniality resolves the problem for me which is looming up like the iceberg did against the *Titanic*, about who's going to conduct the official first night at New Orleans. Rex wants Bob Kriese, the assistant, of which Franz Allers is unaware. He has a problem about not being there himself, and says: 'Rex will hit the roof! He is like a son to me, his first question when he saw me after all those years was "I will only do the show if I can have Franz in the pit at every opening night."' And so he continues in this self-deluding vein, but Don Gregory knows and I know, that Rex is *delighted* that Bob, the assistant director, will conduct the opening, and couldn't care less that Franz is not there. It is ironic and sad – so like love

– the desperate yearning on one side that is met by utter disdain on the other. Complete indifference, in fact, on Rex's part. As Franz himself agrees: 'It is called *My Fair Lady*, or "Fuck The Music".'

But to watch Franz shape the phrasing of the ensemble is every bit as creative and miraculous as Rex winkling laughs out of the audience like the expert trout-tickler that he is. Complimenting (a rare thing) the chorus on the sound they make at the end of Doolittle's 'Wedding Night', a moment of exquisite poetry as with the utmost tenderness they sing 'Daylight Is Breaking', suddenly with delight Franz exclaims with a broad smile: 'Ah, now you can see the difference. Suddenly we have enchantment.'

3 September – Cathleen Nesbitt: New York

Cathleen continues in her fragility to dominate the production in my mind. It's more from my sentimentality, than cynicism, that I let this rather grim charade continue. I can see she would quite like to die on stage, which is perfectly possible aged 92 as she is, and besides, as she says: 'I want to see all my old friends in America.'

Today to my great discomfort, she apologizes to me. 'I don't know where my brain is today,' she says. She seems to have had an accident with her head on the air-conditioning, and has taken her sleeping pills at the wrong time of day, which of course make her dull. It makes me feel dreadful to receive apologies from a 92-year-old. She constantly complains of her failing memory, which is a great deal better than a lot of people one third of her age, 'there's no remedy for that,' she says. And I'm reminded of Philip Larkin's grim poem, which ends:

> *Life is first boredom, then fear ...*
> *and age, and then the only end of age.*

Today she was looking for her address book in her handbag, and as I helped her, because her hands are so arthritic, I discovered that there is absolutely nothing left in it. Everything is lost, she has somehow got rid of all her possessions. No passport, no money, no

154

credit cards, no lipstick, just a vast empty capacious handbag. It's all very reminiscent of the tragic time when Margaret Rutherford suffered the same collapse of faculties as a definitive Mrs Malaprop in a production of *The Rivals* at the Haymarket in the 1950s. She liked to come into the theatre for a rest, but contrived, being of failing memory, to have taken her 'uppers', which stimulated her throughout the afternoon, when she should have been resting. By the time she was getting ready for the performance, she would then take her second lot of pills (which should have been stimulants) but were in fact her 'downers', or sleeping pills, so that by the time she was dressed and made-up and the curtain was ready to rise, she was beginning to fall into a comatose sleep. Ralph Richardson, who was playing Sir Anthony Absolute, used to ask Keith Baxter, who was playing Bob Acres in the same production, 'Is it safe to go down, Cockie? It's Nightmare Tunnel down there tonight, Cockie . . .'

On several occasions members of the audience observed that Mrs Malaprop spoke perfect and logical sense, putting all her malapropisms back to front, and into the original language from which they were taken, so the comic affect was completely nullified. Sometimes she would just fall fast asleep, and there was one memorable occasion when Ralph Richardson had to play the entire scene with Mrs Malaprop, speaking all of his lines, and as many of hers as he could remember, in one extended piece of reported speech. Hermione Baddeley commented that she took a season ticket to see the show at the Haymarket, not so much to see *The Rivals*, but 'to see the funny old lady fall over'.

Perhaps Cathleen is frightened of Rex, like a child is by an angry monster, she certainly gets rattled by him. She beats her withered knuckles against her forehead in frustration when she forgets her lines, or her moves, and is so obviously trying to please, trying to do right. But the theatre is no sympathizer to helplessness, childishness, or reverent old age. Rex snapped at her mercilessly in one of his snake-eyed moods.

'You were very wrong in dropping my cue, you left me dreadfully hung-up.' (And then he threw in a conciliatory 'Darling.') 'You forgot a line, Cathleen,' he said louder, in case she hadn't heard him the first time, 'and it hangs me up.' Cathleen, not hearing, stared uncomprehendingly at him. But she felt, I'm sure, the force of his anger. The gypsies rustled, I saw out of the corner of my eye, like a wave in a cornfield. I decided to set up a smoke-screen to appease the situation if at all possible, and calling everybody together, principals and the ensemble simultaneously, gave a whole lot of fictitious notes which I did not particularly believe in, simply in order to distract attention.

4 September

Cathleen was very good today, significantly in Rex's absence, and when I congratulated her, which was entirely sincere, she very sweetly said to me:

'You remind me of the best director I ever worked with, Harley Granville-Barker. He always found something encouraging to say first, and only later something critical. Dion Boucicault, on the other hand, always found something critical, and negative to say, and then as an after-thought, found something encouraging.' And I bent down to her small frail body, to kiss her, and she placed a little wrist lightly on each of my shoulders, rather like a little squirrel might. Approaching the opening night in New Orleans, however, was very different, and restored to her health I found that Cathleen became as temperamental, as vain, and as demanding as any other star one quarter of her age. When I commented on this curious change of character to Rex, all he said was 'I think of Cathleen, in spite of being a thousand years old, as a bad-tempered, obstinate, old bitch.'

But then, he said that about most people.

5 September – 'Musical Comedy, for God's Sake!'

I can never forget this autumn in New York. Sitting around Harold's television set as if we were all at the tennis ground itself, cheering on McEnroe inexplicably beating Björn Borg in the US Open, one of the great sport events of the century. The view of the Hudson River and restless boating activity – a yellowness in the air now, and at night a softening. A clean wind off the river blows up 79th Street towards Columbus. Sidewalk cafés full of people in their shirt-sleeves late at night – roller-skaters, heads bent against the wind.

> *'Hear the beat*
> *Of dancing feet.*
> *The Avenue,*
> *I'm taking you to –*
> *Is Forty Second Street.'*

A star-studded audience. Dustin Hoffman standing in his smart white shirt-sleeves signing autographs, seemingly rather eager. A lanky Tommy Tune only moderately enthusiastic – but then, his own choreography compared to the old-fashioned hoofing of *42nd Street* is infinitely more complicated and refined. The curtain flies up on the adorable clatter of double-taps – windmills – and pull-backs. Is there anything more exhilarating in the world than forty crack American tap-dancers in full flow! Harold and I took Cheryl, who confided in us that really in her heart she wanted to give up show business in order to be a vet. On stage, life was resembling art, resembling life, albeit ridiculous life. Everything we were busy doing every hour of the day was being represented in front of us on the stage, almost as a form of self-parody. The Director had a wonderful speech at the climax of the show, and it struck me to the heart in all its enchantment, expectation, and monumental silliness:

'I'm not gonna make you any more of those phoney pep-talks – this time I'm telling you right from the heart. Think of the two most beautiful words in the English language – Musical Comedy, for God's sake! Think of Broadway, for God's sake!'

The show actually *is* a living tribute to Gower Champion and the spirit of New York Dance. It has a sort of insane and inspired meaninglessness. Tap-dancing reminds me a little of women's tennis – you watch it with a kind of bored astonishment. Everybody in the audience by the end of the show imagines they can all tap themselves effortlessly – you can see people trying it on the stairs leaving the theatre, on the steps leading down to the sidewalk, and tapping up 7th Avenue to the Russian Tea Room. But of course none of us can tap at all. It's like flying, and imagining you can fly, after seeing *Peter Pan*.

6 September

Uneventful and cheerful run-throughs. Rex is in excellent form, morale excellent. No major crises, except the problem of the New Orleans opening when Franz is going to be in Vienna. Unfortunately the official Press night takes place on Yom Kippur and Don Gregory refuses to appeal against it. 'But there are no Jews in New Orleans,' exclaims Franz, 'except me and Fritzy Loewe. It's full of Spanish Catholics who would like to spend Yom Kippur at a musical comedy.'

Cathleen Nesbitt continues miraculously to grow, she even strides purposefully on and off the stage. Mike Merrick arrives from Los Angeles and says the atmosphere of all the actors on strike fills the pollution with the psychological ambience of poison. A musicians' strike, typically at the New York Metropolitan, takes on a show-business air as pickets parade in shirt-sleeves. As I pass by, a trumpeter plays a poetic solo of Beethoven's 'The Hymn to Joy' which in the New York streets takes on a somewhat melancholy air. Pickets carry rather arty slogans as 'Carmen Shot', 'Othello Sacked', and more humorously 'Tristan Dumps Isolde'. As I make my way home I pass Liu's Laundry and go in to collect some shirts. The old Chinese grandfather, the tiny pigtailed unsmiling girl, the abacus, the smell of pressed clothes, the mother press-ironing the shirts, as if one were not in New York at all, but a back-street in Shanghai.

11 September, Thursday – First Public Dress Rehearsal

So, everything seems in excellent shape thus far. Rehearsal is smooth, affectionate, controlled, eloquent, and funny. Rex seems to be delighted. Cathleen is very good but falls over a chair, the audience are very shocked, but she gets up and receives a generous hand of applause. Rex no longer seems concerned about Cheryl's performance as Eliza, which perhaps for me is the most important triumph of all. Our friendly stage doorman, called John 'The Mayor', has baked an ice-cream cake for all of us and somehow for a day becomes the star of the show, making speeches and generally taking command. After five weeks, in cool September weather we leave New York. I, regretfully, the company, however, cheerfully. Suddenly there are children, and pets at the airport. Arleen's little girl befriends Eric's baby boy, who has his destination label tied to his foot. Three particular favourites of mine from the ensemble, John, Jeff and Judith, all get plastered on the airplane. Rex from his exclusive first-class compartment makes frequent appearances in the tourist part, which is greatly appreciated. It is almost as if he misses our company, and I actually believe he does. Cathleen, true to form, after lunch, makes her way to the lavatory, first struggles with the main exit door and goes to get off the plane, and then in desperation opens the cabin door into the pilot's cockpit. And so, we arrive, with our countless bags at New Orleans and humidity and sensuality are in the air.

Chapter 30

NEW ORLEANS – THE BIG EASY

12 September

A VAST COCKROACH flying in from the terrace of the hotel, lands on my shoulder. I knew it would be a city of oddities. First is a flower seller who announces as a slogan on his tricycle: 'I Am Selling Flowers As An Honest Craft And Not Part Of Any Religious Cult', which puzzles me, until I learn that the rather innocent young people neatly dressed in the middle of Bourbon Street are actually Moonies. There is also a whole group of Born Again Christians, who solicit in Storyville. These glorious names ring in my ears like poems. What is it Philip Larkin writes, in his poem about Sydney Bechet, and the Crescent City?

> *On me your voice falls, as they say Love should*
> *Like an enormous Yes.*

In my hotel room turning on the television I'm confronted by my old friend, Oral Roberts, the notorious faith healer. It's extraordinary to turn on your television in real life and meet something on the screen roaring out of either a film or a book of fiction. Oral was in full flood of Mississippi eloquence:

'Put your fingers on your eyes! The Devil steals those eyes. Now Father, open those eyes! Devil, take your hands off of God's property! Praise God, oh Glory, praise God! I speak in the name of Jesus, look on us now when we have a weight problem!' Certainly, we are in the Mississippi Delta.

'We pray for a financial miracle, oh Lord, and it begins Today – for every heating bill, for every lighting bill, every

160

telephone bill, every air-conditioning bill, oh Lord, we pray to meet those bills . . . !' Oral in swinging swooning Southern rhythms, as expressive in his way as Martin Luther King's famous 'I have a Dream' speech. But vulgar, of course. The hypnotic rhythms of good and bad morality work alike in the Southern States. Americans seem to specialize in their own personal Divinity – I think it must come from the nineteenth-century enthusiasts, from Emerson, Melville, and Walt Whitman. Hence, I suppose, the countless eccentric and individual churches one sees everywhere in America.

14 September – Sunday: First Preview

Unsurprisingly a lot of things went wrong. Terrible, awful crashes and collisions – a computer for the lights breaks down, the technical run-through only finishes by 11 p.m. The scale of the show is so gigantic. Every single six inches of flying space is used right up to the rear wall, there are sixty flying lines hanging. We were rehearsing in Rampart Street. Rampart, Canal and Basin Streets! The extraordinary shock of actually seeing, albeit not on a street-car, but on a modern autobus: 'A computerized A M General called Desire . . .' The famous French Quarter suburbs, altered but intact, Frenchmen, Chartres, Prytania; Lafayette and Beauregard Square, the Crescent City itself, New Orleans.

15 September – Monday: Second Preview

Rex calls me at my hotel at 8 a.m. bad-tempered: 'Patrick, I want to see the technical run-through and I'm not at all satisfied, and I'm going to shout.' Two hours patience, and all seems to be going well with the technicalities, and then the designer Oliver Smith gets angry and he shouts: 'I can be very obstinate too, you know . . .' So as first-class prima donnas in a rage, I've got Rex primarily, then Oliver, then Franz, then Cathleen, and all of them are ready and liable to scream at once. Oliver, for the first time is extremely put out: 'I can be obstinate too, as obstinate as hell.'

16 September – Tuesday: Opening Night

Technically it was a mess-up, the cues all came too late – caution, probably, in the prompt-corner – but for Rex and the actors, to my surprise and great satisfaction, it all turned into a jubilant success. The show, above all, is fireproofed. Oliver, possibly because this is his moment, as we struggle with the technicalities, chose to chastise our stage manager, Jack, when in reply to his: 'I hate that Street traveller,' replied, 'There's nothing wrong with the traveller, Jack, just get it right.' There was a standing ovation at the end, and Rex was extremely cheerful at the curtain calls, in spite of the famous 'Accustomed To Your Face' scene being messed up by the infuriatingly wilful and billowing traveller (a front cloth).

17 September – The Saenger Theatre, Rampart Street, New Orleans

Perhaps characteristic of the ambience south of Dixie, the atmosphere at the early previews altered dramatically throughout the day. The bonhomie and good humour which had generated on the flight from New York to New Orleans dissipated fairly quickly, and quite a number of people got fractious over their hotel rooms and accommodation. We arrived in an evening of grey humidity. The next morning I gave notes, which was easy enough because they referred to the last performance in New York, then Rex arrived, looking dapper, first very good-humoured, happy with his accommodation, which he described to me as 'one of the old Plantation Homes in the French Vieux Carré, with rather attractive Slave Quarters . . .' Later he became extremely irritable, and when the sound man said that the high pitched voices and vowel sounds of scene one, the Covent Garden scene, were perfectly audible to the public, Rex snarled:

'Fuck the customers, *make it loud enough so that the actors can hear it on stage!*'

Regarding a scene-change that I wished Rex to take on the revolve, going from the Pub scene to the Study, he said in front of everybody:

'What! And stand at the top of the stairs looking like a c**t, in full view of the house . . . ? Not on your life – and *Fuck You!*' Which for all its intensity and determination, in fact made me and the Company laugh.

Oliver refers to the slowness of the stage crew as: 'Tippy-Toe Time in Dixie!' I spend a disturbed night at my hotel, not entirely accidentally. One of the gypsies in the chorus, and probably Ron, knowing my obvious predilection for the pretty young women in the company, is sending young men up to my room at various early hours. Declining to open my door, thank heavens, a deeply Southern voice says from the corridor on the other side at three in the morning: 'Ah'm lookin' foah Bert . . .' and this evening at 6 p.m. my telephone rang to say 'Hi, this is Bert, ah met you outside the Broughan Pub las' night . . .'

'Oh, no you didn't,' I said.

'Oh well, okay,' came the plaintive response as I rang off, 'You all have a nice day . . .'

The good old *Louisiana Times – Picayune* had a curious story about a black woman who was suing a supermarket, following a traumatic experience when a thirty-two ounce Coca-Cola bottle exploded in her hand. She maintains that ever since she has had nightmares about being relentlessly stalked by giant Coca-Cola bottles, marching towards her, and when they come close to her, she says, they explode. Once she dreamt she saw a real estate sign with her name on it, and this also changed into a coke bottle and chased her down the street. After the performance we all had a splendid dinner at Le Louisiane, said to be owned by the Mafia, where the *maître d'hôtel* made us a Louisiana shrimp gumbo we simply couldn't refuse.

Rex after a drowsy third-night audience, and a good rousing 'Rain In Spain' said to Cheryl, what he thought was under his breath, 'That will wake the buggers up.' As his microphone was on, it was heard loud and clear over the speaker system by the entire audience. After the show, we went to Bourbon Street to sit outside on the pavement and hear some rather inferior jazz: a pianist strumming, who couldn't play at all. Most of the jazz in the tourist areas, Bourbon Street and the Old City is pretty commonplace.

The names are haunting in their poetry and quite unlike any other city in the United States: some of them seem to me to come from a Shakespearean play, like *Love's Labour's Lost*. Streets are called Dumaine, Piety, Desire, Elysium Fields, Louisa, Ursulines, to rhyme with tramlines, Thalia Hospitalizer, and then exotic slogans like Pappy's Dry Clean, Cabissis Doll Museum, Miss Gay French Quarter (Girls This Is For You!), The London Tea-Rooms on Canal Street, Card, Tarot and Tea-cup Readings are advertised, there are boulevards called Gentilly, Madman, Amen, Theseus, and Socrates, and there are districts called Algiers, Gretna, and Infirmary. An image of exquisite spontaneity was produced by the sight of six sweet looking black schoolgirls in their uniforms with neat pigtails, who passing an open car and listening to the car radio which was playing lively soul music, began bopping all round it. When one of them had had enough, she announced to her friends: 'Waal kids, ah'm boogying off.'.

Over an iced mint-julep, Jack Gwillim told me that for all his off-handedness, Wilfred Hyde-White had the most impeccable and intuitive skill in timing a pause. At the end of his life, wrapped up in a woollen overcoat against the cold in the eighty degree desert, he was asked by Sheridan Morley:

'Wilfred, how is it possible the epitome of an English gentleman like you, can live out here, in Palm Springs?'

'There are two reasons,' replied Wilfred.

'First, I couldn't *stand* the sight of my third wife. Second, I refused to be held to ransom by the English Inland Revenue.'

And then, after a delicate pause, which lasted as long as an intake of breath.

'Do forgive me. That was an inconceivably caddish remark about the Inland Revenue.'

18 September – Rampart Street

A strange and exotic procession marched by Rampart Street this evening without warning. Two street jazz-bands, led by a serpentine tuba which wound itself round its player like a boa constrictor; there were several small horse-drawn carriages, and several Carnival

Queens with huge Inca headdresses. A grey-streaked dusk spread across Armstrong Park. The hotel where most of us were staying, (apart from Rex, who of course is in more stately accommodation) is on the seedy, decayed edge of Rampart Street, bounded by sleazy gay and transvestite bars along its northern edge. After the cheerful little parade passed by, I retired for a siesta, but when I met him later that evening after the performance, Rex told me that he too had heard the band, as it would have passed him half a mile down the street, where he was resting in his dressing-room. He told me: 'I had a little zizz, and woke up thinking I must have died, and that I was now floating in Paradise. Suddenly to my ears came the unmistakable sounds of a distant jazz-band. It seemed to have all the right instruments, and they didn't play very well, but it was all there. And then when I realized that I had merely woken from sleep, I thought I must have been transported back into the 1920s or '30s. It sounded like a little walking funeral band, and after a few moments it walked slowly away into the distance. It was heavenly.'

I walked back past the transvestite bar where some terrible Masquerade was taking place, black transvestites dressed up in black togas as grotesque parodies of Roman Senators. Also on our way back to the hotel, I walked by the old Pestilence Church, where on the side of the chapel the vicar had written in broad letters: 'Thou Shalt Not Park In This Driveway'. And somewhat despairingly, someone had put up a pamphlet in the All Night Dive, where we tend to congregate after the show, announcing: 'Love Is Not To Be Found In The Gay World – Turn To Jesus'.

Autumn cooled us down in New York but as we advanced south, we progress into the same unbearable humidity. The lowest temperature in New Orleans was eighty-three degrees on 17 September and throughout the summer apparently there've been eighty-five days over ninety degrees. Today was a record high at ninety-five degrees, the highest apparently since 1925.

Outside the gay bar: 'No Pets, No Loitering, No Hustling.'

I saw advertised outside a movie house *The Worriers*. I think perhaps they meant *The Warriors*. Seeking the cool inside a movie house, I observed a black man several stall seats ahead of me sitting watching battery television while the film was going on, some sports event presumably, and that same afternoon at Lafitte's In Exile, five gay men talking to one another in deaf and dumb sign language.

21 September – After the First Sunday

An exhausted Company, by all the hard work, the technical run-throughs, the previews, and the insufferable heat, night and day. And, doubtless a bit of partying. Cathleen is puzzled by the running order, she tells me. Complains that I have changed all the scenes round, and totally refuses to believe 'The Rain In Spain' was in the original show. I visit her every evening with various notes, most of them to no avail, and don't know whether she is deaf, senile, or merely cunning. She said to Rex, to his great consternation, after the big street number with all the cockneys, 'Well, if anything will kill the show stone dead, *that* will.'

In Rex's company, we went to a beautiful true Southern party in an old *ante bellum* Colonial house (1806), with four courtyards laid out, and slave quarters, and ancient Louisiana live-oaks in the front. A small four-piece jazz-band, all blacks, came and played heavenly Creole music. It was a present from some of his friends whom he knew in the city for his birthday. The house was seemingly a plantation house of West Indian origin and Rex's eyes slitted into something almost of a trance, as he sat in an old clapped-out cane chair, all by himself, close to the music, hearing the old Creole man play on his battered cornet good, straight, melancholy blues. It had a delicacy to which one could listen all night long. Rex himself lives in a very beautiful *ante-bellum* house also, The Erlanger House, out on one of the bayoux with cool interior, slow winding fan, and his own slave quarters into which I rather think he would like to confine Franz Allers. I asked how he gets on with things once the show is over and he is delivered safely to his door, as Mercia his wife is not with him at the moment. 'I come back late, when everybody is asleep, including the dog, and I do a sort of stumbling Wilfred Lawson act at my front gate, with keys which don't quite fit, then I come into this beautiful, quiet, empty house, pour a good glass of wine, and sit motionless in a kind of pleasurable daze, and contemplate for about half an hour.'

I took a river-trip up the Mississippi, which was rather boring, there were elephant ears along the levee, and the finest sight was the Spanish moss hanging from the ruined trees. Some of the plantation houses that we visited on guided tours had furniture no more antique or valuable than that of my aged aunts when they lived in Bedford Park. Quite a lot less valuable, as a matter of fact. Either the architects used shoddy materials when they built New Orleans, or, more likely, the humidity insinuates itself everywhere.

23 September – Press night and Party

'Wild about your turnip tops
Crazy for your mutton chops ...
I'm your kitchen man.'

The fat, squat black singer poured himself into what must have been a Fats Waller classic, at Brennans, where we spent the party following the official formal Press night. Rex was in a sour mood after the disappointing opening, and it was only several years later that I learnt, partly from the experience of the tour on Broadway, and partly from what other people told me, that Rex suffered acutely from nerves and always took several steps backwards on every opening night. The performance seemed forced and apprehensive, and Rex, as ever, nervous. A poor local review which picked this up seemed to me entirely justified, but didn't help the general morale. It was one of the great Impossibles, touring with Rex, wherever we went. It was no use postponing the Press night, whenever it would be held, he was invariably nervous and off-form. He responded to the generous first-night hospitality of the producers and the general acclaim with sour disinterest, seated next to Cheryl, and unendingly and boringly went over every single minute detail of the play, getting steadily drunker and ignoring the little black trio of musicians to their visible dejection. He almost had his back turned against them. At one moment he turned to me with up-raised finger: 'Patrick, I hear you've been

167

giving the cast ideas about this play behind my back without consulting me . . .' I couldn't help but laugh to myself, but I was sad for him that he was judged on such a disappointing performance.

24 September – Wednesday

Typically, the very next day, there was a startling improvement: all trace of yesterday's fears had gone, and Rex's nervous attacks, sensitivity, disappeared as his confidence came soaring back. How could I describe the poetry and imagination with which he invests Mr Shaw's eloquent sentences? Half-way up the stairs, Henry Higgins captures Eliza, and holds her wrist firmly in his grip:

'Eliza, you are to live here for the next six months, learning to speak beautifully, like a lady in a florist's shop . . .' This was spoken with extreme tenderness, and courtesy. Later on, with vindictiveness and terror, Higgins threatens:

'If you are naughty and idle, you will sleep in the back kitchen among the black beetles, and be walloped by Mrs Pearce with a broomstick . . .' which brought, quite understandably a wail from Eliza of misery.

Changing his tone, a full octave lower by now:

'If you are not found out, you shall have a present of seven-and-sixpence to start life as a lady in a shop.' And, reaching the apogee of his speech, Rex – like a trapeze artist preparing for a triple somersault without a safety net, launched his voice into a magnificent series of arabesques:

'If you refuse this offer . . .' – rising up the scale – 'you will be' – staccato, like a machine-gun – 'a most wicked and ungrateful girl . . .' – here a pause of utter sweetness, and then descending with infinite grace, down, down to his lowest register, concluding almost with a swoon – 'and the angels will *weep* for you.' At which point, the entire audience would break into a rapturous applause, like spectators before a masterly bullfighter, calling 'Olé! Olé!' after a sequence of breathtaking passes. This experience I have never seen before anywhere in the theatre, and it happened invariably, night after night.

25 September – Matinée

Following moderately favourable notices for the production in general, except for the actors, Rex said with delight: 'Everybody gets it in the neck – not excluding Crandall, Franz Allers and yourself . . .' In fact I was quite glad to share the reproaches, as it made him feel vulnerable with all of us. I relished an evening meal by myself at Sean Lartigue's Fish House by the French market. Walked back through the esplanade's romantic boulevard. Lartigue is a house set back behind the willow trees, flat-roofed, said to be haunted (like the La Duire House on Royal, where tragically slaves were chained in contorted positions). There is an interesting house on Decatur Avenue where Bonaparte was meant to be exiled having been rescued by French patriots after St Helena. It seemed to me a good device for a short story, Napoleon in New Orleans, the Emperor of Louisiana, and a decisive change in world history.

Chapter 31

TOURING THE LADY

WE LEFT NEW ORLEANS the night Muhammad Ali took a terrible beating from Larry Holmes, and I remembered walking back along Rampart Street to my hotel and passing the Urban Cowboy Striptease, hearing the raucous voices of sexual hilarity (always a special sound) where outside on the pavement, half-naked, and, I must admit, looking very fetching, girls were riding a mechanical Bronco horse. And, before turning in, I spent a couple of hazy and delirious hours hearing the most excellent jazz at The Blues Saloon.

And so, the *My Fair Lady* tour, in the words of those delightful black schoolgirls I saw jitterbugging on the pavement, 'boogied on' westward from Dixie to San Francisco. The arrival was unprepossessing, since I learnt that the San Francisco Public Library banned all Mary Poppins books because of their being 'out-of-date in moral attitudes, economically old-fashioned, and sexist in views, based on the dependency and inferiority of women.' When I pointed this out to Rex, his eyes narrowed to proverbial slits, and he commented: 'I wonder how they'll take to my treatment of Eliza!'

We were performing in a rather seedy area of San Francisco, fairly close to the famous Haight-Ashbury quarter so familiar in the hippy years, and like our rehearsal space in 42nd Street, unhappily surrounded by pornographic cinemas. One gay film was called *Head Waiter* ('He worked his way up from the Bottom'); and the second, a little more politely, but ominously: *If Mother Could See Me Now*. Resisting the invitation in a shop window further away from the theatre, 'See and Talk to a Nude Girl – $1', I spent as usual most of my working time in the darkened auditorium of the

170

theatre, and my time off in a romantic clapboard hotel on top of Nob Hill. Cathleen was back in hospital. She had had some kind of stroke and a friend of hers asked me to return with some books from her hotel when I went to visit her. Cathleen said to me: 'They are only two old books with black covers, but I would enjoy them. One is a sort of book of notes and jottings, and the other is a French novel I was reading.' The friend went to her hotel, spied the books by the bedside, and the jottings were Rupert Brooke's selected poems, the other, the so-called French novel, 'a bound volume of the poet's original letters to her, naturally all in his handwriting.' From her hospital room there was a magnificent view of the San Francisco Golden Gate Bridge. This time, I thought, we'll have 'to let her go'.

The Hard Hat Area

In the middle of October I left San Francisco, most of my work done, to remain any longer was pleasurable, but an indulgence. The show was now seriously on the road and simply had to play out its number of dates. I returned to New York, and next to my hotel, which I'd observed before had been due for reconstruction, was a mass of scaffolding, and a big sign proclaiming: 'This Is A Hard Hat Area'. The building site, which had been a vast empty hole when I first began to rehearse the show and first arrived in New York, was now miraculously about seventy stories high. When I spoke to my assistant, Harold DeFelice, he commented: 'Things grow fast in New York.' There was a new thriller on in one of the smaller theatres on 46th Street, called *Suicide*. According to Harold, 'The word on the street is people would rather *commit* suicide than see *Suicide*.'

Autumn was back in the streets – a gust of fresh air swept up the East River with a hint of hostility. Saxophone and drums played outside Bergdorf Goodmans. In Central Park fathers were playing with their sons, dressed with baseball caps and bats. Suddenly there was the authentic smell of bagels, and a salty tang in the intersections between the streets, of kebabs and charcoal, chestnuts, and pecans. I saw a diamond in Tiffany's window

171

suspended in a vast oval gold-fish bowl, surrounded by swimming golden fish.

Back to San Francisco, and departure from the Huntington Hotel on Nob Hill with Cathleen Nesbitt in tow. Rex departed in a sort of quaint caravan, an enormous limousine driven by his black chauffeur with the colourful name of Virgil, and behind it a station wagon containing twenty matching pieces of designer luggage; his wife's tiny Yorkshire Terrier, called Terror, was transported in a Louis Vuitton cat-carriage all of his own. The very height of chic, I thought, in the animal world. In the airplane, en route for Los Angeles, Rex said: 'Of course, another twenty-three pieces of luggage went on ahead with the trucks.' Cathleen complained about the informal ceremony of her ninety-third birthday, saying: 'People in this country have an awful preoccupation with birthdays.'

Rex replied: 'I hope to hell I don't have to celebrate my birthday.'

Cathleen said: 'My dear Rex, to me you are a stripling. After you are ninety years of age, whenever a birthday comes round, I'm always astounded to discover I'm still here.' And then, for the ninth time, at least, she reiterated her customary litany:

'When one is seventy, one begins to lose one's sight, well, that doesn't matter too much, one can always use spectacles – when one is eighty, one begins to lose one's hearing, and that's not too bad, because you can find a little machine to put into your ear with a battery – but at ninety one's memory begins to go, and that is something nobody can do anything about, there's no remedy for that.'

Chapter 32

TINSELTOWN REVISITED

REX WAS STAYING in California at Leslie Bricusse's luxurious
Beverly Hills mansion, with two extravagant private wings, separ-
ated by a swimming pool, scathingly referred to by Rex as 'a little
dog kennel at the back'. The peregrinations of Leslie are quite
bewildering. He has grand houses in London's Eaton Square, in
Acapulco, Malta, a villa in St Paul de Vence, a hide-out in Monte
Carlo, and now a new mansion in Lake Tahoe. Rex had collabo-
rated with Leslie on his musical film of *Dr Dolittle*, not one of their
more confident successes.

Looking at Terror, who resembles a diminutive leaf scurrying
about, Rex reminded me of the story I had heard before about the
French family arriving with their prize Pekinese at a Vietnamese
restaurant; pointing to their little dog, and then to their mouths, to
an uncomprehending waiter, in quest for a dish for their little pet
to eat, they were very disconcerted a few moments later, when the
Peke arrived back, served up in a noodle soup.

The descent to Los Angeles on a sparkling November seventy-five degree morning introduced us to a hundred thousand
glittering swimming pools. As we drove in past fat concrete
unsightly studios, camouflaged against some imaginary war,
and a distinct smog which brewed from the annual fires in
the Canyons, fanned by 120 m.p.h. Santa Anna winds, we
descended to the City of Lost Angels, popularly known to New
Yorkers as Tinseltown. On descent, the stewardess said: 'The
time is approximately 2 p.m.,' which struck me as a peculiarly
Los Angelesian imprecision. Almost like a premonition, as the
aircraft descended, I felt a sharp agonizing attack of neuralgic
pain in my left eye, which drew tears, so acute that I feared for a

moment was blood, as if I had been stabbed with a hair-pin like Oedipus.

When I arrived at the theatre, Harold, my assistant tells me the tragic news that Rachel Roberts is dead, and in a frightful manner, having consumed liquid fertilizer. I go straight away to visit Rex in his 'dog-kennel' in some anxiety. Fortunately he was on his own. He had assumed it was suicide, and confessed to me he had visited her the day before. It will be a catastrophe if the press find out. It was announced, embarrassingly, as a 'heart attack'. Rachel had been found in the garden of the house she rented, by the gardener. After a rather depressing run-through, during which Rex commented that performing at the Pantages Theatre, 'was like farting into cotton wool', but throughout which he managed to achieve a successfully jaunty note, he asked me to join him in his room. I had felt his laughter had concealed immense disquiet and anxiety, and all the usual feelings of guilt and responsibility. 'In a way,' he said, and laughed as he said it, 'it's a sort of relief.' After the performance we drank wine together until 1 a.m., and he wept quietly, wiping his eyes. I have never felt closer to him, or seen so sensitive a side. Of course, part of it was guilt, indeed it was, but not all. He had always been very fond of Rachel, very attached to her, loved in his way 'the pilgrim soul in her', and worried (he repeated this several times during my friendship with him) that by taking her away from her original husband, Alan Dobie, and her natural Welsh background, and introducing her to the chic international life of Portofino, he had somehow disturbed her equilibrium, and damaged her natural flow. 'She was happiest as the daughter of a Baptist minister in Wales,' he said. He told me finally that I had helped (I didn't think I had, other than by being there) and even at 1 a.m. outside the theatre there were still twenty or so enthusiastic fans demanding autographs.

Chapter 33

WIVES – RACHEL

'IT IS VERY difficult to be taken seriously,' said Rachel Roberts rather forlornly to a friend of hers, 'when you're introduced at a party to somebody as the fourth Mrs Rex Harrison.' And in a way, Rachel was unlucky enough to feel that sense of not so much inferiority but of discomfort for all of her married life. That Rex should even have been thought to be directly *responsible* for such an unhappy action is out of the question, but that he was implicated, in a very complex and unhappy way, is equally beyond dispute. It is difficult to accept that people kill themselves from love, and Shakespeare, no mediocre authority on the subject, in *Othello* profoundly disputes it, but there are I think exceptions and Rachel Roberts was conceivably one of them.

That night on stage when Rex as Henry Higgins put the key in the door of his grand house in Wimpole Street, and suddenly, almost for the first time, acknowledges Eliza, of her presence around the place being second nature to him, like breathing out and breathing in, as in the words of Alan Lerner's eloquent and poignant song at the end of the show, I felt sure that it was Rachel's face which Rex was singing he had grown accustomed to, rather than the stage Eliza's. His eyes were heavy and grey with tears, his cheeks sunken, his whole body in a state of profound dejection. It was the nearest he could get to an apologia, perhaps, for their love and married life together, and their recent relationship, which had been unnaturally searing and confused. My personal, and amateurish theory of suicide is that a person at the end of their tether only seeks the darkest and most negative way out of self-immolation, when after beating on a diversity of doors he or she finds they are all, one by one, irrevocably closed.

Death by one's own hand, I am convinced, is always on account of more than one thing. With Rachel, it was not that the terrible 'ifs' accumulated but that the possibilities of her life and career and happiness were gradually extinguished one by one. By a strange, and unhappy coincidence, Lilli Palmer was also at Los Angeles, staying at the Beverley Wilshire, when Rachel killed herself, and she was very upset and moved by the fact. Having lived with Rex through one suicide, close to him (and, incidentally, there was another of his wives who also tried to commit suicide at one time, and left him, as he put it at the time, 'shaking in his shoes'), Lilli Palmer was able to imagine what Rex would feel about Rachel. And in a strange way she felt sorry for him, for certainly Rachel's misery was *not* of Rex's manufacture. Rachel was a dissatisfied woman. Not someone who could be happy with anybody.

Lilli felt strongly that Rachel's heart-rending longing for Rex, and as she writes of them in her strange, ungainly memoir, the idyllic honeymoon months in Portofino, were mostly fake. She had good reason to confess such a thing, as she had recently been dining with somebody who stayed at San Genesio at exactly the same time. According to him, the activities of this unforgettable honeymoon, as she describes it, are fairly ghastly, and bear out what the Italian servants had told Lilli when, the following year, it had been her turn to stay there. Her view was that Rachel had no need to have done away with herself, if only she had understood Rex as he was, and not as she imagined him to be, or hoped he might become. And Rex takes his share of the blame on the chin, as I had not infrequently heard him say that he had, without meaning to, introduced her to a life of high style and the grand manner, which both intoxicated, and at the same time, destroyed her. Lilli Palmer, sometimes one thinks perhaps the most reflective and wisest of his glittering wives, wished she had been able to reach the unhappy Rachel and had the freedom to say to her, 'Look you have got it all wrong!' Rex, in her view was not at all the man of power, and sophistication, and domination Rachel believed him to be. She felt that Rachel mistook the Rolls Royce, for the man driving it. To her, Rex was rather simple and fearful, and when he was not dominating the world on the stage, unsure of himself, and profoundly alone.

And yet, there was something about Rachel which held the greatest lure for Rex, and he felt for her probably more intensely than any other of his six wives. It might be called a neurotic tendency, it was presumably to do with their own strange tormented erotic sexuality, heightened by argument and alcohol, generated by competition and jealousy, compounded by fear of failure and loneliness. I well remember Rex, one evening when we were dining together, struggling to explain why it was that he was happy to go on seeing Rachel, although deeply intent that they should never continue their catastrophic relationship, and in the end almost giving up on his quest to put his finger on whatever that chemistry was, by saying quite simply – and this, rather unkindly, in comparison with the new wife he already had – that what he *really* liked about Rachel was that she was an actress. It was the only phrase he kept returning to, repeating it almost as if it was a kind of rune: 'Rachel, you see, is an *actress* . . . Rachel is an *actress* . . .' Something unique, tribal, like a Romany.

On the night Rachel died, Rex stumbled, where formerly he was always sure-footed, on the line: 'The moment I make friends with a woman, Pickering, she becomes jealous, exacting, suspicious, and a damned nuisance . . .' It was altogether too near home. Did Rex acknowledge the unhappy coincidence that Carole Landis had swallowed an overdose of sleeping pills, on account of him, thirty-five years earlier, also in Hollywood, in her home on Capri Drive?

There was something forlorn about Rachel's view of Rex also. In her diary she had written: 'Rex is a scamp. Always was. Impossible to live with, I suppose.'

To Don Gregory, the producer, at a later stage, Rex was even more revealing. Obviously, by now, his life with Mercia was deeply unhappy. 'What can I do, Don?' he asked. 'What will become of me, if Mercia leaves me, or I leave her? Where would I go? I can't live on my own. How can I ever marry again? An *eighth* wife? Where is there for me to go?' Don felt truly sorry for him, as he confronted loneliness, declining powers, old age, death.

Chapter 34

THE AZTEC PANTAGES, LOS ANGELES

STARING IN AWE around the vast acres of the highly decorated 1920s architecture of the old movie house, The Aztec Pantages (aptly named, it looked ideal for mass sacrifice of appropriated virgins) Judith (Cookie) commented: 'I wouldn't be surprised if the entire chariot race out of *Ben Hur* came galloping through this foyer right now.' There were haughty Egyptian goddesses astride the stairs – one rather confusingly wearing goggles, and bearing an airplane on an outstretched hand – a second deity, opposite her, with a fashionable thirties shingle haircut, operated a primitive Mitchell camera. Rest-rooms, bars, staircases, box-office, all were decorated in the same characteristic silent-movies style. But for all its expensive decoration, there was something slightly fascist and tasteless about the whole thing, as if it had been under the personal supervision of Albert Speer (exteriors) and Baldur von Shirach. When the gypsies assembled for the first practice *sitz probe*, with the band, to hear what Bob Kriese promised would be 'the exciting Los Angeles sound' (as the orchestra was made up of the sound-studio movie-veterans), they had taken on a New Look, appropriate for LaLa Land, with T-shirts scrawled with vivid slogans: 'Will You Be My Fred', 'Hotsie Totsie', 'Stage-Hand Dan', 'Fondle With Care', and 'I'll give you a Gypsy Good-Time!'

Rex was characteristically unimpressed, and expressed, I thought, the not entirely sincere world-weariness of the Hollywood 'old soldier'. 'It's your first time in Los Angeles, Patrick,' he said, disparaging my enthusiasm for the 1920s kitsch of The Aztec Pantages. 'My dear boy, I assure you Hollywood's a grave. Everybody's half-dead – all the cinema-people go to bed at nine o'clock – there's a breathless hush over Bel Air – the residents are all

178

asleep in their ghastly homes.' Which was partly true, as so many of them were tuned to an early start at the Studios, but we were soon to discover LaLa Land, or Nowhere City as it was perceptively called, had a special life of its own. Bob Kriese said: 'Oh, don't write off the City of Lost Angels – it has something going for it – I mean, it's not New York, it's Tinseltown, but it's kinda Glitzy.' While we sat in the habitual darkened stalls, which proved to be the great leveller, whether we were in Boston, New York, New Orleans, Los Angeles or Chicago, all these cities looked the same from the half-illuminated, wholly air-conditioned auditorium, I had a small passage of arms with the producers. We sat looking at the so-called frontcloth of Covent Garden, over which St Paul's Cathedral mysteriously towered; Don Gregory, Mike Merrick and the designer, Oliver Smith. Since its respraying, the show-curtain had come back to us, not enormously different, but the curious and unwanted colour of an aubergine. 'You say it's better, Oliver,' I said, 'with a note of apprehension in your voice. Have you managed to make it a little less like Pittsburgh?'

'Yes – it's a lot less like Pittsburgh. Now it looks like Edinburgh.'

'Remember the premise of this production,' interposed Don, 'I always said to Rex, we want to polish an old diamond – not cut a new one.'

'Maybe we can redo it to look like Paris,' suggested Oliver, 'and you can take us all out on a tour of *Gigi*.

'That's not a bad idea,' said Don, 'and Rex can take me back to Madame Claude's. It would be cheaper. Not a lot cheaper, but definitely cheaper.'

Chapter 35

CATHLEEN FOR EVER

I WAS TEMPTED to regret the day I took Don Gregory's advice and telephoned Cathleen Nesbitt in order to ask her to play the part of Mrs Higgins, the role she originally played some thirty years ago, in spite of her being now ninety-three, and logically the oldest actress still working on the English-speaking stage. We had first met in Chichester several years before, when she appeared as the Claire Claremont character in *The Aspern Papers*. At the time she had asked me: 'What year did Henry James write this story?'

'1888,' I answered.

'Oh I should remember that,' said Cathleen, 'it was the year I was born.'

But this time understandably she had forgotten my face. She had told me not long before that she had met this man, who appeared to her totally unfamiliar, but he seemed to have some acquaintance with her. 'I was prepared at ninety to go blind and deaf, but I didn't realize old age makes you lose your memory as well. I said to this stranger – "Look here, I do apologize but I'm afraid I must ask you your name." He said to me, "I was your doctor for the past seven years."'

So I should have been prepared for the moment, when Rex telephoned me one night after the performance, in a terrible rage about Cathleen:

'Do you know what she said in the Conservatory scene? – there she was, I came on, drew a complete blank, said in desperation: "Ah, mother, there you are!" to try to get the scene started, and all she said was: "Now everybody's trying to say goodbye to me . . ." What, in fuck's name, was I supposed to answer to that!'

By this time the show was in Los Angeles, we were sinking

180

deeper and deeper into the water, as poor Cathleen sank into ever-growing Alzheimer's. It was what I called 'unkind to Old Ladies' time. We could hardly fire her, without beastliness, her agent, keen on the commission, refused to permit her to withdraw, she didn't want to go, never missed a performance – in fact, I think, at this stage, 93-year-old Cathleen as Mrs Higgins, was the only member of the *MFL* company who had not missed a performance and had an understudy on, and the producers and Rex felt her family were secretly rather relieved the old lady was safely on the far side of the Atlantic.

'I don't seem to remember anything at all these days,' she said to me one evening, 'except the one word "Alzheimer's".' In fact, this was by no means the entire truth. Apart from surreal lapses of memory, frequently off-stage, like forgetting which hotel she was living in, or what show she was appearing in, her memory of the dialogue was fairly consistent. Aside from selected moments, entrances and exits especially, she was pretty accurate once the scenes were running. These anomalies were alarming, though. Once she got very angry with me, and summoned me to her dressing-room – and she truly *was* angry: 'Patrick, you've been very naughty – you've changed the running-order of the show.'

'Oh, Cathleen, how could I have done? The scenes are written down in letters of stone.'

'But you *have*,' she insisted. 'First of all you get me down for the Ascot scene far too early, and then you put in a lot of new material. While I was waiting during that endless study scene, you had Rex singing some extraordinary song about the rain.'

There had previously been more than a hiatus over the arrival of the snooty Eynsford-Hill party, when Eliza regales the grandees at Ascot with tales about her aunt dying of influenza, or, more correctly, about it being her belief the family 'done the old woman in'. In Mr Shaw's printed original Mrs Higgins' introductions should go something like this:

'Ah, Colonel Pickering, you're just in time for tea . . . May I introduce . . . Mrs Eynsford-Hill. Miss Doolittle. Lord and Lady Boxington. Miss Doolittle. And Freddy Eynsford-Hill.'

Straightforward enough, one might think, especially as each

character stepped forward on cue, to identify themselves with a how-de-do, or a light tap of their Ascot grey topper. Under Cathleen's influence, this invariably turned into something infinitely more eccentric – nobody on stage or off knew who would be presented to whom, and some evenings the entire personnel of the Ascot gavotte would be jammed in the wings, anxious to see how it might turn out. Once we got:

'Ah, Colonel Boxington – you're just in time for tea – now, have you met Mrs Higgins-Hill? Miss Pickering. Lord and Lady Pilkington. And . . . Colin.' But Cathleen remained indomitable, and defeated all our efforts to reduce her character, or her authority.

'The trouble is,' said Rex, after a particularly bad afternoon, 'the more you take the lines away from Cathleen, the more she remembers them.'

And he himself occasionally had lapses; in the recitative between the choruses of 'I've Grown Accustomed to her Face', he put a foot into space, and improvised:

> *'Poor Eliza!*
> *How simply . . . something!*
> *How something else . . .!*
> *How delightful!'*

And once, getting lost in a circular maze at the end of 'Ordinary Man', unable to remember whether he was an ordinary, very gentle, or very simple man, and as he said, 'terrified I was of going back to the beginning, and having to sing the whole fucking thing all over again,' he settled for:

> *'I'm a very SOMETHING man,*
> *Who – dee-dum-de-dum-de dum*
> *And – de-dum-de-dum-de-dum*
> *And – de-da-de-da-de-DA!'*

And I'm not sure anybody in the audience ever noticed the difference.

182

We also had a lot of fun at the start of the Ascot scene; if it ever got started. Cathleen used to enter after all the pretty girls wearing their Cecil Beaton hats for the Ascot Gavotte, generally make a hash of the introductions, then would sit down comfortably drinking her cup of tea, and forget the opening line – not so much the opening line, but the key line, which triggered the entire remainder of the scene, as in:

Mrs Higgins (handing Eliza her tea): 'Will it rain, do you think?'

As nothing seemed able to break the silence, I proposed to Rex, he gave Cathleen a subtle, but silent hint by miming an imaginary umbrella. In fact this became so elaborate, and at the same time, so brilliant, it was incorporated into the scene. First Rex coughed softly to attract his mother's attention, held out his hand for imaginary raindrops, pulled up his collar, opened the invisible umbrella, sheltered beneath it, shook it to dislodge the water, and finally vibrated it in and out like a bicycle pump, in a loud undertone: 'Rain, mother . . .'

'Oh, yes, of course, Henry – will it rain, do you think?' and, justifiably, the house fell in. When the laughter eventually subsided, Rex would take off his familiar Higgins' tweed hat, bow to Cathleen and say: 'Thank you, mother,' to end the episode – and thus the play continued. I cannot emphasize enough, how beautifully it was done – nor how much Rex looked forward to it. And it revealed brilliantly that both Higgins and his mother conspired together to show Eliza off in front of the socially conscious Eynsford-Hills. Although once, on leaving, she floored everybody on stage, by saying: 'Oh, and Henry – I want you to remember two things. Talk about the weather – and the other thing.'

Once she commandeered Rex's car, in order to go home, but drove instead to Sak's 5th Avenue, buzzed all round the store, made a stack of purchases, while the chauffeur waited on the street with the engine ticking over; and, on another occasion, when we were rehearsing at the New Amsterdam, on 42nd and 5th, and in her lunch hour, wandered scattily off into a brothel on the corner of 9th Avenue, where fortunately our two stage managers, set as bloodhounds to keep an eye on her, eventually retrieved her unscathed. Rex was unimpressed when I told him I respected her as a great survivor. 'Underneath all that whimsical charm, I think she's a feisty Northern Irish cow,' he snarled. He was probably half right, but it kept her going. When we flew from San Francisco to Boston, I sat next to her on the plane, and was not too worried when she said she had left in her locker the plastic carrier bag she always took with her as hand-baggage. 'Anything important?' I asked breezily.

'Only Rupert Brooke's love-letters,' she said. I nearly had a heart attack: I thought it was full of Kleenexes, pocket-batteries and sleeping pills. Happily the two splendid stage managers succeeded in tracking them down. I plucked up the courage to ask her what she remembered of her remote love-affair with the gorgeous-looking but rather petulant poet.

'Rupert was extremely beautiful,' she admitted, 'but on the subject of the theatre, he was extremely idiotic. Virginia Woolf always said to me, "you should discourage Rupert, if you can, about writing poems to you: he'll never last as a poet. But I'm sure, if you can persuade him to take up politics, he'll end up as Prime Minister of England!"'

When I last visited her in hospital in Los Angeles (after a severe stroke) she seemed very confused. I went with Jack Gwillim. 'And what are you doing in Los Angeles, dear?' she asked him.

'I'm playing Pickering, with you and Rex, at the Pantages Theatre, in *My Fair Lady*,' he replied gently.

'You mean with Richard Burton, don't you?' she said.

'No, Cathleen, with Rex Harrison, as Henry Higgins,' he insisted.

'Nonsense,' said Cathleen, in some indignation, 'with Richard Burton. Rex was only in the film!'

Chapter 36

ON THE BACK LOT OF UNIVERSAL

ONE EVENING FRANK O'CONNOR and his wife, Bambi, drove me out to Westwood, to the famous restaurant where the movie stars used to go in the forties, and still go now, Marcos Italian Restaurant. We were not disappointed. To my intense pleasure, a heroine of my dodging school-in-the-afternoons-in-order-to-see-a-matinée was eating at a corner table. Esther Williams, star of a dozen swimming and diving pictures, usually with Ricardo Montalban. The face was pretty as ever – and instantly recognizable – I suppose it was all that swimming, but she had got immensely fat. Mountainous.

As well as forties film-stars, the restaurant was also frequented from time to time by forties gangsters, and I was not to be disappointed there either. A sudden tension in the room, the unmistakable slow turning of heads, the lowering of voices, the unfathomable frisson, and Frank muttered quietly: 'We got company.' As if at a signal we stayed heads bent over the Linguini alle Vongole, as four obvious heavies moved to a table just across the room from us and sat down. I felt half in, half out of, a George Raft film, especially as one of the torpedoes, in raincoat and fedora, hovered between our table and theirs, watchful, hands in pockets, quite clearly on guard. The object of their attention, a little old hunched-up figure, like a shuffling grandfather in a tenement doorway, barely able to support his soup spoon, and dribbling helplessly at the corners of his mouth.

Frank whispered to me, leaning right across the table until his mouth almost brushed my ear: 'Just keep on eating and speaking natural. It's Mickey Cohen and his bodyguards. He often eats at Marcos.' My God! – Mickey Cohen – one of the most ruthless of the 1940s mobsters. He ran the drugs and hookers in L.A. right through the war, and into the 1950s. His hired gun was Lana Turner's lover, Johnny Stompanato. Now bent over his soup bowl, and dribbling, a funny little old guy, seemingly paralysed and gaga. In the Prohibition days he always claimed to have great respect for Mr Al Capone, 'because he was such a man and carried himself so nicely.'

'I'm amazed he's still alive. What kind of threat can he be, to be so ancient and helpless, and so well-guarded?'

'They gotta take care of him,' said Frank, 'he knows where the bodies are buried. There's a lot of secrets he knows, that a lot of people want him to take to his grave.'

At Marcos, while Mickey Cohen, the sinister inspiration of the movie *L.A. Confidential,* sucked at his soup, Frank told me of the story of Hollywood and St Teresa. 'St Teresa pleads with God to give her a chance, and come back down to earth. He's against the idea, but eventually he yields to her wishes. But he tells her, no more Italy – she's gotta go this time to America. So, she goes, but with God's approval promises to keep in touch.

' "Dear Father," she says, "it's Teresa. I'm in New York, and it's cruel." '

'A little later, "Dear Father, it's Teresa. I'm in Chicago, and it's torment." '

'Later on, she reports: "Father, it's Teresa. I'm in Detroit, and it's the outer circle of hell." God remains unmoved.

'Finally, she says: "God dear, it's Terry! And I'm in L.A." '

Chapter 37

PROBLEMS

WE WENT ON to Washington, Louisville, where Rex commented 'I look out on to a sea of blue hair,' and then Miami. By the time the show arrived in Boston, to which I had returned, urgently, from my new job at the Chichester Festival Theatre, in July 1981 we faced big problems. The producers warned me they had received critical letters, telephone calls, and simply listened to the voices of the public as they came out of the theatre. Doctors, unasked for, rang in to offer practical help and assistance. The warning signals could not be ignored.

The problem was Cheryl Kennedy. Her voice was wearing down.

Not only could she no longer sing the numbers like 'Danced All Night', which she always found difficult with its murderous top G, now she couldn't sing the ones she *used* to be able to dominate. It confirmed the remark Don Gregory said to me over the telephone from Boston, 'She can no longer cut it. She can't sing "Luvverly" with conviction, she can't sing "Spain", she capsizes in "Danced All Night", and goes completely under the waves with "Show Me" and, even worse, drowned with all hands, in "Without You". She is not only exhausted,' said Don, 'she is battling on helplessly with exhaustion.' Rex, he told me, refused to let them put the understudy on.

The only moment of lightness when I saw a very disgruntled Rex after the performance, he knowing full well that I have been sent for (almost as ominously as Rosencrantz and Guildenstern), was when I told him that the musical *The Mitford Girls* was a tremendous success at Chichester, in spite of one of the critics calling it 'a crypto-fascist-racist show', and he replied,

'In Chichester, I would imagine that counts as a go-and-see-it notice!'

Forgetting our differences about Cheryl's voice, I drove way up along the Maine coast to a dinner theatre known as the Whispering Oyster with Rex, to Orgonquin, a charming boat-scattered, former fishing harbour, built in typical Nantucket style clapboard. We enjoyed an excellent Puligny-Montrachet. We sat at supper with a view of the harbour, a few jostling sailboats, and some attractive clapboard houses. The object of our visit was for Rex to see his son, 'Noel is playing Professor Higgins in a field somewhere.'

Noel, was charming, and relaxed, and desperately eager to see his father. The three of us enjoyed a really delightful, easy-going, supper, and I felt almost as if I was a friendly cousin, or old family friend. Everything went perfectly to end nostalgically, affec-tionately, but there was a heart-rending conclusion. As we finished supper, Rex to my surprise, suddenly announced that he and I had to return to Boston as we had work to do the next morning. This was a Sunday night. Noel said, immediately, and with a real look of panic in his face: 'But surely, Father, you are going to stay and watch me in my cabaret show, aren't you?'

To my great dismay, Rex's answer was short and to the point:
'Oh, no, Noel, I couldn't possibly do that. It would be frightfully boring for me.'

I wouldn't have looked at him deliberately myself, but it so happened I was actually facing Noel at that moment, and I saw the contours of his face fall, as I have no doubt they had fallen countless times before throughout his childhood, and with the look of a deflated small boy, returning alone to the miseries of boarding-school. Noel took sad leave of us, and an unconcerned Rex sailed off to the car, where his chauffeur was waiting. I was too cowardly to protest, besides there was nothing really I could protest about, it was not *my* son, and the wound had already been inflicted. We must have driven about 150 miles up the coast, possibly longer, for Rex to see his son and spend the afternoon with him; and Noel was so obviously delighted to see his father, and laid on an enchanting supper both in the quality of the food, and the atmosphere of the conversation, like two old chums. He didn't seem profoundly put out, as obviously he was accustomed to such a rejection, but I shall never forget the sorrow in his face at that moment. It was difficult to arouse any animation in the spacious limousine as we drove all the way back towards darkness and Boston; after a few desultory words, Rex dozed, and when he woke, he announced: 'Extraordinary that Noel should even think that I would want to watch his show. Most of it is a parody of the stuff I do, in fact he's made quite a living out of pretending to be me. Occasionally he sings those rather milky songs of his, that he writes, but I've even seen him billed as "Professor Higgins in *My Fair Lady*, with Noel Harrison, son of the famous Rex".' It made me recognize that neither Carey, 'my Communist son', nor Noel, 'the entertainer', could ever have enjoyed an easy time in their childhood, and it surprised me to some extent that they were on speaking terms at all, let alone as welcoming.

15 July, 1981 – Running Out Of Steam: Boston

These are critical days for the show. And after all this time of being so good. It has lost all its class. The first performance I saw, flying in from England, arriving in the afternoon, and being driven directly in a black limousine, as if there was some kind of funereal emergency, to the theatre, was a profoundly dispiriting experience. The audience was restless and inattentive. Poor Cheryl Kennedy's voice was so distorted and strained, the result of over-use and exhaustion, and too many shows in too spacious auditoriums, even when it wasn't suffering the extra demands of the high notes which Rex resented so much, had lost all its tone and warmth, was flattened out, hoarse, and 'scooping'. Cheryl never had much volume, but she had a sweet tone. The phrasing was wrong as she struggled to get in control of her instrument, and this cruel sensation of physical discomfort communicated itself immediately to the audience. A woman in the stall seat in front of me awkwardly fondled her throat. We are now in a desperately serious situation, as well as adding the poignant irony, that after so many dates in regional theatres in America, in which Cheryl has been splendid and at times triumphant, and always scoring huge points in the comedy scenes, that in the last lap as we struggle towards Broadway (our next date) the performance is rapidly running out of steam.

What is worse, is that Rex is equally intent on *not* acting with anybody else other than Cheryl, because he maintains, 'none of the others can play the comedy'. Now it is no longer joke-time, and the situation we wrestled with (rather successfully as it happens) in rehearsal days back at the Trafalgar; those times when over a friendly Budweiser, Jack and Harold and I would describe the show as '*My Fair Lady* or Fuck the Music' were well and truly finished. Candidly, we and the audiences are the ones being fucked now. Rex continues to make life hard, no, impossible, as he resolutely refuses to let me hear the first understudy (uncomfortably married to our Alfred Doolittle, Milo O'Shea) and so the resentment caused by putting on a second and *unofficial* understudy is unthinkable. And even if we could, because there is a perfect candidate in the cast, he will not accept her, Nancy Ringham (a joyful exuberant all-American girl), whom he crushingly describes as 'a tall strident Ohio horse'. As for Kitty Sullivan, the legitimate understudy (pretty, red-haired Irish girl), he refers to her as 'the Dublin mouse'. Given that he will accept neither 'the Ohio horse' nor 'the Dublin mouse', we seem to be paralysed between a Scylla and Charybdis of inactivity and obstinacy.

Cheryl visits yet another doctor, and he diagnoses arthritis around her cheeks and jaw, and the dreaded discovery of nodes in her throat. Sitting with her in Rex's glamorous trailer, which for all its vastness, is parked in the even vaster areas backstage of the theatre, stranded as it were in the middle of a huge aerodrome hangar, I sadden for Cheryl's pale, exhausted face, and her list of woes with which she acquaints me, her plate, her 'bite', her valium, her period, her nodules, her arthritis, her tension, her lack of morale, in a single word her total collapse.

As if all of this were not difficult enough, there's the very real problem with Milo O'Shea; he has given the show devoted service and is a superb performer, but the fact of the matter is (a serious production error way back in May or June of last year, of which I am as much responsible as are the producers, never thinking it would ever happen), Milo is married to the understudy; and with the Eliza in a staggering tail-spin and plainly unable to continue for many days longer, it is completely reasonable that the official understudy would be expecting to take over.

Milo and I have always been on the best of terms up till now, but dropping in to his dressing-room, partly to say hello, partly to give him a few distracted, and profoundly unimportant notes, he is clearly irritable and indignant against me. I feel underneath his generally genial disposition, and black bushy eyebrows, and Alfred Doolittle flushed make-up, that he is silently threatening to walk off if his wife isn't formally invited to step in. Not unreasonably, he asked me: 'Why won't you see Kitty?' He knows perfectly well, I'm certain, of Rex's attitude, but then nobody is speaking to Rex at the moment, or rather Rex isn't speaking to them, so he obviously looks to the director and the producers to take some kind of action. The only action we could take, by insisting that Kitty Fitzgerald takes over from Cheryl would mean the instantaneous walking-out of the star of the show, and the immediate collapse of *My Fair Lady* here, now, this very evening, in Boston. We are bound to try to find some other solution, if after this long tour, we are to taste the fruits of Broadway.

Next door to the Copley Plaza, where the indoor theatre is contained, is a vast building made of glass; towering above it, a gigantic mirror which reflects neighbouring skyscrapers in the foothills, and the clouds, and sunrise and sunset, and last night a spectacular full moon. Visually it is very beautiful, but glass panes have been known to fall from it occasionally, slicing their victims below in two equal slivers. Looking up at it, it astonishes me that it remains standing at all, and with my state of mind, and the inescapable dilemma facing me, the prospect of its collapse on top of me, slicing me into two equal pieces appals me. The precincts near the theatre are extremely sleazy and inhospitable, and the company refer to the area as 'the combat zone'. On a wall beyond the stage door a defiant sign is chalked up hopelessly: 'I'm Going To Marry You, Cindy'. One of the ensemble, Jeff, was mugged as

191

he returned from the theatre last night, and he put up a big fight, and managed to get away with his life and his wallet. 'I must have been deranged,' he said wryly to me. Morale at Headquarters was not helped in the Harrison department when he received a telegram today from his old adversary, Richard Harris, concerning the tour of *Camelot* (in which he had replaced Burton, successfully, as King Arthur). He had just played San Francisco, and to our immense chagrin and his delight had broken our staggering box-office record. Harris's telegram read, not unwittily, 'You took away my wife – I took away your box-office record. Money stays longer than wives. Yours Dickie Harris.'

All Rex said, by way of reply, was . . . you've guessed it.

17 July – Friday: In The Caravan

Rex is in recalcitrant mood, one of the worst I've ever seen. It was extremely delicate for me to remain on any basis of communication whatsoever, and at the same time to try doggedly to stick to my guns over the situation we are in. He is at his most suspicious and irritable concerning the nodes on Cheryl's throat. Cheryl, almost in tears, was begging me to release her for the final three performances in Boston, which at least might give her some hope of resting her throat before Broadway. Rex was incensed, and at his unyielding, obdurate worst.

'No way, Cheryl, will I let you off. It is those arseholes, those bus and truck merchants' method of giving you the push, and I *insist* you carry on, and *croak* your way through the last three performances.' This threw him into a rage for the rest of the night. In the performance, a fragment of his real self emerged through the character, when Milo, as Alfred Doolittle, makes himself cosy on the sofa opposite Higgins and asks him, rhetorically:

'What am I? I ask you, guv'nor what am I?'

To which Rex replied (as Higgins), 'A dustman.'

When I had been speaking alone with Rex, after Cheryl left his trailer, and I recognized at last that no amount of reality, or common sense, or instinct for survival, or friendship, or theatrical intelligence, or indeed *anything* was doing any good, I began to understand why there were those prodigious losses on the Western Front, and the Somme in 1916. It was because of decisions made by old irascible men, alone and mad, sitting in empty rooms.

We went through the motions of auditioning, that is listening to, other members of the ensemble, all having a shot at Eliza without much confidence or success, simply in order to appear democratic. We auditioned unnecessarily some good Alfred Doolittle's, and even a potential Pickering from the company. All this was part of an elaborate, and I thought, deeply doomed strategy. Suddenly Rex came in, shouting from the back of the auditorium, not angrily, but just making his presence felt, and probably suspecting we were all conspiring against him:

'Patrick, I must say I prefer watching the show from this side.'

'Well, Rex,' I replied, calling back to him in genial frame of mind, as at least we were not on the edge of argument, 'the problem is you miss from the sides all the acting on the staircase.'

'Thank God,' said Rex, 'I can't stand looking at Allison – oh, is he there?'

I felt small relief from a comical exchange with one of the better looking of the ensemble, Ned Reterron, who in answer to my casual, 'How are you doing?' answered 'Very well, can you imagine I'm still straight, and after such a long tour.'

We all discussed together the perilous and in a way ridiculous idea of Rex disguising himself in the moustache and white wig for the second Saturday matinée performance, in order to see Nancy Ringham's debut with Michael Allison from a hidden position in the second row of the circle. But apart, as previously explained, from being an exercise in style, it was all pretty pointless. And sad.

An extraordinary glimpse of Rex's sexuality, and primitive hostility. Even the delectable Wa-Wa committed something of a blunder. We were obviously in a kind of dramatic situation that everything was going to go wrong both on and off the stage. Rex had always revealed a sweetness for her, but it must be said, in a fairly innocent way, more for companionship, until Wa-Wa suddenly declared a perfectly rational interest in his handsome twenty-five-year-old chauffeur. The seventy-three-year-old Rex spotted this at the company party, and not finding Wa-Wa demurely gracing *his* table, but another table, and with the chauffeur, bristled and left early in a huff.

Next morning, first thing, he called the producers, and insisted that all limousine trips when Elizabeth Worthington was with him should be deducted from the account, and paid for by the chauffeur. And meant it. As a further illustration of the mood he was in, he told me gleefully, that upon leaving the Arie Crown Theatre, Chicago, in March he had said to the press, when they asked him what he thought about the theatre, that it was awful and unplayable. I remembered when I was there with him some months before, the rather nice woman-manager asking him to be generous enough to say a kind word about the newly built theatre on its behalf, if asked by the press. At that time he concurred, and was charm itself. Later, he said to me delightedly, 'I absolutely fucked them.' The choreographer, Crandall, told me that around this time, but before I had flown over from England, a great confrontation scene took place with Rex presiding in his hotel suite, at his side his rather agreeable lawyer, Harold Schiff, and one of the voice coaches (who had also been flown over from England). While horrid abusive arguments took place among them, Rex sat down contentedly, first ordered, and then ate an entire three-course dinner, with the finest wines, at his table, while the others sat around famished. He didn't even offer them a cup of coffee.

Back at the theatre, I stood in the wings, what I called 'the Degas View', and even with all the misery around, enjoyed the marvellous atmosphere of the smoky early morning mist of the Covent Garden flower market, and the dancers limbering up behind the front-cloth in the dry ice; wonderful mysterious shapes, angular, poetic, obscure, and rhythmic. But only a few moments later, still entranced by the magic of the early market scene, Milo O'Shea as Doolittle fell lopsidedly on his ankle, and hobbled off in great pain. It emerges that he has seriously sprained his ankle and will be out for the last four performances in Boston.

With three of the principals off on the afternoon that Rex was going to look at the understudy, Higgins, Eliza, and Doolittle, Rex murmured to me, as he saw Cathleen sitting in the wings in her wheelchair: 'All we need is for Cathleen to feel sick, and we might as well all go home. There won't be anybody in the house!' In fact, later that day, it was absolutely extraordinary. Obviously we had to tell the truth, and advertise the fact that Rex Harrison would not be performing that afternoon and there were queues around the block demanding their money back as long as there had been earlier for advance booking to buy their tickets to see him perform. Beyond the theatre were officials with bullhorns and loud hailers, and no less than four tough-looking Boston cops standing around the box-office window. Outside the foyer, keeping the queues in line, as they threatened to get out of control, were several other Boston cops on horseback wielding night-sticks. When people asked me, as from time to time they do, what is the definition of a star, I often think of that image outside the box-office of the Boston theatre. A star is when you are not appearing at the matinée, and the local police force has to send out uniformed cops on horseback to stop the crowds from rioting. Even in extremity, I confess I had to hand it to Rex.

18 July – Saturday: Breakfast Meeting

The much lauded encounter with the magical voice coach took place this morning. A nice, homely middle-aged woman sat in front of me, and talked about as much mindless gibberish as I could bear at that hour. Her theory regarding Cheryl's voice was that *nothing* was wrong other than that she was a little tired, and mentally somewhat deflated. Her voice is perfectly all right, the high notes are there just as they have always been, but she has been pushing too hard and for too long. If she can rethink the entire performance there's no reason that everything could not return as it was, satisfactorily, in New Orleans six months ago. It is not the first time that I have noticed these marginal figures around the edges of the theatre, claiming to be experts in either movement or voice or psychology, defy reality with an unwisdom that takes the breath away. And she was probably flown in at great expense and put up in a luxurious hotel simply to waste one's time.

Bluntly, although not totally inconceivable I suppose, falling over backwards, or standing on my head to try to be optimistic, it would need a miracle for Cheryl to recover in a mere three weeks, as at the moment she droops with vocal exhaustion like a wounded athlete around the track limping and swaying. The effect on the audience, however sympathetic they may be, is painful in the extreme – the sensation is of a drowning, suffocating girl. It's unfair to Cheryl, and threatens her career. It represents to me a form of sadistic cruelty. People fondle their throats anxiously, or there is a ripple or sway as they mutter mutinously, sometimes a grimace, and a sense of anxiety disperses all over the house. The applause at the end of 'The Rain In Spain' is at best muted, and I'm astonished that Rex doesn't notice it; his hearing is not of the best any more, so I can only assume he *doesn't* hear it, or, possibly, perhaps, he is arrogant enough not to listen to it. I have to bring Cathleen Nesbitt on *early* for the Ascot applause, after the pause which follows 'Danced All Night'. The stage manager hissed to me: 'It's bring on the old lady time!' Have we come to this, I wonder, that the aged, unremembering, dear old lady of 93, is now propping up the show.

Friends in the ensemble told me that when Nancy Ringham sang the role she apparently drew three rounds of applause after 'Danced', and *bravos* coming down the staircase, and uniquely after 'Goodbye Professor Higgins', which our original Eliza never gets. Company morale must be thought of, their common sense has to be taken into consideration. This afternoon I gave notes, with a heavy heart, trying to create a smoke-screen of enthusiasm and concern for the performance. As I looked round their affectionate faces, I thought to myself they must think I have taken leave of my senses. Here is the Director, flown all the way over from Britain, giving notes on this and that, on infinite and unimportant detail, and in their heads they must be thinking: 'What on earth is he talking about? *This* inflection, *that* pause, and there's this vast gaping hole in the centre.' I fear that under such circumstances I too genuinely earn the soubriquet of Rex's favourite pejorative word. It's 'fire the maid' time. But at the same time the decision appears easy, apart from the reality of those who are in the position of dealing with it. Rex Harrison has contractual casting control, he refuses to accept either of the legitimate understudies, and our only hope in salvaging the show by the time it gets to Broadway is to find an alternative third candidate, obviously who can perform the role, preferably who comes out of the company, and above all who manages to reach Rex's approval. Cathleen, in Rex's fruitful phrase 'drew a complete blank' yet again in the Ascot scene. She had been worrying about how she would get to a company party which was being held afterwards, and finally managed to run Jack Gwillim to earth on stage, and decided to confront him.

'Ah, Colonel Pickering,' she began correctly, and then, 'do you know where this party is being held later tonight?'

'I *do*,' said Jack, after a moment's pause, and then with admirable presence of mind concluded, 'but first of all I thought you might like to accompany me to Ascot,' and thus held the scene safely on course.

August – New York At Last

In the event the only compromise we could achieve was that while Cheryl took time off to recover, and for her voice to be rested, and with a faint glimmer of hope and optimism, that she would be well enough to sing the role for opening in New York, we made do with the weak alternatives open to us. Rex accepted that we could ring the changes, he refused to perform opposite 'The Irish Mouse', which was unfair, as she probably would have made quite a good shot of it. Even more reluctantly he accepted Nancy Ringham, 'the Ohio horse', but generously refused to rehearse with her. So I went through the ludicrous pretence that all was well, and rehearsed all day with the substitute Eliza, and Rex would perform the show with resentment in the evening, and of course his resistance showed. The wonderful atmosphere of friendly sparring between Higgins and Eliza vanished, and a leaden hand of humourless antagonism developed on stage. Nancy told me that at the end of the First Act when she yells out at Ascot:

'Come on Dover, move your blooming arse ...!' as the

curtain fell and the company broke up to return to their dressing-rooms, Rex hissed in her ear, clutching the copy of Sporting Life which he holds in his hand: 'I'd like to stick this up your blooming arse!'

Chapter 38

CURTAIN DOWN ON *MY FAIR LADY*

August to October – 1981: New York

SOMEBODY ONCE TOLD me, when he was present at a nightmare dinner party following a show, which Rex Harrison had come expressly to see, in order to take over a starring role and take it triumphantly into London and New York, as he systematically set about criticizing and ultimately wrecking every positive aspect of the production: 'You can never underestimate the enormous powers of self-destruction which Rex Harrison, when he was on form, could exhibit.' This cruel reality fermented in my brain, in the last pressing days when I and the two producers, Don Gregory and Michael Merrick, with, I honestly believe, some degree of valour, and idealism, tried to salvage the production of *My Fair Lady* on Broadway. The truth of the matter is, without any doubt whatsoever, that if Rex had, even out of a sense of survival, agreed to allowing Nancy Ringham, from the ensemble of the show, to take over the starring role of Eliza, we would have had, not only a success on Broadway (because after all the rest of the show was impeccable, and the casting of Doolittle, Pickering, Mrs Higgins and of course the incomparable Rex as the Professor, perfectly cast) but it would have turned into a *Star is Born* story. In addition (unlike London, which is more muted, and mercifully more rational), the Cinderella story of plucking an unknown one night out of the chorus and presenting her firmly centre-stage, would doubtless have gratified the standards of hyperbole so typical of New York and Broadway. A generosity of spirit, often misplaced, frequently over-exaggerated, but somehow heart-warming and life-enhancing for all that. Rex was negative, stubborn, arrogant, and

199

wildly impractical. The two producers and I were steadfast in our great affection and admiration for him, even if it cut against the grain, but we so longed for just a fraction, a glimmer, of humanity to enter his spirit, and to enhance the passionate loyalty and dedication of a large company (possibly as many as seventy-five, even a hundred if you include the orchestra) who had trudged all round the provincial touring dates in America, and merited a well-earned success on Broadway. As did the original authors, Lerner and Loewe, and all the production staff, investors, technicians, publicists, casting-directors, who had worked so hard, and indeed with such friendly enthusiasm. Capable of standing out against everybody, Rex was determined to do so, and in a sense, we could do nothing but stand idly by, as our stately ocean-travelling galleon sank without hope of salvage. This is how it all happened:

Eliza's voice did not (as I knew it couldn't) recover and after a miserable band-call, and an even worse treacherous session in the recording studio, when I and the sound supervisor – as if in an effort to console ourselves with some source of oracular proof – took a solo tape recording of her voice, without orchestra backing, which was disastrous, the English Eliza was fired. I absolutely refused to take this action, as is traditional, via telephone calls, typewritten letters, messages to agents, and decided to go round to see Cheryl personally in her apartment. The confrontation was obvious, she knew what was about to happen as soon as she opened the door, and received my news with dignity, and only a few tears. It was a rotten evening altogether, but there was absolutely no alternative. The only crumb of consolation I could just about rustle up was the alternative reality that had Cheryl in fact opened on Broadway in her vocal condition, the critical reaction would have been murderous, and I would have thought that her career would have been terminated on the spot. Americans take their musicals very seriously. Certainly the news would have reached England in the very next edition of the morning papers. Our meeting was extremely succinct, sadly unaffectionate, and profoundly depressing. Even her customary prettiness seemed to have deserted her. As I left to go, I could not help but see her cage of friendly white mice, which had accompanied her from the early days of rehearsal at the Trafalgar, from dressing-room to dressing-room, from Dixie to Tinseltown to the Big Apple, and would presumably accompany her on the airplane back to London, which she took in a few days.

But even after that brutal confrontation, so far as the producers and I were concerned, we were not really much better off. We still had no Eliza. Grudgingly Rex agreed that he would perform with Nancy in the part (Milo was still off) and his hostility to me was apparent, almost as if I had deliberately sabotaged things. So far as the producers were concerned, they were all on non-speaking terms with Rex. The charade of rehearsal continued. My struggle to make Nancy's Ohio vowel sounds seem either remotely cockney, or classy, for the Ballroom scene, and to try and play these delicately crafted comedy scenes, with an understudy from the ensemble performing Professor Higgins was ludicrous. However, we all did our best, the good American spirit rallied round, which I cherished, they would not be beaten, and Nancy was valiant. It was really so frustrating, because all that was needed was one afternoon's rehearsal with Rex, and a bit of loving kindness and enthusiasm and encouragement on his part, Nancy would have blossomed, morale would have flooded back into the company, and I believe (but of course can never prove) we might have all enjoyed a great Broadway hit. Oddly enough, we almost did.

At the final preview – the *last* performance before the opening night, and the glamour of trumpets and drums and high-pitched hysteria which accompanies any fashionable first night in New York, and the first revival of *My Fair Lady* with Rex Harrison reclaiming his crown as Professor Higgins was such a festival – Rex chose to perform at his savage worst. His reaction towards Eliza from the first scene in the study right through to Ascot was ferocious and competitive. His eyes were deeply etched and viperous. Several quite cheerful previews, and some really rather optimistic rehearsals, where Nancy managed to play her own game, unmoved by the wall of hostility on stage opposite her, gave us all grounds for hope. I actually believed she was going to come through. But on this night, even Nancy quailed. It was too much for her. Rex was like a basilisk. She moved around, lifelessly, without humour, without the necessary vivacity and spirit (Eliza Doolittle, like Viola, like Mimi, has to be completely adorable) she hit all the high notes, sang all the words of the songs, but the inner fire was completely extinguished. Frantic with worry, I rushed round at the interval to visit her in her dressing-room. It was like a funeral-parlour. The room was in complete darkness, blinds drawn; Nancy was lying backwards on the couch, with pads over her eyes, the sensitive dresser had perfumed the room with gentle unguents, and soft transcendental music played, but it was more like visiting a hospital bed than a star dressing-room. This Eliza was completely and utterly defeated. In the battle between Higgins and Eliza, Higgins had cut down his antagonist remorselessly and finally. I used all my energies, summing up every fraction of confidence and enthusiasm that I had, to rally her spirits: all was not completely lost, I told her if she could raise her game for the second half. Nancy turned to me and said with infinite sadness and inner weariness: 'Patrick, I vowed I would go out there to do my best, but Rex looks at me with such absolute hatred, and with eyes of such cruelty, that my hopes and spirits are completely abashed. There is nothing else I have left to give.'

I left the room, and its ambience of the condemned cell with a genuinely sinking heart. Returning to my seat, I discovered to my dismay, that Nancy was unable to raise her game, and let Higgins wipe the floor with her, in the all-important scene when Eliza returns from the Ball, and hurls the slippers at him. The slippers never even reached his feet. She was a defeated army on the run, and there was nothing anybody, least of all the director sitting in the stalls, could do about it. This was the first time that my spirits quailed, since watching a performance of *Billy* (the show which rocketed Michael Crawford to stardom in the seventies) when we performed it in Vienna, before an audience who regarded it as if they were watching an orchestral concert by Arnold Schoenberg. On that occasion too, after bearing the misery for about thirty-five minutes, I preferred to leave the box in which I was sitting, and stroll alone around the corridors of the Theatre an der Wien. So too, on this occasion, I slunk away from my seat, and 'misérable comme les pierres' I exited to breathe the less claustrophobic air of the lounges, and theatre bars.

Then, miraculously, my spirits perked up; after all, I thought to myself, why am I getting so upset? This is not the first night, this is the final preview. We are not being critically judged, there is no ghastly after-show experience to be undergone at Sardi's, and tomorrow is another day. Genuinely, I looked forward to tomorrow. Nancy Ringham was a girl of indomitable spirit, she was a good, straightforward, attractive, self-confident, American girl. Tomorrow we would rehearse again. Tonight had been a great shock, but she was not bound to yield to Rex's ill-temper and unpleasantness. True, Rex was unlikely to alter within twenty-four hours, but I would appeal to her colonial spirit, to her strong sense of nationality, which I knew I could count on, to her natural exuberance, even to her own competitive nature. She would tackle Rex Harrison toe to toe, and just as the song has it in the show, 'Just You Wait, Henry Higgins, Just You Wait', she would triumph. Not even Rex in all his morose glory could prevent her shining forth with a radiant light, banging off all the high notes, those maddening top G's, with serenity and aplomb on an opening night on Broadway. She would rub Rex's nose in C's above G's, to G's above C's! Fuck the Music, indeed? Fuck him!

Even during that short walk, probably emphasized by the sheer relief of getting away from the performance, and Rex's brooding malignancy, I had rallied my spirits, and it was with a sure stride that I walked purposefully towards my two friends, Don and Mike, the Flying Wallendas, who were always sympathetic in adversity, as I saw them also in the foyer, sitting with their wives.

Mike came up to me and put a friendly arm around my shoulder: 'Ah, my dear boy, you too have fled the scene! Well, who can blame us. Rex is behaving like a real pig up there on stage. Let me get you a good, healthy drink, come and sit with us, and we'll all go out to dinner afterwards.' I accepted a large glass of Château Bargain Basement and rejoined them:

'After all, Mike,' I said, 'it isn't so very bad. Watching it is as depressing as hell, and almost unbearable, but I have great belief in Nancy; I am convinced that tomorrow, after getting over the shock of tonight, she will be restored, and invigorated, and raring to go. It's the character of Eliza to fight back at Higgins, and our girl has all the necessary vitality, and good old-fashioned Ohio grit. I shall let her sleep all morning, call rehearsal for the whole company in the afternoon, bring everybody together on stage, have a good rousing sing at 'Get Me To The Church On Time', and work quietly, but passionately with Nancy, and lift her game to battle cheerfully on the first night, and, *Fuck Rex Harrison*!! After all,' I concluded, 'tonight is only the final preview. Tomorrow is the opening night, and that's when all the critics will be there, tomorrow night is the one that counts!

Don Gregory stood up, put both arms around me, and enfolded me with one of the most comfortable embraces of affection and complicity that I have ever experienced:

'Patrick, I have some news for you. Everything you say is right, and I'm sure that's what you're going to do, but you misunderstand *one* thing. This is not London, this is New York, and the tradition here is that the critics, in order to get their copy out into the first editions, have the right to see the show on the final preview. All the major critics, all the television reviewers, all the late-night radio critics who count, and above all the *New York Times*, are sitting there watching it tonight.'

My face as much as my heart must have shown a gradual but conclusive relapse. It was the end of our great adventure, because I knew there was no possibility we could overcome the perform-ance tonight. Ruefully, I told myself, well at least Nancy hits the proper notes, and our own Eliza would have been even more disastrous, and would have been thrown to the wolves, but there is no hope for us in capitalizing on our much-longed for Cinderella story. And so it proved. Tonight was indeed the night.

Oddly enough, and mysteriously to my mind, the notices were not all that bad. Not as bad as they deserved to be. Rex, perhaps getting exactly what he had connived for, received rapturous reviews, and we were able by and large to capitalize enough on them, and at one point looked like having a truly established success. The box-office, also to my surprise, did really rather well. The next night, the official opening night, was a totally different affair. Rex mollified, performed elegantly and beautifully, there was no trace of the vindictive hatred he had shown on the previous night. Nancy Ringham did exactly what I thought she would do. She did respond to my collegiate pep-talk, rallied her spirits, lifted her game, hit all the top notes with assurance, and performed with gusto and radiant charm. At the end, there was the customary standing ovation (but this time, deserved) and – I could have killed him on the spot – Rex led his Eliza forward, and gracefully presented her to the audience, which only increased the roars of applause waving over the proscenium. None of this euphoria could wash on the shores of myself, or Don or Mike, who sat with all our wives in increasing gloom, concealed by public smiles.

The public reaction of a first-night audience on a Broadway show is relatively unimportant. It is whatever is written in the *New York Times* at one in the morning that counts. The notices, as I have said, were much better than they deserved to be. I think that a lot of the critics were actually over-awed by the legend and myth of the show. For example, I didn't think that Rex was particularly good at the final preview; perhaps he too knew that the critics were in, and suffered his customary collapse of morale. Or, perhaps he was saving himself. But his performance on the opening night had all the majesty and charm with which the world associates him, so in a bizarre sense, I suppose he deserved the congratulations he received. The flaw in all his thinking was simple, and I confess, the one point that none of us could make to him. Alan Lerner, the creator of the show, always knew it, and beat it into my head repeatedly; but even he admitted that it was quite unsayable to Rex Harrison. The point always was that *My Fair Lady* is not *Pygmalion*, that it is a musical comedy, and not a straight play, and that there are three leading characters, Higgins, Doolittle, and above all Eliza. And the original creators were always right in centring their effort on having an inspirational Eliza, who, above everything else, could knock off those soaring high notes without effort and, for all the high comedy in the world, without those songs being sung imperiously, the show actually fails. In his supreme arrogance, Rex would never acknowledge this, and his deeply held philosophy that the show was called '*My Fair Lady* or

205

Fuck The Music', rebounded on him fatally. We concluded our three months, and did well at the box-office. It was always meant to be a limited season, but secretly Rex knew, just as much as I and the producers hoped, to say nothing of all the rest of the company, that we would run for six months, possibly even a year. After all, Rex was comfortably at home in his beautiful riverside apartment, and he would have enjoyed, as he put it 'pottering along to the theatre in the evening'. There was no hope of extending the season, because the aura of the Eliza Doolittle was never really there. Rex had managed to turn it into a one, or two-man show, always allowing for the estimable Milo O'Shea, but that is not what *My Fair Lady* is all about. Sometimes I even wondered how Rex managed to agree to so obviously feminine a title. He would have settled for 'My Fair Professor Higgins' no doubt. After that first week, by which time all pigeons had come home firmly to roost, and I knew in my heart that short of a miracle (which in fact was not to be) the show would only run its expected three months, I returned to England, and thence to Chichester, where a great number of extraordinary events were to befall me.

Appointed the Artistic Director of the Chichester Festival Theatre, I enjoyed a somewhat schizophrenic first season, with a disastrous *Cherry Orchard*, a so-so documentary drama about the verbatim trials of Oscar Wilde, a glittering successful musical of *The Mitford Girls*, and an equally jubilant music-hall show, *Underneath the Arches*, which was graced by the legendary, albeit fragile presence of the last survivor of the Crazy Gang, Chesney Allen. I was fortunate enough the same year to marry Alexandra Bastedo (Peter Dews, my predecessor, said it wasn't necessarily part of the contract), and we bought together a beautiful seventeenth-century farmhouse, with a large Sussex barn, which over the years she filled with various rare breeds of countless animals; these proved to be both a blessing, and a miracle, to our pastoral lives. My father, a distinguished, but always very modest, veteran ace of the Royal Flying Corps lived with us until his death aged eighty-nine some years ago.

The memories of the tour of *My Fair Lady* begin to recede,

but never the sharpness, and the extraordinary ambiguity of what I now look back on as 'The Years with Rex'. It was Bernard Shaw, who bowing out of his daily dramatic criticism on the *Saturday Review* with a graceful nod in the direction of Max Beerbohm, commented 'I now make way for The Incomparable Max'. So thinking back over those years, I will always remember 'The Incomparable Rex', because there was really nobody one could ever compare him to.

I tend, I suppose, now after these years to recollect more the fun, the humour, the grace, and the charm, rather than the intolerable unpleasantness of my association with Rex. And, I believe rightly so; it is not always true when Shakespeare declares the evil alone lives after men. I for one shall never forget Rex's extraordinary elegance, capacity for laughter, artistry and unique sense of style.

Chapter 39

C**TS

When Rex Harrison was awarded a knighthood in the summer of 1989, his old friend Harold French commented: 'What has Rex ever done for England, except live abroad on his illegal income-tax and call everybody a c**t?' There was a substance of truth in that, even if it was a little harsh. Certainly the latter was his favourite term of disapprobation. Not that he ever, in my mind, used it crudely against women, in the literal sense of *pudendum mulieris*, which he held, presumably, in deep regard. I never once, on any occasion, recall him using jargon of the barrack-square, or the locker-room, or indulging in dirty jokes. Clearly, he used the word in the alternative sense, as for 'cretin', or 'moron', or, more likely, 'arsehole' – and always directed it towards men.

Even the actual investiture ceremony itself came under his harsh scrutiny. When I asked Rex how the Palace had gone, apart from sniffing abrasively that 'the Queen wasn't properly briefed, she didn't seem to know who I was', he said, the occasion had passed off more or less all right. 'Mind you,' he said, 'you'd have to be a complete c**t *not* to get it right – there's always somebody out there with a white moustache, and rows of medals, in full fig, to tell you the form. Although, as a matter of fact, one of the old busters *was* a complete c**t and got tangled up between his tail-coat and his footstool and fell arse over tit . . . !'

Used as a constant source of opprobrium for directors, producers (with whom he seemed almost destined to do battle), actors who offended by dropping a cue, an inflection, or trod on a laugh, he applied the term liberally and frequently to politicians. When Saddam's war, in Iraq, loomed up, I remember well – when, inexplicably, idiotic politicians were still trying to appease – Rex protested it was pointless to do business with such an obvious c**t, but that Edward Heath was an even bigger c**t in flying all the way to Baghdad to try.

I remember, one morning, arriving at his apartment and finding Rex engaged in a tirade against his gentlemanly lawyer, Harold Schiff, to see him yelling down the telephone: 'What I want to know is, are you *my* lawyer, or are you a c**t-lawyer?'

Although he liked the company of Edward Fox, playing the Admirable Crichton, Rex, as Lord Loam – at the end of the Second Act, when the aristocratic family is shipwrecked on the uninhabited island, and Crichton takes command – in the rather atmospheric silence, punctuated by wild animal cries, and jungly sounds, while Crichton refuses to grant the family security of his camp-fire, the audience at the Haymarket was somewhat astonished to hear Lord Loam whisper, just about audibly: 'Well, if he isn't going to allow us to join him, I suggest we should just leave him all on his own, the silly old c**t . . .' Which was hardly what J. M. Barrie had in mind, when he wrote his family play.

Many an actor, fairly and indeed, unfairly, has found himself on the end of a similarly phrased tongue-lashing, or a stage manager, inadvertently coming in with a prompt too soon, and if ever he was feeling ill-at-ease in an unhealthy stage-position, his first recourse to the director would be: 'I couldn't care less about the blocking, all I know is, I'm standing up here, looking like a c**t.' But he said that so often, he frequently accompanied his complaint by a healthy explosion of laughter; for to say Rex lacked humour, is a foul heresy.

Gayle Hunnicutt suffered a terrible experience one weekend, in 1978, when she inadvertently agreed to take a trip to the Isle of Wight with Rex, at a point in her life when she was being wooed with a degree of gallantry and charm, and both she and he were acting together (but not in the same play) at Chichester. The owner of the yacht and his wife, robust Sussex sailors of no little expertise, had not realized that Rex Harrison's idea of a yacht was some eighty foot long and preferably motorized, and that a sailing picnic was caviar, Pol Roger, smoked salmon and strawberries. His hosts prepared a plain hamper of chicken sandwiches and a couple of

bottles of honest Médoc, on board a glorified dinghy. This rough
sailing had not been what Rex had originally in mind, and on the
way back, as the wind rose, and it became increasingly clear they
would not get back to Chichester Harbour before the tide stranded
them on some mudflat or other, the more inflamed his temper
grew. In order to placate his anger, the desperate sailors plied him
with more and more vodka, until Rex, stranded, frustrated, pow-
erless and drunk, grew almost deranged with fury. Gayle describes
how she tried to keep the party going, by lifting her voice with gay
laughter and idle chatter, while bottles and thermos flasks and
plastic plates and 'fucking c**ts . . .' flew in the direction of the
stern. As Rex's obscenities wailed above the wind, Gayle frantically
attempted to drown them out by screaming louder and louder:
'How did you get on with Stanley Holloway?' and 'Was Julie
Andrews driven home in an ambulance?'

Eventually, the stalwart sailors, Christopher and Lindy Purchase, who owned at that time the oldest traditional wine-
merchant's in southern England, gratefully deposited the explosive
actor on a jetty in the Birdham Pool. When he got to the car-park,
apparently Rex was unable to find his car, and lying on his back
on the gravel, literally howled like an animal, kicking his legs in
the air, bewailing to himself: 'Help me, help me! Oh, for God's
sake, please will somebody *help* me!' Lindy Purchase told me at the
time, it was without doubt the single most horrible day of her
entire life, and haunts her to this day.

Perhaps the most telling of these confrontations took place at
the conclusion of a trying, contentious period of rehearsals at
Theatre Clwyd for the above-mentioned *Admirable Crichton*, in 1988.
As fond as I was of him, by this time, I felt his great powers were
gradually leaving him, and dreaded that he would ask me to direct
the play. As did Clifford Williams, who had worked with him
probably more times than I had (most directors only worked with
him once), above all in his profound interpretation of Pirandello's
Enrico IV, after Henry Higgins possibly his finest creation. But if
Clifford shared my anxieties, and I believe he did, we needn't have
worried: 'For my new production of Crichton, who will I choose
as director? Will it be my old chums Clifford Williams, or Patrick

Garland?' he proclaimed. 'Well, I think both of them have had a fair crack of the whip, so I think it is time to break new ground, and I would like to have Michael Rudman as director . . .'

Ultimately, Clifford and I were wise to have steered clear, because early on it became apparent, just as I had anticipated, that Rex had great difficulty in memorizing the lines. Even though he was playing the relatively minor role of Lord Loam, he found it hard to master, and still dominated rehearsals, demanding a lion's share of the rehearsal time. He hated being away from the Ritz, and his traditional series of comforts, all within walking distance, and disliked as well the Welsh habit of spelling their local places with nothing but consonants. 'I'm working in a theatre mysteriously called Clod,' he said to me when I telephoned him, 'in a curious little town which goes by the name of Moule,' referring to Mwld's civic Theatre Clwyd. Neither the place, nor the director, was his cup of tea, which was unfair on both, and Rex, when rehearsals became trying, referred to Michael Rudman, in the same way he always called Carey his 'Communist son' (mildly liberal views), as 'that left-wing oddity'.

Relations between them were never very good, even from the beginning, and Rex virtually ignored any helpful direction Rudman might have given him, which was extremely unjust, as he clearly had given a lot of thought as to how to make the old warhorse relevant, gracefully written though it is, to a contemporary audience. By the end of the rehearsals, they were barely on speaking terms, and most of the rehearsal time was taken up while Rex struggled to remember his lines, to the detriment of those trying to perform around him. When I saw the play at the Haymarket later that summer, rather than about an opportunistic butler, it seemed to me about an old Scottish peer, who was about to go under from Alzheimer's disease, and everybody else in the play was very worried about him.

What followed after the Saturday night of the first week, I learnt from the Associate Producer, Peter Wilkins, who accompanied the director backstage to cheer everyone on for the weekend. Obviously, it wasn't much good, but there was enough for Michael Rudman to encourage and hang on to, especially from

Rex, who by Saturday night, had at least created a small oasis of confidence, and above all, accuracy. I've frequently been in the same position, and psychologically it is possible to build on this shaky structure, and eventually create a solid performance, especially from the older generation of actors, now past their peak. After all, I think fearfully, forgetfulness will come to us all. So, with a certain degree of assurance, and friendliness, and a great deal of honest professionalism, Michael Rudman went round to the great man's dressing-room and congratulated him warmly on a good week's progress.

'This was the best performance of the week, and you've created something substantial to build on.'

It fell on stony ground. Rex was grouchy, unforgiving and sour-faced. Receiving Michael Rudman's genuinely meant compliments, just as he was retreating from the room, Rex grumbled under his breath:

'No thanks to you, *Mister* Director.' Rudman had had a week of unalloyed harshness, exhausting technical rehearsals, and great strain from Rex not knowing his lines, and ganging up against him with Edward Fox. And there had been four weeks forced labour in Clwyd with an old-fashioned and recalcitrant play. He was near breaking point.

'What', he said, as he reached the door, 'what did you say?' 'I said,' repeated Rex, make-up towel in hand, unrepentant, provocative, 'that it was no thanks to you, Mister Director', and then, after an imperceptible, but well-timed pause, the one, monosyllabic limpid word.

'C**t.'

That did it. Rudman by the door turned abruptly round on his heel, and all the suppressed rage, and frustration of the last weeks poured out of him:

'Don't you call me a c**t, Rex, you're the c**t if anyone is, and you've acted like a c**t ever since we started. When you were young, and at your peak, and a great movie-star, you could do just about whatever you wanted, and all your life, you've treated people abominably. You treat your fellow-actors like shit, you treat the producers like shit, your agent like shit. You have no respect for anybody, and no concern for anybody, other than yourself, your own needs, your own selfish wants. You have no respect for the play you're in, or the audience who pay to see you. And above all, you treat women like shit, just as you've treated your wives, all your life. But now you're old, and you're nearly blind, and nearly bald, and you're vulnerable and you can't remember your lines, and you're no longer a big, rich movie star, it's about time you started to treat people a little differently, and stop calling everybody who stands in your way, a c**t because if anyone's a c**t round here, it's *you* . . .'

And slamming the dressing-room door, he stormed out. After a shocked silence – there was nobody else in the room – Peter Wilkins, himself, always a kind man, realized he was looking accidentally in the mirror at Rex's unmade-up face, ashen-white bald head, sunken cheeks, listless eyes. That Rex was deeply shaken, was unmistakable. And seeing his collapsed countenance in the stage-mirror, even Peter felt very sorry for the old crestfallen actor. But he needn't have worried too much.

'I think, perhaps, I might have gone a little too far over the top,' was all he said.

Perhaps the last word on the subject might come, not from Rex, nor the world of theatre, but from the Houses of Parliament. A member of parliament had been heard to complain over a large glass of Scotch on the terrace of the House of Commons:

'The trouble with this country is it's being governed by c**ts.'

And the other member of parliament, who was drinking a gin, replied:

'Quite frankly, old man, there's an awful lot of c**ts in this country, and they deserve representation.'

Chapter 40

CAREY

WHEN REX WENT into hospital in June 1990 for tests to explore
his liver and kidney area, to see whether anything was serious or
needed operating, malignant or not, Rex had made it absolutely
clear to Mercia that he did not want to hear about it. What the
surgeons discovered was malignant, inoperable, and patching him
up as well as they could, Rex was returned to his riverside
apartment where, without rallying, he declined gradually towards
a quiet unpainful death. It was reminiscent in some ways of the
famous life of King George VI, 'peacefully drawing towards its
close'.

An ironic conclusion, it has to be admitted, for Rex to die
gracefully at home in his bed surrounded by his loving wife, albeit
the sixth, and both his sons, after a life of such turbulence,
irritation, provocation, and sometimes downright beastliness. It
was as if there was no particular justice, but then in death there
seldom is. Towards the end, his son Carey told me, Rex's face
collapsed with his strength. Without his toupee, his reduced tem-
ples blanched and his cheek-bones sunk, with one long-dead eye
and the other failing in sight and illumination, without his false
teeth, which allowed the wrinkles around his mouth to etch into
ever deepening incisions, his face in repose looked like nothing
more refined than that of a dying, exhausted, musical-hall comedian. I had noticed this quality in Rex several times before, and
always with a kind of relish, although it seemed so unlikely for the
celebrated sexual icon of the fifties and sixties. Nevertheless it was
touching to see how his face resembled an old vaudevillian, the
sort of ancient character-man who might emerge from the ranks of
Vincent Crummles's Company, or indeed one of the last gener-

214

ation of The Crazy Gang, or, most likely, a film by Federico Fellini. It was those wonderful deep lines that tunnelled from the corners of his eyes down to his cheeks that created this special effect, as of Grock or Grimaldi once the motley and the make-up had been discarded. It was about this time, during what turned out to be the last vigil, that Carey made the mistake of leaving for a half-hour's fresh air, and a well-deserved cup of coffee, when he leant forward to his father, propped up by now on the pillows, and said to him: 'I'm just going out, father, for a few moments, but Mercia is in the next room, and Noel is still here; is there anything I can do for you?'

Almost immediately, the sightless eyes opened and their original glare animated them into life; and the poor weak voice which had truly descended to thin pipish trebles adopted its familiar rasp: 'Yes,' barked out Rex, '*Drop Dead*! That's what you can do for me.' And gesturing to his younger son, to approach him, Rex murmured: 'And by the way, Noel, there was something I always wanted to tell you. I could never stand the sound of your fucking guitar.' And then he died.

It has to be said, that there was something wonderfully consistent that Rex should conclude his life on a note of vituperative rage, even directed against his two sons. There was nothing hypocritical or sentimental, and it can faithfully be said of him, as it was of the traitor Cawdor, 'that nothing became his life like the leaving of it.' When he came to speak about his father in the Memorial Service that was held at the Little Church Around the Corner, in New York, Carey Harrison spoke somewhat glowingly of his recollections, in retrospect, admitting to himself, and to me in conversation, that as in war, so in memorial services, Truth is usually the first casualty.

In January 1991, Carey and I had a long and pleasurable lunch together, genuinely in celebration of Rex, and chose Wilton's of Jermyn Street as the appropriate rendezvous. We selected good white burgundy carefully. We both chuckled at the memory of many another lunchtime spent there, usually with some row or other going on between Rex and either the wine-waiter, or the *maître d'hôtel*, or indeed one of the fat comfortable matronly waitresses in their white aprons who even still preserve that rich atmosphere of the English public school in London restaurants of distinction.

He admitted to me that he had great unease in committing himself to contributing towards a portrait of his father, a little to protect the feelings of surviving family, and obviously to avoid the inevitable ill-feeling, but more because of his own diffidence with regard to his father's memory. It was apparent that he had very mixed feelings about his father as a man, not just as a father, but as a human being, and that he had difficulty in separating his feelings about Rex as father, or as 'man'. There was no doubt at all that he delighted in the idea of him as an artist; not so much a great artist, which (in the company of, say, Bach, Monet or Flaubert), he could not reasonably be thought of, but as a most original and remarkable talent, even a unique one in his own sphere. Certainly there is nobody around today, since the death of Cary Grant anyway, with whom comparison can be made. Even Ralph Richardson said of him, and the Du Maurier-Hawtrey 'high style', 'after him, there is no one left to show us.' And alongside this genuine delight and respect and admiration and affection, Carey had to balance his own feelings of sadness at the sheer pawkiness of his humanity. Obviously this reaction was coloured by a son's particular disappointment at this perceived pawkiness. Carey said to me that he always felt of himself that he was compulsively and by temperament an observer (he is an excellent novelist and playwright), and that it was as a studious observer of his father that he felt sadness, as well as joy at the prospect of celebrating Rex's seductive irascibility, relatively harmless though it was.

He it was, after all, who had the humiliating experience to introduce his girlfriend to his father, and see her marry him some months later. To be truthful to himself, and at great pains not to appear priggish, the qualities that Carey would look for and admire in somebody else, and in particular a father, would contain qualities of human feeling which might prove less theatrical in action, and not harmful at all. In other words, he could not help but feel that what made Rex a 'star', as the world will have it, a glorious high comedian, a celebrity and the source of many delightful anecdotes were qualities rooted in what he called the thin, sad soul of a shallow humanity – 'like an undernourished plant, to pursue the metaphor, gangly and overgrown and seeding in mad display.' While Carey felt there was nothing surprising or dreadful about his view of his father, some months after his death, it obviously made him sad. He felt conscious of an unhappy and pious tendency in this, feeling that such a viewpoint led towards the argument that perhaps all biographies should be about Mother Theresa or Charlotte Brontë, or better still some unsung anonymous servant of humanity, rich in love. But, he admitted, if those were the biographies that ought to be written, the ones he would rather read would be about Lord Byron and Rex Harrison.

He found it hard to forget, he said, what a poor fish in reality Rex really was, how lonely he must have felt, and, sharing this perhaps with most of us in some degree, how unable he was to learn the simple lesson of life that what you give is frequently what you get.

I, too, have constantly felt that it is something of a cosy belittlement of life to reduce it to the kind of character-study of Mrs Do-As-You-Would-Be-Done-By, from *The Water Babies*, but sometimes as a pretty generalized basic rule of thumb, even to be found in Shakespeare's plays, that does seem to be a fairly rough and ready instruction manual for the way we all ought to behave. Like Democracy, it's flawed and hopeless, but find something better. Carey felt this out of a compulsive fondness for his father, certainly as both of them grew older, as much as out of filial disappointment. It was a fondness a lot of people, including myself, – disenchanted misogynists though we be – John Standing, Doug Hayward, Mick Gough, Terry O'Neill, shared (I don't think I dare speak for any of the wives). It was Doug Hayward, I recall, who on the occasion of Rex's seventieth birthday, suggested we should invite all his friends to a party, and hire a telephone-box. 'How we love our cripples!' smiled Carey, as we finished our fish pies at Wilton's, and drained the last of the most excellent Pouilly Fumé, ordered especially in honour of the old boy, 'how we feed those who habitually short-change us, who have so little to give us back; how we water this barren ground.'

Even allowing for the glorious truth revealed by John Cleese, that the fact of the matter is that rampant egocentricity is gloriously, joyously funny, even allowing for all of this one cannot help sighing at the thought of all those futile decades of adulation and wealth, presumably sex, and certainly devotion, crowning the poor withered stick of his lonely soul. And then again, what a glorious flower miraculously emerged from it! The paradox of glow and glory distilled from such hollowness, and occasional mean-spiritedness, reveals especially in the case of Rex Harrison, something of the nature of the pure artist. Perhaps, I should temper my reflections with the limitation of the *theatrical* artist. Although writers and poets, I believe, come pretty close to it. The best we can hope for is to thank God that this make-up is not necessarily the precise composition of every artist's nature, or indeed of the best of them. As Carey said as we rose to leave the restaurant, he was not quite ready to succumb to the theory that all-geniuses-are-egotistical-bastards . . . At any rate, he didn't think he was.

Some months later, having returned to New York and flown back again to London, bearing his father's ashes in a wooden cabinet, as well as a small plastic bag of 'extras' (the funeral director on handing them over said he suspected that there was always a little too much of Rex Harrison to ever fit in quite tidily), Carey, arriving somewhat sheepishly at Laurie Evans's house, his devoted agent and friend, admitted that he had been somewhat embarrassed, having flown over on British Airways depositing the box of ashes beneath his seat, aware that he was guilty of flying with his father on a second-class excursion ticket. Something Rex, in his lifetime, had never done.

There is a small coda to this. When a year before it was agreed between them, Carey would take out Rex's ashes and scatter them in Portofino, he asked his father if he wanted the instructions written in the will. 'If you like,' replied Rex, 'provided of course I haven't already been out there myself, to scatter *your* ashes.'

Chapter 41

SCOTTY

THE DANCE CAPTAIN of the show when we were on tour, and during its run on Broadway, was given, rather as his name implies, to an attractive and well-disciplined, although very young member of the company, unmistakably officer-class. Scot Harris began as one of the ensemble, but was rapidly singled out as being a fastidious and precise figure, who was an instinctive leader of men, in particular of dance-gypsies. Rex had always taken a great shine to him from early days, partly I suspect because he dressed quietly and conventionally, and didn't whirl around wearing T-shirts with insane statements written across his chest. As Lord Gowrie once said on a memorable occasion at the *Evening Standard* awards, that he recognized these days the world was divided into two kinds of people, those who wore name-badges on their jackets, and those who didn't. Well, Scot Harris was clearly one of those who didn't.

I remember we were sitting together, with a group of the youngsters in the company, and Rex, all very relaxed and happy, drinking coffee out of cardboard cups one break, during technical run-throughs. One of the ensemble in an ill-advised moment turned casually to Rex and asked him if David Niven had ever played Henry Higgins. Rex turned his cobra-lidded eyes on the questioner, saying: 'What! With those thick, Scottish legs!'

Something like a decade later, after witnessing a version of *Pygmalion* at the Shaw Festival at Niagara on the Lake, Scot reminded me that he was finally able to comprehend his meaning. The actors, he told me had no rhythm to the speech, everything jerked forwards and backwards in fits and starts and splutters and holes, and there was no music to the language. The actor playing

Higgins was doubtless a good actor, but there was no trace of the aristocrat in him either physically or emotionally. Rex, said Scot, was sadly missed, although on this occasion he was very glad that Rex hadn't come along. He had always felt that although he might have been Dance Captain at the time, Scot was mindful that he was too insignificant an adversary to have merited the full and terrible force of Rex's broad-sword. But when you were in his good graces, Rex could be as charming and magnanimous as anybody, and even though he was the star, and Scot was at the bottom of the ladder, Rex always treated him with respect.

He felt that Rex's mistake in taking on the revival of *My Fair Lady* was possibly in not trusting myself, or Crandall, the choreographer, and above all Franz Allers, the music director, to do our work in order that he might be freer to do his. This is a situation I've often encountered, and it's wearisome, as director, to find that you have to do battle with your star from morning to night in order to gain authority over him. It is so much better, and obviously so much easier, to be allowed that authority, and the collaboration is always beneficial. So often the stars waste away their energies worrying about what the other actors are about to do all round them, or what their photograph looks like outside the theatre, or whether there are spelling mistakes in the programme notes, when they should be quietly concentrated on giving their performance. And worse, so many of the stars of that nature constantly mistake the one for the other. There was a moment in rehearsal when the girl playing the cook told Franz Allers that Rex had countermanded one of his orders. Franz turned purple in the face and began screaming: 'This is none of Rex's fucking business.'

In Scot's opinion, although it might seem contradictory, he felt that Rex was mistaken to think of himself as the director, simply because he'd been in the show years before with great success, and won an Oscar from the film. His instincts were always brilliant, but they were the instincts of an actor and not a director. He never held the larger view. And it has always been my belief that one of the reasons that great actors are actually great is because they listen to themselves so well, and with such total fascination, and never to anybody else. It's that single-minded purpose that makes everything so concentrated, and focused, and precise. And so, if Rex had decided that the twenty-fifth anniversary production of *My Fair Lady* was going to be the 'Rex Harrison *My Fair Lady*', then it would have been better for everybody if he had somehow found a way to do it by himself, and produce it like one of the actor-managers of the nineteenth century, and not stepped on so many people's faces, or perhaps more dangerously, stepped into areas that were better inhabited by the directors and producers. 'I always believed his intentions were entirely good,' Scot said to me over a drink at Charlie's on 46th Street, but 'as we all know, it is good intentions which pave the path to Hell. But irrespective of my feelings, I adored the man, and ten years later these are some of the tales I can remember.

'Whether actors imitate life or life imitates actors, I don't know, but I do know that like Henry Higgins, Rex had a gleeful, child-like streak in him. When we toured St Louis, we played in a dilapidated barn called the Civic Center. Our stage sat directly behind another stage in the Civic Center, each one sharing a common back wall. During some of the time we played there, a rock concert was going on directly behind us, and all the subtleties that had been preserved by Lerner and Loewe were consistently trashed by an unending, blasting, heavy-metal rock beat. This amused Rex no end.

'One night, stocky David Johnson was upstairs on the third floor, in the chorus men's dressing-room telling a story. While illustrating one of the many subtleties of his story, David sat on a nearby sink in a suave and debonair manner. Unfortunately David didn't realize that suave and debonair raconteurs never exceed 300 lbs, and he managed to tear the sink completely out of the wall. The result was both tragic and hilarious. Apart from crashing to the floor, which was funny, what was not funny was that he had broken the hot water main of the building and hundreds and thousands of gallons of very hot water began to gush out of the wall. In only a matter of seconds, the upstairs dressing-room was twelve inches deep in boiling water. Dozens of pairs of Capezio dancing shoes were floating around like little boats. Everyone grabbed whatever he or she could and ran down the stairs followed by steaming torrents of hot water. In a matter of minutes, the backstage looked like Niagara Falls. Water was flowing down the stairwells, flooding all the floors beneath. To add to the misfortunes, the theatre manager had only the day before fired the senior janitor of the complex, and therefore there was nobody in the building who had the faintest idea how to shut off the water mains.

'Backstage was bedlam, everybody was running and screaming. I can never forget the sight of Milo O'Shea creating a little dam across the doorway to his dressing-room, with socks, and Kentucky Fried Chicken bags. Dear old Cathleen Nesbitt had been moved to a drier room upstairs, which the local stage-hands vacated for her, totally unaware that the room was thick with the smoke from hastily stubbed out marijuana. The waters kept flowing, and soon the ceiling and wall plasters of the dressing-rooms started falling in great sheets. Everybody dressed in the halls with what scraps of Cecil Beaton's costumes they had managed to save from the deluge. If it rains in Hell, this is what it would look like.

'When Rex came off stage after "The Rain In Spain", there I stood with my flashlight in one hand and an umbrella in the other. At this point, water literally was cascading down all three walls of the backstage area, dangerously splashing over and through the electric lights and cables. Simultaneously Cathleen, and the flounced Ascot ladies, were all being carried on to the stage on the shoulders of the local stage-hands over the flood waters to the safety of the elevated dance floor. Rex was curiously composed, and taking a look at all the fantastic disaster collapsing around him, and without missing a beat, said to me quite placidly: "You know Scotty, if this keeps up, we won't have to do Act Two."

'One night, backstage, one of the stage-hands showed us a grotesque picture postcard of a girl with the longest tongue you can imagine, sticking her tongue out at the camera. This obscene tongue was extremely long, and reached well down to below her chin. I suppose the stage-hand showed the picture to Rex in order to shock him. Rex stared at the girl in the photo, almost as if he recognized her, thought for a moment, and in a reminiscent and honest tone delivered his verdict:

' "There was a whore in Venice, who had a tongue just like that." I must say we were all very impressed.

'When we toured Chicago, we played a great barn of a theatre called the Arie Crown. It was vast. It had, I believe, three and a half thousand seats. There was a stage doorman there, who over the years had come up with many resourceful schemes to make money on the side. For instance on Sundays, the doorman would buy cartons and cartons of doughnuts and sell them for twenty-five cents a piece, making roughly a 30 per cent profit. Perfectly harmless, and on Sunday mornings we were all very grateful for doughnuts.

'Another of his sidelines was pimping. One night, after the show the doorman imported a young whore for our stage-hands to play with. Well, it seems they all had a marvellous time, and in a moment of reckless confidence even took pictures of the whore posing somewhat provocatively on the set of *My Fair Lady*. To be precise on the desk in Henry Higgins's study. Well, the stage-hands gave some of the pictures to Walter, Rex's dresser, who promptly showed them to Rex because he knew he would like that sort of thing. Rumour had it that it was one of Walter's jobs to keep Rex's pornography current and copious. Although Rex had nothing in particular against whores, he did not exactly relish the idea of whores sitting on his antique leather-topped desk in the Henry Higgins study. As soon as he saw the pictures, he roared into action, pitched a fit, and the resourceful doorman's profit-making schemes came to an immediate and stark conclusion. The stage doorman was fired, the desk was scrubbed, waxed and polished until it was restored to its original pristine innocence.

'First-class acting, and first-class living, were always very important to Rex, and the fact he was so brilliant in high comedy is most likely because an aristocratic drawing room was where he wanted to be. He had no respect at all for what he thought was vulgar, particularly loud, bombastic, over-acting. One night, standing in the wings with Rex, a group of us were watching the end of "Get Me To The Church On Time". Milo O'Shea, as the celebrated dustman, who was by no means a vulgarian, was out there giving it about 800 per cent. Rex watched for a little while, sighed wearily, and asked: "Is it Saturday?" I said: "No, it's Wednesday." After a pause, Rex said: "Well, you'd better tell Milo, we don't want him to waste any of his Saturday night performances."

'One night, during the early scenes of *My Fair Lady*, for some peculiar reason the revolve refused to turn, and the scene with Doolittle, and his low-life cronies, dancing "A Little Bit of Luck", the Tottenham Court Road scene, took place inside Professor Higgins's study. When Rex came on to play the next scene, he looked studiously at Mrs Pearce, and casually enquired: "Who on earth were all those frightful people who've just been in my study?" It brought the house down. Something along the same lines, an example perhaps of his literal mindedness, reminds me of the time when one of the cast was trying to tell Rex the story of *M. Butterfly*. Rex was completely nonplussed by the thought that anyone could be stupid enough, audience, actors, or characters in the play, to sincerely believe that a boy in drag could ever be mistaken for a woman. It was completely absurd to his way of thinking, and incomprehensible that anyone could possibly bother to write a play about such an imbecility.

'How odd that Rex is dead. I remember one night on the road, Rex telling me that he had just been reading Strindberg's *Dance of Death*. But he couldn't make head or tail of it. He kept asking me: "But what does it mean? What does it mean?" I suppose now, wherever he is, he understands it very well, and presumably somewhere in the cosmos he's performing that very show. And I'm equally sure that he is belittling his leading lady, bullying the artistic director, screaming at the producers, and dazzling the hell out of his heavenly, Sold-Right-Out audiences.'

Chapter 42

WALTER

WHENEVER I THINK about Rex, which I do frequently (but never constantly) I also think about Walter. Walter Massey was Rex's valet for most of the tour of *My Fair Lady*, and on Broadway. To describe him as Rex's 'dresser' is unworthy. If he was a black Sam Weller to Rex's attenuated Samuel Pickwick, it was not in the linguistically contorted way of the Great Inimitable's original, but in the spirit of Sam being 'Mr Pickwick's Gentleman' as much as Mr Pickwick was Sam's Gentleman. Walter was Mr Harrison's Gentleman. No man, the well-known saying tells us, is hero to his valet, but in a curious way, Mr Harrison was Walter's 'hero'. Walter never called Rex anything other than 'Mr Harrison'. Even after he received his knighthood, which Rex considered grudgingly overdue, Walter still called him '*Mr* Harrison'. Rather in the way his actor friends always thought of Olivier as Sir Laurence, and never Lord Olivier. Their relationship reminded me of that exquisite portrayal of master/servant by Henry James, called *Brooksmith*. The aura of the master was seemingly conjured up by his valet. Certainly Walter was more than a professional dresser, although he was very good at that side of things also. He preferred to be thought of as 'one of the family', and so he was. At Rex's Memorial Service in New York, in 'the Little Church Around the Corner', after his two sons, Noel and Carey, and Rex's last wife, Mercia, both in the procession and in the front pew, came Walter.

Alan Bennett has written wryly of how one visits one's closest actor friends backstage after a performance, with them generally seated in their underpants, their trousers flopping around their ankles – in the case of Rex, many were the times I would see him comfortably enthroned, a glass of beaded yellow burgundy in his right hand, discussing some nuance of the play, or merely just gossiping, while Walter on his knees, unbuttoned Rex's trousers, removed them, and carefully replaced them with a second pair of evening trousers, without disturbing the flow of conversation. Two elderly Southern queens of Rex's acquaintance, who witnessed such a sight backstage in New Orleans, admitted to me they had hardly expected to see such a thing in Louisiana since before the Civil War days of the early 1860s. At least Walter was better off than Tosh, his former black valet, who was summoned to bring Rex's three best-loved Herbert Johnson hats to New York. The valet was inconveniently murdered in Los Angeles en route, and Rex's only comment was: 'And now, I suppose I'll never get my hats.'

I last saw Walter at Joe Allen's, a theatrical hang-out on 45th between 7th and 8th, when he was looking after Nigel Hawthorne with great affection and customary solicitude, who was appearing in *Shadowlands*. Walter together with his friend who worked as a chef at the Plaza Athenée, was invited to prepare the cuisine for Mr Harrison's eighty-second birthday, as it turned out, his last. 'My friend and I and Mrs Harrison, we did the whole thing, and it was superb!' Walter liked working for Nigel Hawthorne, he told me, and he had worked with many theatrical stars before him, but none of them ever matched Mr Harrison. Walter lived in a remote neighbourhood of Harlem, so that even in spite of being an indigenous inhabitant, Walter took the frightening subway home wearing a strange kind of elaborate disguise. Rex told me he used to watch fascinated while Walter, at the evening's end, before saying good night, once the dressing-room was tidied for the next day, disguised his face to make himself look like a seedy down-and-out – 'Fright beard, like a worn out Father Christmas, and a ghastly matted wig, the sort of thing you'd see in a stock company production for Fagin . . .' Then he'd cover his visible patches of skin with grease and charcoal to darken it, making use of Rex's carmine-liner. Intrigued, Rex sometimes assisted with the making-up himself, adding a few flourishes he told me, to make the disguise a little less penetrable. Then, covered with patched overcoat and submerged behind scarves, and sometimes a balaclava, Walter would set out for the sinister subway. He had an extraordinary knack of effacing himself whenever turbulence flared on the horizon, by vanishing on the one hand from the actual scene of the row – frequently the dressing-room – and yet, at the same time (no mean feat, this) managing to undress, dress, wash and tidy his volatile star. I can only relate this apparent miracle of sleight of hand to the spectacle on stage of a brilliant farceur from the Comédie Française, who caught in the wrong place, with the wrong woman, at the wrong time, and with his trousers around his ankles, in an irresistible way, succeeded in making his body somehow of single dimension, so that when he turned into profile he seemed to vanish altogether. This is also a quality effected by the scene-shifters of the Kabuki Theatre, who bring on stage furniture and props, and from some negative capability, because you are not *intended* to see them, you somehow don't. All of this was part of Walter's self-effacing talent.

Rex's last performance on Broadway was a deeply dreadful version of Somerset Maugham's drama, *The Circle*, in which he played Lord Porteous, with Glynis Johns and Stewart Granger co-starring. When I went to visit him on the road, Miami, I think, two quaint American queens were chattering with him backstage. After an exchange of congratulations, one of them said, 'We've just seen Glynis in the corridor . . .' 'Glynis?' queried Rex, 'Glynis *who*? 'Glynis Johns.' 'Oh,' replied Rex in a tone of intense wonderment, 'Glynis *Johns*! Now there's a name to conjure with.' His second co-star the seventy-six-year-old Stewart Granger, commonly known as Jimmy (but not by Rex), was considered a disagreeable sort of fellow, even by other colleagues in the play who referred to him as 'Rex, without the jokes'. The two of them were always snapping at one another's throats or heels. On one occasion, a friend of mine was sitting with Rex in his dressing-room, the faithful Walter discreetly in attendance, when Jimmy Granger burst into the room in turmoil. 'You shit, you bastard, you absolute rotten bugger, Rex, if you ever ever tread on one of my laugh lines again, I swear I'll break your fucking leg, even if it's in front of the audience. You do it on purpose, just to slight me . . . You are a rotten shit of the first water . . . !' Rex seemed to be completely unperturbed by this outburst of self-righteous, red-faced indignation, and waited until Jimmy Granger ran completely out of steam, then, pointing to the door with imperious forefinger like a furious prep-school house-master, Rex bellowed: '*You!* Granger! Go to your *Room!*' And Jimmy Granger went.

Three days before the play ended, Walter told me, 'a terrible thing happened'. Mr Harrison had not been himself, he said, not feeling well at all, and the decision had been made, as soon as the play ended its run, for him to go into hospital 'for tests', as he put it. 'Mr Harrison was in his dressing-room after the performance waiting to go home. That night there had been no visitors, and I'd just put Mr Harrison's pants, shoes and shirt on, and I was reaching behind me for his tie, when a sixth sense warned me I should turn about. As I did so, I saw Mr Harrison pitch forwards toward his wardrobe – which was really just a hanging closet, with a metal rail for his suits of clothes, and behind that nothing at all – just a bare, brick wall. So I sprang towards him, and I just kind of caught him under the arms, and I held on to him with all my strength. So I sat him down – he was as light as a kitten by that time – and I stayed with him, holding both his hands in mine, until he got his breath back.

'"Walter," said Mr Harrison to me, "you saved my life there." And do you know, I just about believe I did. You see, there was nothing behind that curtain rail, just a bare, brick wall. Then when he felt good and ready, we walked all the way down the long iron staircase to Mr Harrison's car. Going up was no problem for either of us, but going down . . . Oh, boy! If he fell, you see, it would be forward on to my shoulders, and not backwards. He'd feel his way down those dark stairs, like he was a sort of blind man, and we'd make a joke about it, Mr Harrison hanging on to my shoulders like I was grim death. That's something I'll always remember about Mr Harrison.'

'Walter,' I asked, 'Mr Harrison was notorious for losing his temper; he did with me, he did with Mrs Harrison, he did with the producers, you used to make yourself scarce at such times, do you remember?'

'Mr G, when there was turbulence,' he smiled, 'I was outta there . . .'

'But he was never rude to you, abusive, or bad-tempered?'

'Well, I'll tell you something. To be truthful about that, yes, he was, but only once. If you remember, I joined the show in San Francisco, and I can't quite recall now why it was, or exactly what it was, but suddenly he was standing up screaming at me, and I said to him very quietly, 'Oh, Mr Harrison, there's no need to do that,' and do you know he never did it again. I've worked with all the so-called stars, but there was none of them in the class of Mr Harrison. Oh, no.'

Walter has a slight, gentle figure, with a simple, smiling face, and great sweetness of spirit. He stayed there in Joe Allen's, reminiscing with me about the old days, tapping his fingers on the red and white table-cloth. And then the time came for him to seek out his present gentleman, whom he was dressing at the Royale Theatre, a block or so away, on 48th Street. His devotion for Mr Harrison, and the sincere affection he provoked in a notoriously irascible man does great honour to them both.

Chapter 43

THAT CRAFTY OLD BUGGER, REX

THAT WAS WILFRED HYDE-WHITE's phrase for him, and in so
many ways it will have to do. I miss him, dreadfully, as I miss
many friends these days. Emotional Memorial Services bring an
old colleague, lover, tyrant, fleetingly to life for an hour or so, and
homage is duly paid, 'we are not here to mourn, but to celebrate
the life and works of . . .' 'Let us now praise famous men', and that
over-worked piece: 'Do not think of me as if I am dead, I have
only just gone out for a short walk to Harrods . . .' or whatever,
but I am left these days with a deep feeling of void, of melancholy.
Life is full, friendships are overflowing, but nothing quite replaces
the quality, the mood of *that* particular friend. Even his voice is
absent for me, in high dudgeon, but often vituperative and impas-
sioned in support: 'I sympathize with you, Patrick, but you've only
yourself to blame, I told you the man was a complete C**t . . .'
Naturally I was grateful to have been myself, and not some
vulnerable beautiful woman who had fallen under his spell. But I
cannot forget impressions fleeting by, sometimes memories of my
own, sometimes vignettes of other people. The excellent humorist,
George Axelrod, author of *Seven Year Itch* and other comedies, who
was summoned to speak to Rex about a possible vehicle he might
be persuaded to write for him, told me: 'When I arrived at Rex's
table, the first words he said to me were: "Well, Mr Axelrod, I
understand from my advisers you have written several successful
light comedies, most of them rather SHABBY."' An endearing
vagueness, as when, after a rigorous day of auditions, we stepped
into the lift of the Sherry-Netherland in order to go out to dinner,
and when the elevator-attendant asked:

'Where to, Mr Harrison?' Rex replied,

'Oh yes, La Petite Gavroche, between 5th Avenue and 46th Street, please.'

Or, when Peter Eyre regretted Rex had not found time to play more Shakespeare (one cannot help but think how marvellous a Benedick he might have made) he answered: 'I never had a lot of patience with those Tudor Buggers.' I miss his graceful hetero-sexuality. Sometimes, I even miss feline, destructive, devastating, penetrative, his eloquent misogyny. He was always tough-minded, as Lord Byron was. None other than Marghanita Laski maintained one of her chief problems with modern-day feminists, was that so many of them were so despairingly 'Minnie-Anne'. Rex wouldn't stand for that, and much of what passed for so-called 'political correctness', he regarded as an ideology steeped in the suburban values of the lower-middle class, 'a contemptible egalitarianism,' he said to me once. It could fairly be said of him, with just the change of vowel his second favourite term of abuse was *cant*.

Rex never stopped being contemptuous of our rival musical, *Camelot*, even though he secretly enjoyed and admired 'my friend, Burton'. When Richard dropped out of it, through the illness which ultimately killed him, he asked:

'How's *Camelot* staggering on?'

The producer, Don Gregory said warily, 'The company Manager thinks it will last through until June.'

'With or without the audience?' asked Rex, pointedly.

He still had the erratic potential to send Alan Lerner into panic. We were walking down Bond Street in the direction of the Ritz, when Rex suddenly extolled the virtue of a private hair-dresser. 'You must use him, Alan, he's marvellous, and it costs you absolutely nothing. He'll cut your hair absolutely without charge.'

Alan sounded enthusiastic. 'But is he really free?'

'Totally free, Alan. He just cuts hair out of love of anybody connected with the Show, and that certainly includes you.'

'How do I set about finding him?' asked Alan.

'Just come up to my rooms at the Ritz. He'll follow you, he puts his sheets out on the floor, covers you in a great white towel, and cuts your hair beautifully. It doesn't cost you a sixpence. All you do is just tip him £25 (this was in 1980), and he cleans up afterwards and disappears as if he'd never been.' At the sound of the price of the gratuity, I thought Alan was going to capsize on the pavement.

Rex was delighted to hear from me, during one matinée in Los Angeles, that I overheard a woman at half-time say to her friend: 'Well, it's very entertaining for a Classic!'

And he rang me up to say he'd read a notice for a play called: 'The Vanity of Nothing' in New York, which went: 'The Vanity of Nothing was . . .'

We spoke one afternoon, over a bottle of Imperial Tokay, which had been presented to him by the Hungarian Ambassador, about the first Eliza Doolittle, Mrs Patrick Campbell. In the old days, in Hollywood, Rex had known her, and she used to give acting-lessons to young Americans in the recently discovered industry. She was capable of being extremely cruel and unfeeling, and Rex told me that one day an aged needlewoman came into her dressing-room, and she cried out: 'Stop! That's just what I want – that common, rickety little walk.'

Mrs Pat, as she was known, refused to be parted from her horrid little pet Pekinese, which eluded the Customs officers, for quarantine, on several occasions, as a picnic hamper, a needlework basket, 'and once under my skirt, as a small hip operation'. In London, with the same 'beastly dog', as John Gielgud described it, she was taking a cab to the West End, and the peke dropped a packet. When she went to pay the cabman, he looked round, saw the dog turds on the floor, and shouted out: 'Oi! 'oo the 'ell made that mess?'

Mrs Pat drew herself up to her full height, and declaimed loudly: '*I* did!'

Robert Morley was an uneasy friend in some ways, but Rex genuinely admired him. The two of them met one day in the Burlington Arcade, and Rex said: 'Oh, Robert, I do so admire you. I've made a mess of my career, and my domestic life. All my wretched marriages, and living in hotel-rooms, out of suitcases. And there you are, the same lovely house in Henley-on-Thames, surrounded by the same lovely fulfilling family, married to the

same wife . . .', and after a slight pause, 'and the same performance,' before pottering off in the direction of Albany. They
presumably got on quite well, because they amused one another.
Rex told Robert once that an actor in one of his productions
stormed off-stage complaining:

'There's a man sitting right in the front row, playing with
himself.'

Robert replied 'My dear boy, if we can't entertain them, you
can hardly blame them for entertaining themselves.'

Although she lived in the same fashionable apartment building, Garbo and Rex never terribly hit it off, and he found her
reclusive, unfunny – a great crime – and bad-tempered. So he was
rather delighted to hear my account which I'd been told by Sir
John Gielgud, when he came over to play in *Normansland*, of an
equally unsatisfactory encounter he had had with Greta Garbo
years before in Hollywood, at a party of Rudolph Valentino's. To
his disappointment, being a fan, he found her a terrible bore;
principally because she kept affecting not to know anybody. By
way of conversation, Sir John said cheerfully:

'Of course, you're a great friend of Cecil Beaton's aren't you?'

To his consternation, Garbo replied: 'No, I've never met
him.'

'What do you mean, you've never met him? Aren't you meant
to be one of his closest friends, he wrote that huge article about
you.'

'No, I don't know him at all,' replied the immutable Garbo.
Sir John concluded rather feebly: 'Oh, I'm so sorry, I must be
mistaken, but whenever I see him, he's always telling me you were
both going to get married.'

Sir John had been talking to Peter Shaffer about his play, a
failure in London, transferring to New York. It was called *The
Battle of Shrivings*.

'I'm afraid, when I was having dinner with him, I rather
indiscreetly asked him: "Will it go to New York, do you think? I
do hope so, these pretentious plays usually go down rather well."'

I said that Rex never descended to the language of the locker-
room, nor told dirty stories; nor did he, but this was a sardonic

story, he did tell me (which I remembered) one matinée in New Orleans, between the shows. I think he had heard it from the Czech director, Milos Forman:

'A Russian peasant driving his sleigh in the deep snow hears a faint cheep-cheep, and looking around, discovers a tiny sparrow, weak and trembling with the cold. Tenderly he takes it into his hands, and places it into the steaming manure, recently dumped by his horses, in order to revive it. After a little while, the sparrow does revive, and begins to whistle and sing. Unfortunately, a hungry wolf lurking nearby, lopes out of the tundra, scoops the sparrow out of the horse-manure with his paw, and in a single mouthful, swallows it up. There is a moral to this story. It isn't necessarily your enemy who puts you into the shit. Equally, the one who takes you out of the shit isn't necessarily your friend. And finally, if you're in the shit – don't make a song about it.'

Rex said that he felt the story was an excellent metaphor for the entertainment industry. I thought it was almost a metaphor for himself, but kept the idea to myself.

From Australia and a dissatisfied tour of *Aren't We All* came a gloriously mad postcard with primitive Antipodean marsupials, crocodiles, platypus, flying foxes, possums, wallabies, with a single sentence on the other side: 'Just wait until you see the people!'

One day in the 1980s, Rex went to visit the impresario, Duncan Weldon, at his country house, in Milford, in Surrey. Duncan noticed that during their conversation, Rex was extremely preoccupied looking out of the window at the lawns. Some weeks before Duncan had been plagued by a company of moles which had invaded the garden, and in spite of all his precautions, he found himself quite unable to stem the tide. Mole-traps, poisons, smoke, wire, all were unavailing. He consulted his neighbour, Penelope Keith, who lived nearby. She said: 'Oh, Duncan, the remedy is simple. All you have to do is go to a child's toyshop and buy plastic windmills, you know the sort of thing with little plastic tops and wooden sticks, but not just one or two, you need to buy dozens and dozens of them.'

This, Duncan had duly done and returned with them and, as it were, planted them, liberally all over his front lawn. Evidently it was the sight of these plastic windmills which had so preoccupied Rex. Apparently, when stirred by the wind, the noise they make as the plastic sails revolve, vibrates inside the moles' tunnels and they cannot bear the sound of reverberation. Rex made no comment about this, until much later in the day, when the meeting was ended and they were motoring in Duncan's Bentley down the drive in order to go to lunch. Suddenly Rex aroused himself from his temporary torpor: 'I never imagined, Duncan, that you would be able to generate enough electricity from those little windmills, to run the heating and lighting in your house.'

'Oh no Rex,' said Duncan, 'they are not for the house, they are for the moles.'

There was a pause, as the car continued down Duncan's generous winding drive, and Rex said: 'Oh, for the *moles* . . . I never realized that moles needed electricity.'

When I was in England, rehearsing my first summer season at the Chichester Festival Theatre, the revival of *My Fair Lady* was fairly well established at Washington. Rex told me that one evening President Reagan and Nancy came to see the show, and had supper with him afterwards in the apartment he and his wife had rented. He said it was a most surreal experience, and something of a nightmare. 'Oh, it was a frightful evening,' he said, 'the President was surrounded everywhere by armed security guards, and they were all over the house. A strident helicopter permanently swirled overhead, making a hell of a noise so that none of us could hear ourselves speak, and a large silver "thing" like a fire engine stood outside with the black bags in the hallway – in fact, it was a mobile hospital emergency room. The President could only enter from the back stairs and the garage in an oddly furtive manner, for the President of the United States. We also had in the house the box with the red telephone, and the Nemesis button, in case the Russians suddenly launched a nuclear attack.' When Rex complained to a security guard that it seemed undignified for the President of the United States to scuttle in the back way, the guard said: 'Hell no! A guy out there might rocket the President.' All in all the evening could not be counted a success.

That same summer, in 1985, Rex collapsed during supper at

the Ritz and admitted 'that he was feeling rather decrepit'. He came down to see Alexandra and myself in Chichester, and stayed the weekend: 'I'm awfully wobbly on my pins,' he complained, 'I was going to watch some cricket at Lord's with my communist son, Carey, but I'll chuck that, and I'm afraid I can't possibly manage Goodwood. My eyes are the main problem – can hardly see to read these days – the quacks won't operate any more because they say under the cataracts, I've got glaucoma.'

We had a very cheerful lunch with Richard Briers, who said that in his opinion, in order to get a laugh on the stage of the Chichester Festival Theatre, which was a thrust stage, you had to act like Grock. Rex had acted there for me, in 1979, and agreed with him. 'That Thrust Stage is an absolute fucker!' he said.

When Rex died in 1990, I happened to be reading, entirely by coincidence, Saint-Simon's account of the death of Monsieur – 'there is often something humorous, even on the gravest of occasions . . .' and so there was 'something humorous' about the death of Rex and his extraordinary exchange with his two sons, apparently the very last words he ever spoke. And there being too much of him to fit into the casket of ashes, and the remainder being poured into a plastic-bag, like a surplus of sugar or salt.

It was sometime in the 1980s, but after we had finished *My Fair Lady* that I remembered saying to Rex that I'd once been invited to what I regarded as an extremely seedy and unworthy political occasion at No. 10 Downing Street in the 1970s when I came along more or less as Michael Crawford's 'date', when he'd been asked to Harold Wilson's private residence in London on one of these ghastly get-togethers of various showbiz and political and media celebrities.

Rex weighed in forcefully in agreement, as he had been to one of those equally unfortunate get-togethers at Harold Wilson's. He told me that it was just when he had come back from America and was still suffering terribly from jetlag, so the last thing he wanted to do was to go to a jamboree at No. 10 Downing Street. However, his wife Rachel felt that they ought to go as, however unlikely it might seem, it *was* the Prime Minister of England, and so Rex went along. He told me that he quite enjoyed the company of three rather smartly dressed young American Air Force officers, who were cheerful and larky, and seemed to be very pleased to meet him. 'I had absolutely no idea who they were, and I told them I'd recently come back from New York and landed at London airport the same day; "What about you three?"'

'Oh,' said one of them, 'we've all just flown over the pond the last flight.'

'I see,' said Rex, 'then, like me, you must be suffering from this terrible jetlag.'

Rex said they seemed a little disconcerted at this. 'It wasn't until sometime later' said Rex, 'that I learnt that it was John Glenn, Buzz Aldrin and Neil Armstrong, the American astronauts. The "last flight" they were referring to, of course, was their return from the moon.'

'Comedy' wrote Victor Pritchett, that admirable essayist, 'has a militant, even tragic edge.' Well, it did when Rex performed it, especially in Chekhov, or Pirandello.

Was his talent the cause of his egocentricity, or was his egocentricity the source of his talent? There was always a close connection between the art of high comedy and a capacity for rage. It always played a dominant part in his romantic relationships. Rex seldom spoke of previous lovers. Correctly, he was reserved, but it was claimed that part of his success was because, as John Aubrey wrote of the Duke of Buckingham, 'he had great natural parts.'

Sometime in the 1970s I was at a rather grand dinner party at the Marchioness of Dufferin and Ava's; I can't remember all the people who were there, but I remember David Hockney, Twiggy, Patrick Procktor, Wayne Sleep, a Rolling Stone or two, sundry other glittering guests of that era, and above all, Mr and Mrs John Paul Getty II, an extremely glamorous couple. By the greatest of good fortune I found myself seated between, on my right, a Roman contessa of Italianate beauty, and on my left, quite frankly the loveliest woman I've ever seen in my life, John Paul Getty's wife, the exotically named Talitha Pol. Apart from her own personal allure, I shall never forget that she was wearing earrings made from peacocks' feathers; she had recently returned from Rome, where the Getty's were living at that time, and her olive skin was glowing with the warmth and scent of the South. Her eyes seemed to possess metallic slivers of gold in them, she was exquisitely made-up, a soft full mouth, and she spoke with a most captivating eagerness and vivacity. It emerged she was the daughter of Poppet John, granddaughter of Augustus John. I remembered my mother and father talking about the two John daughters whom they knew intimately in their own bohemian days when they were first married and lived in Paulton Square. Talitha Pol and I spoke warmly and nostalgically of what we remembered from our parents' conversations about the delight of living in Chelsea in those days, when it was a village, and a lively, exotic, and artistic village at that. My parents used to join the John family, watching the old Chelsea Pensioners playing bowls behind the Six Bells, in the King's Road.

Years later, I found myself on a completely different occasion, with Rex, indulging in a conversation which we very seldom shared together, namely about romantic love, our personal love-life, the nature of romantic love, what we felt about it, how much we responded to it, and the haunting memory of past love affairs – if, that is, they were haunting. At one point, we were actually talking about women whom we had been in love with, or perhaps merely had a short passing love affair with, and I asked him if he could remember the most beautiful woman he had ever slept with. He paused for quite a long time, not so much because he couldn't remember, but because I suspect he found it rather difficult to make a decision, the beauties in his life counted for quite a number; to push the conversation ahead a bit, I said that although I had never had the pleasure of seeing her other than once, I could never forget the awesome beauty of somebody I had met at a party at Lady Dufferin's in the 1960s, when London was a heady place to be living in, namely the never to be forgotten Talitha Pol, whose beauty and exquisite peacock earrings had seduced me so long ago. Rex's eyes opened wide: 'Talitha Pol!' he exclaimed, 'My God, I remember her well. And those peacock-feathers! I had a radiant love affair with her during one week in Rome when we

238

were filming *Cleopatra*. I've never known anybody more beautiful than Talitha Pol.' Trust the crafty old bugger to have had a raging affair with her in Rome, whilst I at best had only sat next to her at dinner in Holland Park.

Chapter 44

THE POET AUDEN

SOME MONTHS AFTER the long tour of *My Fair Lady* (which had brought us together in the first place), Rex was involved in discussions with producers about a possible revival of *The Man of La Mancha*. It didn't seem a very practical idea, as Rex was too old to do justice to the heroic music, although he had the slender physique, sculptured head and rasping voice for the Knight of the Woeful Countenance. What I did not know, however, was that Rex had almost been involved in the original version of the musical when it was in an early stage of pre-production and still called *Don Quixote*. He was even invited to record three songs from the show, when the lyrics were composed by the then greatest poet in the English-speaking language, Wystan Auden. Rex told me he went along one morning to a disgusting recording studio, somewhere in downtown New York, and with Auden actually there, 'grunting and smoking cigarettes non-stop' as Rex describes, recorded these songs in his habitual *Sprechstimme*, or 'talking on pitch', that he created for Professor Higgins. And that was the last he heard of it, because afterwards, for some mysterious reason, the great poet was dropped from the project. Too poetic, presumably. And the world of musical-comedy, it must be said, is that little bit the poorer. Furthermore, somewhere, in somebody's mouldering archive, in a downtown recording studio, these tantalizing tapes must exist still, of Rex Harrison playing Don Quixote, book by Cervantes, lyrics by W. H. Auden.

In a curious way, W. H. Auden cropped up several times in spirit, or, at the very least, in quotation, throughout the tour that year, 1980, of *My Fair Lady*. Remembering faceless airport-lounges, rehearsal-rooms, and press-conferences, Auden's lines 'Upon the

240

Reading Circuit', comforted me. And when later on, I grew to know, and enjoy the company of, our legendary designer Oliver Smith, he would delight me with anecdotes about the time he shared the famous house, 7 Middagh Street, on Brooklyn Heights in the war, with distinguished tenants such as Benjamin Britten, Peter Pears, and Wystan Auden, who, he declared, 'played the landlady, called himself Mother, bossed us all around, and made himself responsible for organizing the rent. Sometimes wielding a bread-knife.'

In fact, Rex no more played his part in *The Man of La Mancha* than Auden did, and nothing further was heard from the producers concerning Cervantes's masterpiece as a musical revival. But it was not the last to be heard of Auden or Don Quixote.

In 1990, at Rex's Memorial Service in St Martin's in the Fields, both Carey Harrison and myself, read from *Don Quixote de la Mancha*, both believing it somehow fitting. Self-delusion, ancient charm, vainglorious dreams, battles with windmills, pursuit of fair women . . . Perhaps there was a connection somewhere, although Rex was less inclined to wear a woeful countenance himself, as to give one to other people. Carey read a passage from Hugh Whitemore's version for television of the great original, I from Auden's lost lines of the musical, and friends in the congregation swore they could hear the Master's voice rasping, caressing swoops and barks – his highs and lows, his ups and downs:

'Who is mad and who is not? What is a dream and what is not? . . . Whatever huge machines we may construct, or whatever mighty empires rise and fall, nothing will surpass the imagination of man. In the human brain you shall find madness, *and* the secrets of the universe.'

Rex Harrison had a perverse resemblance to Don Quixote, even that part of his legend and allure, and the television performance remains one of his finest characterizations. His curious character, the mixture of tenderness and rage, of artifice and occasional sincerity, the glimpse of secret dreams, of romance, and, alas, the capacity to smash things – and people – into smithereens, had long preoccupied me.

Auden's lyric ends:

241

It shall not be! Enchanters flee! I challenge you to battle me –
Your powers I with scorn defy, your spells shall never rattle me.
Don Quixote de la Mancha is coming to attend to you,
To smash you into smithereens and put a final end to you!

EPILOGUE

'It is odd how vanity supports the man who succeeds, and ruins the man who fails.'

La Rochefoucauld

IN A WAY, a surprising way, perhaps, Rex defeated the old-fashioned star-system. This meant you either have a life, or, you are a star. And for a long time, in the Hollywood system, the studio-system, the movie Czars, the Zanucks, the Goldwyns, the Louis B. Mayers were able to command that from their glamorous employees. There were others as well, of course, Chaplin, Keaton, Pickford, who bucked the system, but out on his own, from the day he arrived in LaLa Land, Rex was always a star, but he had a life as well. If you don't want fame, then for heaven's sake, don't be an actor. Rex achieved acting and fame, which is not given to so many.

Recollecting his life, even the somewhat penny plain revised version Rex permitted us to celebrate, was oddly pleasurable, where we filmed him over the course of a week, at the Haymarket Theatre, interspersed by long, nostalgic lunches around the area of St James. The director was Richard Mervyn, an immensely sympathetic figure, who got on well with the star, the more so as his father, William, or Bill Mervyn, was a former colleague of Rex, an esteemed character actor of similar quality. Until the last day, that is, when Rex mysteriously lost his spectacles, and a search-party took place, he being virtually blind without them. They were found, eventually, as I thought they would be, in the top pocket of his tweed jacket, on the back of his dressing-room chair. But not before his bedroom at the Ritz was searched by two *femmes de chambre*, the wardrobe-lady, the supervisor of the luxury suites, the manager of the hotel (of course), the first and second assistants from the television company, my personal assistant, the director's secretary, and researcher.

'Is something the matter?' I enquired mildly, when Rex wandered rather distractedly on stage, for his final shot of the morning.

'Well', answered Rex, '*everybody's* lost my glasses.'

People have often asked me, did Rex never receive a comeuppance, and the truth is, in a way, frequently. Large numbers of things failed to come through quite the way he wanted them to, and for anybody as sensitive to his own indecisiveness as he was, and the many examples of the road not taken, his life was always strewn with disappointment and dismay. But, it probably has to be admitted, that most of the time events and indeed, people, went the way he wanted them to – he always had riches enough and power enough to ensure they did. He bested most of his wives, who somehow yielded to him; his representatives, managers, agents, producers, and above all – having scarred hundreds of associates and relatives, not excluding his sons – he died peacefully, in his bed at a good age, honoured by the nation, wealthy, and without much pain. So there is evidence of a certain degree of injustice. Not however entirely. During the war, Lilli Palmer was accompanying Rex to luncheon in the best hotel in Nottingham, before he began rehearsing a play. They were darkly estranged at this time, and Rex was already inclined to philander. She was worried at such times about her alien status (she was a Viennese Jew), and did not feel, as she might have expected, her husband's entire support. The situation was not helped by Rex's appalling behaviour to the young hotel-waiter, which continued humiliatingly throughout the lunch. By the end of the meal, the young man, in some agitation, came over to the Harrisons' table, and said, urgently: 'Oh, forgive me sir, but there's something under your chair.'

Rex, scowling, rose to his feet swiftly, whereupon the young waiter leant back on his heels, lifted his fist, and swung Rex such a haymaker, the great star ended up flat on the floor, wiping blood from his mouth.

'If it's the last thing I do on earth,' said Rex, 'I'll have you fired from this hotel, and any other hotel in the country.'

'You can do whatever you like, Mr Harrison,' said the waiter, 'but I'm going to enlist in the Army this afternoon, so it won't do you much good!'

Lilli Palmer said it was the happiest day of her life.

While I was in New York in the winter of 1990 with the successful tour of *A Room of One's Own* with my great friend, Eileen Atkins, I met the producer and writer (author of several Broadway shows), Jay Presson Allen. Knowing that I was a friend of Rex, she told me this very curious story. Years ago, when they were working with Woody Allen on a picture, he had requested them to try to locate a boxing kangaroo, which he had heard, existed somewhere in a British seaside resort. He needed it for some movie or other, and indeed, this kangaroo did end up in one of his own films, boxing with Woody. Jay Presson Allen eventually found the creature, in a really down-at-heel sawdust ring, at the end of the pier in Brighton. The owner was an Australian woman and far from being apologetic about the seedy atmosphere of her menagerie, flea-bitten dogs and under-nourished horses, and of course, frightful kangaroo, she was defiantly proud of it. 'This kangaroo has been in several motion-pictures,' she said, 'including *Dr Dolittle*. Now, there's a funny story about this film. There was a most exceptional man in that film, a big film-star who was meant to be starring as the main character, Dr Dolittle. Well, it so happened that the weather was terrible that summer, and we were on location with all the animals down in a little place in the country called Castle Combe. Because it wouldn't stop raining we were losing a lot of time, and the producers were naturally in a terrible state about it. Day after day, this peculiar man, very well dressed, used to come out to the location, where we were all waiting, and when his car drew up – it was a grey Rolls-Royce – every morning, the chauffeur would open the door, and this man would place one leg outside the vehicle, look up at the rain-clouds and announce in a loud voice: "Too Wet!" Then he'd step back in the car again, and be driven back to his hotel. And the First Assistant would say, "Sorry everybody, it's a wrap! Come back tomorrow!" This happened day after day after day, and we never did any filming for ages.' The owner looked round at the shivering ponies, the threadbare monkeys, the emaciated dogs, and the depressingly squalid lodgings, which they all shared, with the boxing kangaroo.

'I didn't know his name,' she said, 'but I can tell you, a man like that would never survive one week in the circus.'

INDEX

Entries under Rex Harrison have been confined to those not readily found under other headings. RH has then been used.

My Fair Lady is referred to throughout as *MFL*

ACKNOWLEDGEMENTS

The author acknowledges the help of Adrian Rigelsford in finding the photographs.

The author and publishers are grateful to the following for giving permission to use copyright material: Faber and Faber for permission to quote from 'Dockery and Son' from *Collected Poems* by Philip Larkin, 'For Sidney Bechet' from *The Whitsun Weddings* by Philip Larkin, 'On the Circuit' and 'Don Quixote' from *Collected Poems* by W. H. Auden; B. Feldman and Co. Ltd, London WC2H 0EA for permission to quote from the song 'Forty Second Street' by Harry Warren and words by Al Dubin © 1932; M. Witmark & Sons, USA; REDWOOD MUSIC LTD (Carlin) Iron Bridge House, 3 Bridge Approach, Chalk Farm, London NW1 8BD in respect of 66.67% interest in the Estates of Maceo Pinkard and Alex Bellenda and B. Feldman and Co. Ltd, London WC2H 0EA for permission to quote from the song 'Kitchen Man' words and music by Maceo Pinkard, Alex Bellenda and Andy Razaf © 1929 by Clarence Williams Publishing Co. c/o MCA Music Publishing, California, USA; Christopher Fry for permission to quote from his letter.

Every effort has been made to trace all copyright holders, but if any have inadvertently been overlooked, the author and publishers will be pleased to make the necessary arrangements at the first opportunity.